Ebenezer Burgess

What is Truth?

An inquiry concerning the antiquity and unity of the human race; with an examination of recent scientifc speculations on those subjects

Ebenezer Burgess

What is Truth?

An inquiry concerning the antiquity and unity of the human race; with an examination of recent scientifc speculations on those subjects

ISBN/EAN: 9783337063603

Printed in Europe, USA, Canada, Australia, Japan

Cover: Foto ©ninafisch / pixelio.de

More available books at **www.hansebooks.com**

WHAT IS TRUTH?

AN INQUIRY CONCERNING THE

ANTIQUITY AND UNITY

OF THE

HUMAN RACE;

WITH

AN EXAMINATION OF RECENT SCIENTIFIC SPECULATIONS ON THOSE SUBJECTS.

BY

REV. EBENEZER BURGESS, A. M.,

MEMBER OF THE AMERICAN ORIENTAL SOCIETY, AUTHOR OF A MAHRATTA GRAMMAR, TRANSLATOR OF THE SURYA SIDDHANTA, ETC., ETC.

PUBLISHED BY

ISRAEL P. WARREN,

52 WASHINGTON STREET,

BOSTON.

Entered, according to Act of Congress, in the year 1871,
By MRS. A. T. BURGESS,
In the Office of the Librarian of Congress, at Washington.

Stereotyped at the Boston Stereotype Foundry,
No. 19 Spring Lane.

TO THE

AMERICAN BOARD OF COMMISSIONERS

FOR FOREIGN MISSIONS

𝕿𝖍𝖎𝖘 𝖂𝖔𝖗𝖐

IS RESPECTFULLY DEDICATED,

BY THE AUTHOR.

TESTIMONIAL.

The following testimonial was adopted at the close of the author's twelve lectures, as expressive of the opinions of the auditors respecting their interest and value: —

"We, the ladies and gentlemen of the city of Boston, who have attended the valuable and highly instructive course of lectures on the Antiquity of Man, delivered at the Lowell Institute, by the Rev. E. Burgess, do hereby express our hearty thanks and unqualified appreciation of the same.

"We would also express the hope that our worthy and much esteemed friend, the Rev. E. Burgess, will at an early day publish the said lectures, in order that all may have the benefit of the important facts therein contained.

"Ordered, That the foregoing resolutions be published in the daily papers in the city of Boston.

"Boston, February 23, 1867."

PREFACE.

A DISTINGUISHED American scholar has recently put forth the following declaration respecting the subject discussed in the present volume: —

"It has been supposed that the first introduction of man into the midst of this prepared creation was distant six or seven thousand years from our day, and we had hoped to be able to read the record of his brief career even back to its beginning; but science is now accumulating so rapidly, and from so many quarters, proofs that the current estimate of his existence must be greatly lengthened out, — even perhaps many times multiplied, — that universal acceptation of this conclusion is not, it appears, much longer to be avoided."

The opinion here expressed is — it may be safely said — that entertained by a large class of professedly scientific, semi-scientific, and literary men of the day; that is, judging from the yearly reports of the meetings of the various scientific bodies, American and European, and papers frequently found in certain prominent quarterlies and other periodicals.

The object of the present volume is to show what science does teach in regard to the antiquity of man on earth.

Science, in its true sense, is based on actual facts and established principles; and a scientific conclusion is one that is fairly deduced from such facts and principles, though it is admitted that the words "science" and "scientific" have an appropriate use in connection with *supposed facts*, or in reasoning about things that are confessedly only probable, or possible. And there is no objection to the phrase "scientific speculation;" for every science has connected with its true domain a margin — more or less wide — within which all things are, to say the least, not settled, and in which she must be allowed to speculate with the utmost freedom. It is only by allowing this freedom that the domain of true and real science can be enlarged. But always and everywhere great caution is to be observed in regard to taking a fact or principle belonging to this doubtful margin within the field of true science. The non-observance of this caution, it is well known, has been the occasion of endless and bitter disputes among scientific men.

Another caution is needed in this connection. In adducing scientific evidence in any discussion, it should be kept in mind that it makes a difference whether the alleged facts are derived from the speculative margin of the science concerned, or from its positive domain; e. g., when a demonstrated fact in astronomy or chemistry is brought forward, it should have the weight of scientific truth; but when the alleged fact is a part of some theory or hypothesis not yet established, it certainly is not entitled to the same weight. Is not this principle, though so very obvious, often overlooked in so-called scientific reasoning?

Has it not especially been overlooked in the discussions of the subject treated of in this volume?

This suggests another important fact, viz., that indicated by the very common and trite remark, — so common that an apology almost is required for introducing it, — that all the sciences harmonize among themselves; that one science can not conflict with another; that a truth in one of her departments is consistent with all truth in every other department.

Science! *Scientific* KNOWLEDGE! Not supposition! Knowledge of things in heaven above, in the earth beneath, and the waters under the earth! Knowledge of God, of angels, demons, and men! Knowledge of matter and spirit! Knowledge, in short, of whatever can be known in this wide universe, whether connected with matter or mind, or the abstract principles of things! It is true that there are things in the universe — or it is probable there are — respecting which so little is known that they have not yet been assigned their true place in the realm of science. But in general, it may be said that the realm of science embraces the whole universe. But this universe is one, having one Author, and all its parts constituting one harmonious whole; and these parts, as represented in the various sciences, properly understood, perfectly harmonize with each other.

When Alexander's generals first saw the river Indus in the far east, they supposed it to be identical with the Nile, with which they were familiar in the west. This was in accordance with the well-known principle of the human mind to generalize all its knowledge. It was well enough, only they were a little hasty in their generalization. It is true the Nile and the Indus belong to the same system, as we may say, the facts connected with them being discussed by the same science. Does not this incident often find a parallel in the scientific speculations that have been recorded since the time of Alexander to the present day? How often is the gap between a meager premise and the conclusion as wide as that between the Indus and the Nile!— the interval being unexplored, and as unknown as was that which separated those ancient rivers. The literature of the subject discussed in the present volume abounds in such cases.

In order that the importance, drift, and application of these general remarks may be appreciated, a few specifications are called for.

It has been said that all the sciences are parts of one whole, and consequently must harmonize together; that the facts of one science, rightly interpreted, can not conflict with those of another. This being the case, it follows that no one science has a right to decide a point, or regard a point as decided, — though it be clearly within her domain, — until she has obtained the concurrence of all her sister sciences.

As illustrative of this principle, let us take one or two obvious cases.

Philology, according to some of her students, says the great diversity of languages proves that these languages could not have had a common origin, or that the great diversity in the languages spoken by mankind proves the plural origin of the human races; and with a parade of facts makes out a plausible argument. But here other sciences, as ethnology, mythology, physiology, and natural history in some of her departments, step in and claim a right to have a voice in the discussion. Ethnology and mythology prove, or render highly probable, e. g., the common origin of the Semitic nations with those called Indo-European, and the same with other peoples speaking diverse languages, affording strong analogical ground for extending the argument to all mankind; and physiology and natural history claim that they prove the common origin of the human race. On whichever side the weight of argument may be thought to be by the opposing advocates, it is evident that all the sciences named above, and perhaps others, have a right to be heard in the discussion. Other illustrations of the principle here contended for might be adduced.

The author is deeply sensible of the imperfections of his work. As the reader sees these imperfections, he is asked to call to mind that the field traversed in the argument is very wide, and that one mind, unless it be of uncommon grasp, could not be expected to be equally familiar with every part of it, and do equal justice to all the points that are discussed.

The author does not profess to have done justice to any point, but hopes, imperfect as it is, his work will be found of some value as a part of the literature of the subject under discussion, and especially in the presentation of the facts upon which a correct decision must be based.

With these remarks, and with great diffidence, the work is submitted to the judgment of the candid public.

NOTE BY THE EDITOR.

The excellent author of this work was called to his rest before he had completed its preparation for the press. It was a work which had occupied his attention more or less for many years, and believing it called for by the growing skepticism of the times, — a belief confirmed by the opinions of many scholars and divines whom he had made acquainted with his plan, — he ardently desired that it might be given to the world, as the last labor of a life which had long been devoted to the service of divine truth. It was in accordance with this desire that the manuscripts were placed in the hands of another for revision and publication.

It was not the expectation of the author to offer the fruits of his own independent investigation, except, perhaps, when discussing the literature and religion of India, where he had spent many years of missionary service. He aimed only to gather up the results which had been reached by the best authorities on the various branches of the subject, and present them in a popular form for the benefit of those who have not time nor opportunity to study it for themselves. His book, therefore, is a book for the *people*, rather than for *savants*. We believe it will be very valuable to clergymen, teachers, and others, for that purpose.

NOTE BY THE EDITOR.

The work was left by the author in its original form, comprising Twelve Lectures, with copious materials designed to be placed in an Appendix. So great, however, are the inconveniences of that form for the discussion of such a subject, compelling a reduction of the most important topics within the single hour of the lecture, and involving repetitions and recapitulations not needed in a written work, that, with the approval of his family, the lecture form has been dropped, and the subdivisions arranged in chapters, as is customary. Many of the materials which had been designed for the Appendix have been brought forward and incorporated into the body of the work. This has, of course, necessitated some rearrangement and some revision of the language of the lectures. In some instances ampler citations from authorities have been given, and in a very few cases, a fuller elaboration of the positions taken has been ventured on, to give more completeness or clearness to the discussion; but in no case has anything been advanced differing from the author's well-known views. For those views, of course, he would hold himself alone responsible.

The editor regrets that he has not in all instances been able to verify the quotations introduced into the work. They are from a very wide range of reading, and many of the books referred to are not within present reach. He has done what he could to secure entire accuracy, both in form and language; but it is possible that some errors exist which have been overlooked.

W.

CONTENTS.

	PAGE
PREFACE,	5
NOTE BY THE EDITOR,	11

CHAPTER I. INTRODUCTORY.

The Subject recently come into Notice,	19
Former general Assent to the Bible Chronology,	20
Origin of recent Doubts on the Subject,	21
Modern Geological Discoveries,	22
Ethnology and Comparative Philology,	23
Systems of Chronology,	24
System of Bunsen,	24
System of Boëckh,	25
System of Rodier,	27
Call for a new Consideration of the Subject,	30
VIEW OF THE SCRIPTURE CHRONOLOGY,	31
The three Versions of the Pentateuch,	32
Period I. From the Creation to the Flood,	33
Period II. From the Flood to the Birth of Abraham,	34
Period III. From the Birth of Abraham to the Exodus,	35
Period IV. From the Exodus to the Foundation of the Temple,	36
Period V. From the Foundation of the Temple to its Destruction,	38
Period VI. From the Destruction of the Temple to the Birth of Christ,	40
Dates according to various Authors,	42
Testimony of Megasthenes,	45
Testimony of Abu-Màshar,	45
Testimony of Demetrius Phalereus,	46
Testimony of Eupolemus,	47

CHAPTER II. THE ARGUMENT FROM HISTORY.

I. EGYPT.

Sources of our Knowledge of Egyptian Antiquities,	49
1. The Temples and Monuments,	49
2. Literary Remains,	50
3. Greek Historians,	50
I. Testimonies relating to *Pre-historic Times*,	52
Diogenes Laertius,	52
Diodorus Siculus,	52

Herodotus,	53
Pomponius Mela,	53
The Old Chronicle,	53
Eusebius,	53
Julius Africanus,	54
Castor,	55
Practical Value of this Testimony,	56
The Accounts not to be taken literally,	56
The Accounts inconsistent with each other,	56
Months reckoned as Years,	57
The Zodiac of Denderah,	61
Stobart's Wooden Tablets,	65
II. Testimonies relating to *Historic Times*,	67
Egyptian Chronology without Dates,	67
MANETHO, his History and Writings,	68
His Lists of Dynasties,	69
1. Their Sources unknown,	71
2. Their present Form corrupt,	71
3. Internal Evidence against them,	72
4. They are contradicted,	73
a. By the Old Chronicle,	73
b. By Eratosthenes,	74
c. By Josephus,	77
d. By the Monuments,	79

CHAPTER III. THE ARGUMENT FROM HISTORY.
(Continued.)

II. GREECE AND ROME.

Identity of Origin between the Greeks and Romans,	85
Practical Character of the Greeks,	86
The highest Date in Grecian History B. C. 776,	86
The Siege of Troy mythical,	87
The alleged Date of it,	88
Its Value as an Era in Chronology,	88
The Greeks did not claim a remote Antiquity,	89
Date of the Founding of Rome uncertain,	89
Three principal Theories,	90

CHAPTER IV. THE ARGUMENT FROM HISTORY.
(Continued.)

III. THE CHALDEANS.

Extravagant Claims of the Chaldeans,	91
BEROSUS, his History and Writings,	92
His Annals of an Antediluvian Kingdom,	93
The ten Kings,	94
The Account mythical,	95
Elements of true History contained in them,	95
Chaldean Measures of Time,	95
Earliest Historical Dynasty B. C. 2458,	102

CHAPTER V. THE ARGUMENT FROM HISTORY.
(Continued.)
IV. THE HINDUS.

Importance of the Discovery of the Sanskrit,	103
View of the Sanskrit Literature,	104
The Vedas,	104
The Upavedas,	105
The Vedangas,	105
The Upangas,	105
This Literature has no historical Value,	106
Comparison between the Hindus and Greeks,	109
Origin of the Vedas,	111
Contents of the Vedas,	112
Antiquity of the Vedas,	113

CHAPTER VI. THE ARGUMENT FROM HISTORY
(Continued.)
V. THE CHINESE.

First Explorers of Chinese Literature,	118
Jesuit Missionaries,	118
Protestant Missionaries,	120
1. View of the Chinese Chronology,	120
The Ante-historic Period,	121
The Semi-historic Period,	122
The Historic Period,	122
2. How far is this Chronology reliable,	123
Views of Pauthier,	124
Views of Amiot,	124
Views of Williams,	126
Examination of the Elements of Computation,	126
The Chinese Year,	127
The Cycle of Sixty Years,	129
Statements of Rev. J. Chalmers,	130
Statements of Dr. Legge,	132
The Cycle of Sixty borrowed,	133
Chronology dates only from the Christian Era,	134
The Materials of it unreliable,	135
Portions of it mythical,	136
The Shu-king, how compiled,	137
Its Destruction and Recovery,	139
Earliest historical Date B. C. 2637,	142

CHAPTER VII. THE ARGUMENT FROM ETHNOLOGY.

Descent of all known Nations from Noah,	144
The tenth Chapter of Genesis,	145
Descendants of Shem,	146

Descendants of Japheth, ... 147
Descendants of Ham, ... 149
Agreement of this Account with History, ... 151
The so-called Aboriginal Races, ... 152
Scripture Language not to be pressed too literally, . . 153
Earlier and later Departures from original Seats, . . 155
Alleged Aborigines of Egypt, ... 158
    Evidence from Names of the Country and People, . 159
    Evidence from Physical Characteristics and Language, 160
    Evidence from the Monuments, ... 162
Alleged Aborigines of India, ... 163
    Of Northern India, ... 164
    Of Southern India, ... 165
Alleged Aborigines of Western Europe, ... 166
Historic Times but little before J. Cæsar, ... 167
These Aborigines were of Celtic Origin, ... 167

CHAPTER VIII. THE ARGUMENT FROM PHYSIOLOGY.

Rise of the Doctrine of a Plurality of Origin, . . . 170
La Peyrère, his Character and Writings, ... 170
Voltaire and Rousseau's Espousal of it, ... 172
Its supposed Bearings on Slavery, ... 173
AGASSIZ's Theory of Natural Provinces, ... 174
    Theory of Unity of Species, ... 177
Estimate of this Theory, ... 179
  I. It is a mere Theory, ... 179
  II. Alleged Inconsistency with the Bible not real, . 180
    The Case of Cain, ... 180
    The Case of Cain's Wife, ... 181
    Diversities among Races, ... 182
      1. Man is of a single Species, ... 183
        a. Identity in Mental and Physical Characteristics, ... 184
        b. The single Head of the Animal Kingdom, 186
        c. Intermixture of Races fertile, . . . 189
        d. Unity of Species proves Unity of Origin, . 193
      2. Changes are now constantly taking place, . 195
      3. Analogous Changes among Animals, . 202
  III. This Theory contrary to Analogy, ... 202
  IV. Is opposed by Theological and Moral Science, . 206
    All Men possess the same Moral Nature, . . 207
    All Men sustain the same Moral Relations, . . 208

CHAPTER IX. THE ARGUMENT FROM LANGUAGE.

The Hebrew once thought the Primitive Language, . . 209
Discovery of the Sanskrit, ... 210
Views of Stewart, ... 210

Views of Lord Monboddo,	211
Labors of Sanskrit Scholars,	213
Key to the Classification of Languages,	214
Three great Families of Languages,	215
I. The Aryan Family,	215
II. The Semitic Family,	216
III. The Turanian Family,	218
Classification according to Structure,	221
1. Monosyllabic Languages,	222
2. Agglutinative Languages,	222
3. Inflectional Languages,	223
Bearing of the Diversity of Languages on the Argument,	223
1. The Miraculous Confusion of Tongues,	224
2. Languages have still much in common,	225
3. Differences diminish as our Knowledge increases,	227
4. Languages subject to rapid Changes,	229

CHAPTER X. THE ARGUMENT FROM TRADITION.

Traditions of Primitive Ages to be expected,	235
Such Traditions exist,	236
Independent Traditions only valuable,	237
1. Traditions of one God,	238
2. Traditions of the Creation,	239
3. Traditions of the Garden of Eden,	243
4. Traditions of the Temptation and Fall,	244
5. Traditions of a Sevenfold Division of Time,	245
6. Traditions of the Deluge,	246
Among the Mexicans and Peruvians,	246
Among the Greeks,	247
Among the Phrygians,	249
Among the Chaldeans,	250
Among the Chinese,	252
Among the Egyptians,	253
Among the Hindus,	254

CHAPTER XI. THE ARGUMENT FROM MYTHOLOGY.

Mythology, its Nature,	261
All Myths founded in Fact,	262
Examples of modern Myths,	264
Characteristics of Greek Writers,	266
Specimens of their Mistakes,	267
I. All Mythologies had a common Origin,	270
The Roman and Greek Mythologies,	271
The Egyptian,	271
The Phœnician and Chaldean,	272
The Hindu,	272

CONTENTS.

II. That Origin in the Bible Narrative, ... 273
    Myths of the Creation, ... 274
    Myths of the Flood, ... 275
    Myths of the Antediluvians, ... 276
    Myths of Noah, ... 277
    Myths of the Ark, ... 280
    Myths of the Dove, ... 282
    Myths of the Rainbow, ... 284
    Myths of the eight Persons saved, ... 286
    Myths of Noah's three Sons, ... 288

CHAPTER XII. THE ARGUMENT FROM GEOLOGY.

Alleged Facts proving a Remote Antiquity, . . . 287
  1. Fragments of Brick and Pottery from Egypt, . . 287
    The Data not verified, ... 290
    Changes in the Nile Valley, ... 291
    Burnt Brick unknown to the Ancient Egyptians, . 292
  2. Human Fossil in Mississippi Valley, . . . 293
  3. Skeleton found near New Orleans, . . . 295
  4. Remains in the Florida Coral Reefs, . . . 300
  5. Flint Implements in the Valley of the Somme, . 300
    Geological History of the Valley, . . . 302
    No Proof that the Remains were contemporaneous, . 304
    No Proof of their extreme Antiquity, . . 306
    Geological Changes in the Valley, . . . 308
    Assumed to be wrought by existing Agencies, . 311
    The Assumption rejected by various Authors, . 312
  6. Human Remains in Peat-bogs, etc., . . . 320
    The Stone, the Iron, and the Bronze Age, . . 321
    The Remains belonged to the Celtic Race, . . 322

APPENDIX.

A. CHRONOLOGY OF BUNSEN, ... 327
B. CHRONOLOGY OF BOËCKH, ... 348
C. CHRONOLOGY OF RODIER, ... 349
D. MANETHO, ... 357
E. MANETHO'S LISTS, ... 359
F. THE OLD CHRONICLE, ... 377
G. ERATOSTHENES AND APOLLODORUS, . . . 378
H. MANETHO, ACCORDING TO JOSEPHUS, . . . 383
I. CHINESE ASTRONOMY, ... 391
J. SUPERFICIAL CHARACTER OF DIVERSITIES BETWEEN RACES, ... 393
K. VARIATIONS IN SPECIES AMONG DOMESTIC ANIMALS, 401
L. VISIT OF DIONUSOS TO INDIA, ... 412
M. CHINESE THEOLOGY, ... 413
N. THE CELTS IN EUROPE, ... 417

ANTIQUITY

AND

UNITY OF THE HUMAN RACE.

CHAPTER I.

INTRODUCTORY.— VIEW OF THE BIBLE CHRONOLOGY.

The Subject recently come into Notice. — Former general Assent to the received Chronology of Man's Creation. — Testimony of Hitchcock and Lyell. — Origin of recent Doubts concerning it. — Geological Discoveries. — Ethnology and Comparative Philology. — Systems of Chronology. — System of Bunsen. — System of Boëckh. — System of Rodier. — These Systems never critically examined. — Call for a new Discussion of the Subject. — View of the Scripture Chronology. — Three Versions of the Pentateuch. — Period I. From the Creation to the Flood. — II. From the Flood to the Birth of Abraham. — III. From the Birth of Abraham to the Exodus. — IV. From the Exodus to the Founding of the Temple. — V. From the Founding of the Temple to its first Destruction. — VI. From the Destruction of the Temple to the Birth of Christ. — Statements of heathen Writers.

THE Antiquity of Man is one of those subjects which have very recently come into prominent notice among learned men. It is scarcely a fourth of a century since the apparent teachings of the Bible chronology, which fix his creation at less than six thousand years ago, were generally received without question. For a little time, indeed, the discoveries of the new science of geology had disturbed the commonly received views on this subject, as astronomy in the days of Copernicus and Galileo had so greatly modified the ancient theories of the physical structure of the universe. But a re-examination of the sacred text, with the aid of a broader philology, soon demonstrated that there was no necessary discrepancy between it and the new science; nay, even derived fresh evidence from the very facts adduced by the latter in support of its own correctness. It was seen that the first verse of Genesis, "In the beginning God created the heavens and the earth," would permit the date of the creation to be carried back to any indefinite antiquity, leaving the subsequent account to cover successive periods in which the earth was fitted for human abode, stocked with the present species of vegetable and animal life, and lastly, crowned with the introduction of man, the destined lord and proprietor of all. In this fact of the comparatively recent origin of man, Genesis and geology were entirely agreed. Says Dr. Hitchcock, "As to the period when the creation of such a being by the most astonishing of all miracles took place, I believe there is no diversity of opinion. At least all agree that it was very recent; nay, although geology can rarely give chronological dates, but only a succession of events, she is able to say, from the monuments she deciphers, that man can not have occupied the globe more than six thousand years." Sir Charles Lyell also, in his "Principles of Geology" (vol. i. p. 240), a work published before the recent discoveries of fossil human remains, remarks, " I need not dwell on the proofs of the low antiquity of our species, for it is not controverted by any experienced geologist; indeed, the real difficulty consists in tracing back the signs of man's existence on the earth to that comparatively modern period when species now his contemporaries began to predominate. If there be a difference of opinion respecting the occurrence in deposits of the remains of man and his work, it is always in reference to strata confessedly of the most modern order; and it is never pretended that our race co-existed with assemblages of animals and plants, of which all, or even a great part, of the species are extinct."

Until very recently, therefore, the researches of science, and the supposed teachings of the Scriptures respecting the age of man on the earth, had been in entire accord. But within the last twenty years a series of investigations has been made which to some extent have again awakened doubt on this subject. Human bones and implements of labor and defense, together with domestic utensils, and even rude attempts of art, have been found in ancient peat beds, in bone caverns, and in the shallow lakes of Europe, in such geological connections as seem to demand for them a much higher antiquity than has hitherto been claimed for the race. Professor H. D. Rogers, of the University of Glasgow, writing in 1860, remarks, " Geologists and archæologists have recently somewhat startled the public by announcing the discovery, in the north-east of France and the adjacent corner of England, of supposed indications of the existence of the human race in the remote age when these tracts were inhabited by the extinct elephant, rhinoceros, hippopotamus, and other animals whose bones are preserved in the diluvium, or great superficial deposit attributed to the last wide geological inundation." *

These researches have been pursued with great industry and zeal, and are already giving us a new science, not yet twenty years old, called "prehistoric archæology." " It is," says Lenormant,† " like all sciences which are still in their infancy, presumptuous, and claims, at any rate in the case of

* Blackwood's Magazine, October, 1860, p. 422.
† Manual of the Ancient History of the East. Vol. i. pp. 24, 25.

some of its adepts, to overturn tradition, to abolish all authority, and to be the only exponent of the problem of our origin. These are bold pretensions which will never be realized. Prehistoric archæology, moreover, is yet but in its infancy; it still leaves great gaps, and many problems without solution. There is too often a desire to establish a system, and many scholars hasten to build theories on an insufficient amount of observations. Finally, all the facts of this science are not yet established with perfect certainty."

These claims for the high antiquity of man, derived from his fossil remains, have been fortified by similar claims deduced from the related sciences of ethnology and comparative philology. It is argued that the present races of men, with their great diversities of feature, color, and language, could not, according to any known rate or law of change, have descended from a single pair within the period that has elapsed since the received date of the creation, or rather of the deluge of Noah. Some, indeed, go further, and deny altogether the Bible doctrine of the unity of the race, insisting both upon its plurality of origin and its vast antiquity. As these views will be considered hereafter at length, it is only necessary to remark here that they are advocated with great zeal, and a display of learning which is well calculated to confound, if it does not convert, the believers in the Mosaic narrative, especially those whose time and attainments will not permit them to examine the subject for themselves.

In accordance with these claims of recent scientific research, numerous elaborate systems of chronology have been constructed, all of enormous reach. Some of these systems, indeed, are not new; but inasmuch as they never before acquired any credit beyond that of mere speculation, they did not seriously disturb the faith of mankind in the chronology of the Bible. It may not be inappropriate to give an outline of these speculations in this place, partly because they will not need any extended consideration further, and partly since they will serve to show us, at the outset, the extravagance of those speculations, as contrasted with the moderate and reasonable teachings of the Scriptures.

It has been remarked * that not less than *ninety-seven* systems of chronology have been put forth, some of them professing to be derived from the Bible, but most of them avowedly and irreconcilably differing from it. There are three of these which are specially worthy of notice, viz., the systems of Bunsen, Boëckh, and Rodier.

The system of Baron Bunsen is too elaborate to

* Iteler, in Halma's Almageste, vol. iv. p. 165.

be fully set forth here. In this system the creation of man is placed at B. C. 20,000, the flood of Noah at B. C. 10,000, the founding of the Egyptian empire by Menes at B. C. 3623, the birth of Abraham at B. C. 2870, the exodus at B. C. 1320, &c. For his reasons for these dates, and for a consideration of the value of his system, see Appendix, A.

The chronological system of Boëckh * is confined to Egyptian history and antiquities. According to this writer, Hepæstus, the first god-king of Egypt, began to reign on the 20th of July, B. C. 30,522. He reigned nine thousand years, and was followed by other gods, as Sol, Typhon, Horus, Jupiter, &c., then by demigods, heroes, and manes. Of the gods there were three dynasties, of demigods three, together extending through nineteen thousand and twenty-four years. These were followed by a dynasty of manes, ruling five thousand eight hundred and thirteen years. The whole period thus embraced under the government of the gods, demigods, and manes, which he styles *tempus mythicum* (the mythic period), amounts to twenty-four thousand eight hundred and thirty-seven years, reaching down to July 20, B. C. 5702. Then follow historic times.

* See Müller's Fragmenta Hist. Græc., vol. ii. pp. 599-606, at the close of a *résumé* of the fragments that have been preserved of Manetho.

Menes, the first mortal king of Egypt, begins his reign July 20, B. C. 5702. The chronology of thirty-one dynasties of kings is then given, extending to the conquest of Egypt by Alexander, November 14, B. C. 332, in the thirty thousand two hundred and twelfth year of the world. Of ten or twelve dynasties he gives the date only of the beginning and the end; of others he gives that of the individual kings; so that from Menes, July 20, B. C. 5702, to Alexander, November 14, B. C. 332, a period of five thousand three hundred and seventy years, we have one hundred and sixty-five dates, assigned with a precision that extends *to the very day of the month!*

This feature of the chronology, as it seems to me, is alone sufficient to stamp it as utterly unworthy of confidence. The first god-king begins to reign precisely on the 20th of July, thirty thousand five hundred and twenty-two years before Christ! Then follow gods, demigods, and manes, i. e., demons, for exactly twenty-four thousand eight hundred and thirty-seven years, till the accession of Menes, July 20, B. C. 5702! The first dynasty of human kings, eight in number, lasts from July 20, B. C. 5702, till May 18, B. C. 5449! And so on to the end of the chapter. Surely the student of history has a right to know on what grounds an author bases such definiteness and precision in periods of high antiquity. The unlearned and credulous are likely to receive all this as the simple truth, when they see it so confidently put forth by an author of acknowledged eminence. For a more comprehensive view of the system, and of its real value, see Appendix, B.

In 1862, a work on chronology was published at Paris by Rodier, entitled, " Antiquity of the Human Races; Reconstruction of the Chronology and History of the Primitive Peoples, by an Examination of the original Documents, and by Astronomy."* In a second edition, which appeared in 1864, the author says, in his preface, that he has neglected no occasion and no means of eliciting criticism for the detection of errors; but as no criticisms of consequence have been offered, he issues the second edition as a simple reprint of the first. He evidently has increased confidence in the soundness of his work from the favor with which it was received.

The following paragraphs from the Introduction, showing the author's claims for his work, are all I need quote in this place: —

" To show clearly the field of discussion, let us an-

---

* Antiquité des Races Humaines; Reconstitution de la Chronologie et l'Histoire des Peuples Primitifs, par l'Examen des Documents originaux et par l'Astronomie. Par G. Rodier. Deuxième éd. Paris, 1844, 8vo., pp. 454.

nounce, in the outset, that we are able to demonstrate with precision (*en mesure de demontrer*), both chronologically and astronomically, the following epochs, viz. : —

" The epoch of the year 14,611 B. C., the Egyptian period called *Ma*.

" The epoch of the Egyptian calendar at the end of the seventh dynasty, in the year B. C. 4266.

" The epoch of a reform of the Babylonian calendar, about the year B. C. 2783.

" The epoch of the reform of the Iranian calendar, by King Djemschid, about the year B. C. 7000; according to the chronology, or precisely in the year 7048, according to the cycles and astronomical verifications.

" The epoch of the commencement of the period, called the *Satya Yuga* of the Hindus, in the year B. C. 13,901.

" The commencement of the *Treta Yuga* of the same people, in the year B. C. 9101.

" Several other epochs are capable of verification by astronomy, but with less precision ; for example, the era of the Manavantaras in India, corresponding to the year B. C. 19,337, the era of Thoth in Egypt, corresponding to B. C. 17,932, &c., &c.

" All these eras constitute a complete whole (*ont entre elles une solidarité*), more or less perfect, but undeniable and characteristic ; they proceed one from another by a filiation which becomes evident as soon as one has caught a glimpse of it. There are thus revealed, among the primitive peoples, connections and reciprocal influences of which history has lost the remembrance.

" We well know that to announce that our researches

lead to such results is to mark them for the contempt, perhaps even the hostility, of our readers. Every new truth assails at its birth old opinions, which never disappear without offering a resistance more or less active and determined. Reason always ends, however, by triumphing over opposition. Profoundly convinced that our work re-establishes in their ancient rights very important truths which have been long obscured by a fatal misapprehension, we present it with confidence to the small number of readers who may be disposed to examine it without taking sides in advance." Appendix, C.

Such are the leading features of three elaborate systems of chronology, which profess to extend the period of man's existence to from twenty to thirty thousand years before Christ. They fall in with and seem to strengthen the geological and ethnological arguments for a high human antiquity. And I am not aware that the principles and details of either of them have been subjected to a critical examination. The consequence is, that our common system (or systems, for there are several, according to the different versions used) of Bible chronology is rejected as unworthy of credence. Many devout believers in inspiration, indeed, who till recently had never doubted its correctness, already feel their faith in it shaken. A professor in one of our colleges writes me that very recently he was visiting the geological cabinet in company with a friend and professed geologist, when, as they were looking at a stone adz, his friend remarked that it was certainly the work of man, and "gave unquestionable evidence, by the situation in which it was found, of being at least one hundred thousand years old." Similar opinions are finding frequent expression in our current popular literature. One of our most respectable daily papers, after giving an account of a late meeting of the British Association for the Advancement of Science, in which the discoveries in the river-drifts and caves of France and England were related, remarks, "The results of these researches thus far must revolutionize the long-accepted theory of the age of man, and add many thousand years (we dare not venture to say how many) to the period when it is believed he first trod the earth." *

In view of these things, is there not a call for a new and thorough discussion of the question thus involved? If man has existed on the earth twenty, fifty, or a hundred thousand years, what, precisely, is the evidence of it? What traces of his existence during that long period has he left behind him? Do the facts adduced in opposition to the common view, when carefully and candidly weighed, prove what is claimed for them? Do they invalidate the

* Providence Daily Journal, October 4. 1866.

authority and accuracy of the sacred Scriptures? Especially is it important to ascertain what *are* the facts. In dealing with these matters, writers have substituted speculations for facts, until the reader often knows not what to attribute to the one and what to the other. He who can eliminate the one from the other, who can show distinctly what is properly substantiated as truth, and what is hypothetical and imaginary, will perform a real, though it be humble, service both to the cause of science and the Bible. Such is the object which I have proposed to myself in this work. And if in some instances, as will unavoidably be the case, it shall, from a deficiency of the data, be necessary, in order to bridge over a chasm, to make suppositions and draw inferences, — in other words to *speculate*, — I shall endeavor to do it in such a way that my readers shall know I am speculating, and not reciting facts.

Inasmuch as the question before us implies a comparison between the Bible Chronology and that alleged to be demonstrated by Science, there will be an advantage in exhibiting the former in this place.

WHAT, THEN, DO THE SCRIPTURES TEACH US AS TO THE AGE OF MAN ON THE EARTH?

It is well known that there are considerable discrepancies in the conclusions which have been reached by different authors on this subject. The ages of the patriarchs who lived before Abraham are variously given in the three ancient versions of the Pentateuch, the Hebrew, the Samaritan, and the Greek of the Septuagint, the variations amounting in the aggregate to about fifteen hundred years. We have not space to go at length into the origin of these discrepancies, or attempt to decide positively which of them is most accurate. Each version may have been subject to alteration, perhaps by accident, perhaps also by design. I will only say that the numbers of the SEPTUAGINT appear to me the most probable, and best give the true chronology as recorded by Moses, — a little indefiniteness being admitted as. possible in consequence of various readings.

The following is an outline of the chronology of the Septuagint, according to our most approved texts of that version of the Old Testament Scriptures. These texts are, (1) that of Cardinal Mai's edition, which is after the celebrated Vatican MS., and, (2) that of Tischendorf, which is from a collation of most ancient MSS., the Vatican being the basis.* We make Mai our basis, giving the various readings of Tischendorf.

* Tischendorf says in his title-page, "Textum Vaticanum Romanum emendatius edidit, . . . omnem lectionis varietatem

While it is not within our object to enter into any discussion in regard to the comparative claims of the Septuagint and Hebrew chronologies, still, in order to afford the facility of comparing the two, I shall notice the points of difference between them, and give a parallel synopsis of both at the close.

PERIOD I. FROM THE CREATION OF ADAM TO THE FLOOD.

		Years before Birth of a Son.	Residue of Life.	Whole Life.
1.	Adam,	230	700	930
2.	Seth,	205	707	912
3.	Enos,	190	715	905
4.	Cainan,	170	740	910
5.	Malaleel,	165	730	895
6.	Jared,	162	800	962
7.	Enoch,	165	200	365
8.	Methuselah,	(167) 187	782	969
9.	Lamech,	188	565	753
10.	Noah to the flood, 600			

(2242) 2262

The above table differs from a corresponding one drawn from the Hebrew in this: The lives of the

Codicum Vetustiorum Alexandrini, Ephraemi Syri, Friderico-Augustani, subjunxit." And Mai says (title-page), "Ex antiquissimo Codice Vaticano." But as the first forty-six chapters of Genesis are wanting in this MS., we can easily account for the difference between Tischendorf and Mai in regard to some of the patriarchal numbers hereafter noticed.

first five and the seventh patriarchs, before the birth of the son who succeeded in the patriarchal line, in the Hebrew, are just a century shorter, which century is added to the residue of life, making the whole life precisely the same; the years of Lamech before the birth of Noah are, in the Hebrew, one hundred and eighty-two, his residue five hundred and ninety-five, and his whole life seven hundred and seventy-seven years, instead of as above. In the Hebrew, then, the duration of the period is sixteen hundred and fifty-six years.

The various reading of one hundred and sixty-seven, in the life of Methuselah, is edited by Tischendorf.

Period II. From the Flood to the Birth of Abraham.

		Years.
Shem, after the flood to the birth of Arphaxad,		2
1. Arphaxad, to the birth of a son,		135
2. Cainan,		130
3. Sala,		130
4. Eber,		134
5. Peleg,		130
6. Reu,		132
7. Serug,		130
8. Nahor,	(79)	179
9. Terah,		70
10. Abraham born,	(1072)	1172

According to the Hebrew, the lives of the first seven patriarchs (excluding Cainan) are just a hundred years shorter before the birth of a son, Cainan is entirely omitted, and the years of Nahor, previous to the birth of Terah, are only twenty-nine, making the period two hundred and ninety-two years.*

The reading seventy-nine, in the life of Nahor, is found in many MSS., and is edited by Grabe, and by Field in an edition of the LXX recently published by the Society for Propagating the Gospel. But one hundred and seventy-nine is edited by both Mai and Tischendorf, and, in fact, by almost all editors of the LXX.

PERIOD III. FROM THE BIRTH OF ABRAHAM TO THE EXODUS.

In regard to the duration of this period there is no difference between the Septuagint and the Hebrew. By a wonderful agreement of almost all chronologers, both ancient and modern, this duration is estimated at five hundred and five years. The texts upon which this estimate is based are the same in the Septuagint as in the Hebrew. These texts are, Gen. xii. 4 and Ex. xii. 40, 41.

Abraham was seventy-five years old at the " Call,"

---

* Usher and some others — Hebraists — make this period three hundred and fifty-two years. This is done by making Abraham to be born in the one hundred and thirtieth year of Terah, comparing Gen. xi. 32 with xii. 4.

and the exodus was four hundred and thirty years after. For, by the consent of all the chronologers, the four hundred and thirty years began when the patriarch, at the divine call, left his land and kindred. And Paul corroborates this in his statement that the law came four hundred and thirty years after the promise. (Gal. iii. 17.) This interpretation is strengthened by the particular reading of the Septuagint in Ex. xii. 40, this translation adding, after the words "who dwelt in Egypt," the words "and in Canaan."

The chronology of this period, then, according to the Septuagint, is the same as in the Hebrew, viz. : —

Abraham to the "Call," 75
From the Call to the Exodus, . . 430
Total, ... 505

Period IV. From the Exodus to the Foundation of Solomon's Temple.

This period is shorter according to the Septuagint than it is according to the Hebrew, and that whether we determine the duration by the single text, 1 Kings vi. 1, or by the details of the current history. In 1 Kings vi. 1, it is said that the temple was begun four hundred and forty years [*] after the chil-

---

[*] Five MSS. collated by Holmes and the Compl. Ed. have four hundred and eighty in 1 Kings vi. 1.

dren of Israel came out of Egypt, and in the current history only twenty years are assigned to Eli instead of forty, as in the Hebrew. In all other respects the details are the same in both.* And both are alike indefinite in regard to the time of Joshua and the Elders, and that of Samuel and Saul.

The duration of this period, then, according to the Septuagint, if we adopt the present reading of 1 Kings vi. 1, is four hundred and forty years; but if we adopt the details in the current history, giving to Joshua twenty-seven years, according to the ancient chronologers generally, and to Samuel and Saul forty, according to Paul (Acts xiii. 18-21), it is six hundred years, as follows:—

		Years.
Moses in the desert,		40
Joshua,		27
1st Servitude (Mesop.),	Judges iii. 8	8
Othniel,	" iii. 11	40
2d Servitude (Moab),	" iii. 14	18
Ehud and Shamgar,	" iii. 30	80
3d Servitude (Canaan),	" iv. 3	20

* Clinton (*Fasti Romani*, vol. ii., Append. p. 226) says the details from which the chronology of the period is determined are precisely the same in the LXX as in the Hebrew; and he presents the details in parallel columns in which forty years are assigned to Eli in the LXX. Parker (in a recent elaborate work on Chronology) says the same. See next note.

		Years.
Deborah and Barak,	Judges v. 31	40
4th Servitude (Midian),	" vi. 1	7
Gideon,	" viii. 28	40
Abimelech,	" ix. 22	3
Tola,	" x. 2	23
Jair,	" x. 3	22
5th Servitude (Philist.),	" x. 8	18
Jephthah,	" xii. 7	6
Ibzan,	" xii. 9	7
Elon,	" xii. 11	10
Abdon,	" xii. 14	8
6th Servitude (Philist),	" xiii. 1	40
Samson,	Judges xv. 20, and xvi. 31	20
Eli,	1 Sam. iv. 18	20*
Samuel and Saul,		40
David,		40
Solomon to foundation of the Temple,		3
Total,		580

Or, according to 1 Kings vi. 1, 440.

PERIOD V. FROM THE FOUNDATION OF SOLOMON'S TEMPLE TO ITS DESTRUCTION BY NEBUCHADNEZZAR.

There are some difficulties in the chronology of this period on account of discrepancies in the sacred

---

* This is forty in the Complut. Aldine and Georg. Slav. editions of the LXX, and some two or three MSS., as noted by Holmes. But all our present editions have twenty.

text; but these discrepancies are the same in the Septuagint as in the Hebrew, and the details in regard to numbers upon which the duration of the period rests are precisely the same in both, as follows: —

		Yrs.	Mos.
1.	Solomon,	37	
2.	Rehoboam,	17	
3.	Abijam, current 3, complete,	2	
4.	Asa,	41	
5.	Jehoshaphat,	25	
6.	Joram, current 8, complete,	7	
7.	Ahaziah,	1	
8.	Athaliah,	6	
9.	Joash,	40	
10.	Amaziah,	29	
11.	Azariah, or Uzziah,	52	
12.	Jotham,	16	
13.	Ahaz, current 16, complete,	15	
14.	Hezekiah,	29	
15.	Manasseh,	55	
16.	Amon,	2	
17.	Josiah,	31	
18.	Jehoahaz,		3
19.	Jehoiakim,	11	
20.	Jehoiachin,		3
21.	Zedekiah,	11	
	Total,	427	6

Or, as we may say, 427 years.

A close examination of the history of the period shows that the numbers of some of the reigns should be reduced by one to denote complete years. Such we regard the third, sixth, and thirteenth reigns. The grounds for this conclusion will be seen on comparing 1 Kings i. 1 and i. 10, 2 Kings viii. 16 and viii. 25, and xvi. 1 and xvii. 1. We have put down the time of those reigns accordingly.

PERIOD VI. FROM THE DESTRUCTION OF THE TEMPLE BY NEBUCHADNEZZAR TO THE BIRTH OF JESUS CHRIST.

The duration of this period cannot be determined by any scriptural data alone. For its commencement and chronological details we have to resort to profane history. In reference to this point, the Septuagint and the Hebrew occupy the same ground. For, as we have before intimated, all essential difference between the two is confined to the first two periods, or the patriarchal ages, there being only a slight discrepancy afterward, viz., in the fourth period, the years of Eli or the statement in 1 Kings vi. 1. Since, then, our object is to give the chronology of the Septuagint, we, without discussion, remark that the destruction of the temple by Nebuchadnezzar has been fixed by means of Ptolemy's canon at about B. C. 586, by the ablest chronologers,* some varying two or three years on one side or the other of that date. Waiving the discussion of that point to another place, we assume that as the date of the destruction of the temple.

The chronology of the Septuagint, presented in tabular form, stands thus (that of the Hebrew being added for convenience of comparison) : —

	THE SEPTUAGINT.				HEBREW.	
	Mai's Ed.		Tischen. Ed.			
	Yrs.	B. C.	Yrs.	B. C.	Yrs.	B. C.
1. Creation,	2262	5532	2242	5512	1656	4066
2. Flood,	1172	3270	1172	3270	292	2410
3. Birth of Abraham,	505	2098	505	2098	505	2118
4. Exodus,	580	1593	580	1593	600	1613
5. Founding of Temple,	427	1013	427	1013	427	1013
6. Destruction of Temple,	586	586	586	586	586	586

The first column of figures in each system denotes the length of the periods, and the second, the date

---

* The author of "The History of the World," Philip Smith, B. A., one of the principal contributors to Smith's Dictionary of Greek and Roman Biography, in his Note on Chronology, p. 10, says, "The epoch of the destruction of the temple is fixed by a concurrence of proofs from sacred and profane history, with only a variation of one, or, at the most, two years, between B. C. 588 and 586. Clinton's date is June, B. C. 587." This margin should be extended a little on each side of 586, as some, as Bede, have 589, and some as low as 583.

of the epochs beginning them. It should be remarked, in regard to the Hebrew computation in the above table, that Hebraists generally make the second interval three hundred and fifty-two years, by regarding Abraham as the youngest son of Terah, and born when his father was one hundred and thirty years old, instead of seventy, and the fourth period, four hundred and eighty, from 1 Kings vi. 1, instead of six hundred, making the time from the creation to Christ sixty years less than it is in our table, placing the creation at B. C. 4006. The sum four thousand and four, as indicating the date of the creation in our received chronology, is made up, in addition to the above modifications, by shortening the fifth period. But our table presents what we regard as the correct Hebrew chronology.*

---

* Dates according to various authors : —

	Petavius.	Usher.	Hales.	Jackson.	Poole.	Bunsen.
Creation, . . .	3983	4004	5411	5426	5361	Ab. 20,000
Flood, . . .	2327	2348	3155	3170	3099	Ab. 10,000
Birth of Abraham, .	1961	1921	2078	2023	2157	
Exodus, . . .	1531	1491	1648	1593	1652	1320
Founding of Temple,	1012	1012	1027	1014	1011	1004
Destruction of Temple,	589	588	586	586	586	586

It should be further remarked, that most Septuagintarian chronologers make the first period twenty-two hundred and fifty-six, out of deference to Josephus; they likewise make the second period only ten hundred and seventy-two,* by putting the years of Nahor at seventy-nine instead of one hundred and seventy-nine; or nine hundred and forty-two,† by leaving out the second Cainan with his generation of one hundred and thirty years; or ten hundred and two,‡ by giving Terah one hundred and thirty years to the birth of Abraham. We simply remark that our object is to present the chronology of the Septuagint according to the most approved texts. This we have done. We would state, however, that we think this version should be corrected to make it harmonize with Josephus in the length of the first period, since, by giving Methuselah only one hundred and sixty-seven years before the birth of Lamech, we make him survive the flood fourteen years; and the one hundred and eighty-eight years of Lamech should doubtless be corrected by the Hebrew and Josephus, and made one hundred and eighty-two; we would likewise give to Eli forty instead of twenty years.

* As Jackson. † As Eusebius.
‡ As Hales. Hales, a Septuagintarian in chronology, gives Nahor seventy-nine, leaves out the second Cainan, and makes Terah one hundred and thirty at the birth of Abraham.

Thus it appears that the highest date of the creation of man, according to the Septuagint, — and that is according to Mai's edition, — is B. C. 5532, and the lowest (arrived at by taking the lowest numbers found in any text, of Methuselah, viz., one hundred and sixty-seven, and Nahor, viz., seventy-nine, and the four hundred and forty of 1 Kings vi. 1, for the fourth period) is two hundred and sixty years less, i. e., B. C. 5272.

The difference between the Septuagint and the Hebrew, according to our computation, is fourteen hundred and sixty-six or fourteen hundred and forty-six. This difference, by taking other numbers of the various readings, might be increased to sixteen hundred and twenty. It may be remarked, however, that the amount of difference, which is to be set down as the probable result of designed alteration in one or the other, is thirteen hundred years, or, if we include Cainan's generation in this class, fourteen hundred and thirty,* viz., six hundred in the period before, and seven hundred or eight hundred and thirty in the period after the flood, the lives of thirteen patriarchs before the birth of the son who succeeded being shortened or lengthened a century

---

* We are inclined to the opinion, however, that the interpolation or omission of the second Cainan, whichever is adopted, is the result of mistake of copyists.

each, and the second Cainan being interpolated or left out. Other differences are probably the result of mistakes by copyists.

These results, deducible from the sacred history alone, receive some remarkable confirmations from early heathen writers, which may properly be exhibited in this place.

1. We have a fragment of a work on India, written by Megasthenes, a Greek historian contemporaneous with Alexander the Great, about B. C. 323, in which he gives an account of the institutions and customs of the people of that country. He says, "The Hindus and the Jews are the only people who had a just conception of the creation of the world and the beginnings of things." And he adds, "The Hindus did not carry back their history and antiquities above five thousand and forty-two [some manuscripts read six thousand and forty-two] years and three months from Alexander's invasion of India,"* — viz., 327 B. C. This would place the creation at B. C. 5369, differing less than two hundred years from the date now given.

2. In an Arabic work, attributed to Abu-Mâshar, in the conjunction of the planets, the author remarks that the Indians reckoned three thousand seven hundred and twenty-five years (Persian) and

* Hales' Chronology, vol. i. p. 195.

three hundred and forty-eight days between the deluge and the Hegira (A. D. 622), which would bring the date of the former at B. C. 3102. This is the date of the commencement of the celebrated *Kali-Yug*, an historico-astronomical epoch of the Hindus, which doubtless had its origin in that great event, the Flood, of Noah.

3. Demetrius Phalereus, a Greek writer, born B. C. 345, is quoted by Alexander Polyhistor, another Greek author, as making the period before the flood to be two thousand two hundred and sixty-two years, and from thence to the birth of Abraham, one thousand and seventy-two years.

4. Another heathen writer, named Eupolemus, said to have flourished about B. C. 160, who wrote several works on the history of the Jews, has a paragraph to this effect: " That from Adam to the fifth year of Demetrius, and the twelfth of Ptolemy, king of Egypt, are five thousand one hundred and forty-nine years." Reference must here be made to Demetrius Soter, king of Syria, who began to reign about B. C. 163, and Ptolemy Physcon, who began B. C. 170. The fifth of the former and the twelfth of the latter concur in B. C. 158, which makes the date of the creation, according to this writer, to be B. C. 5307. The numbers given, both by him and Demetrius, were evidently originally derived from

the Mosaic records, and can not, therefore, be regarded as independent testimony in support of those records. Their testimony, nevertheless, is valuable, as showing how the Jewish chronology had found its way into heathen writings many years before the Christian era.*

* Demetrius and Eupolemus are both mentioned by Josephus (Cont. Apion, i. 23) as foreign writers who had "not greatly missed the truth about our affairs; whose lesser mistakes ought, therefore, to be forgiven them, for it was not in their power to understand our writings with the utmost accuracy."

CHAPTER II.

THE ARGUMENT FROM HISTORY.

I. EGYPT.

Source of our Knowledge of Egyptian Antiquities. — I. The Temples and Monuments. — Afford little Help in this Inquiry. — No monumental Date earlier than B. C. 2500. — II. Literary Remains. — Art of Writing early known. — Number of Egyptian Books. — These contain no Chronology. — III. Greek Historians. — Their Study of Egyptian Antiquities. — Divided into two Classes. — Testimonies relating to PRE-HISTORIC TIMES. — Diogenes Laertius. — Diodorus Siculus. — Herodotus. — Pomponius Mela. — The "Old Chronicle." — Eusebius. — Julius Africanus. — Castor. — These Accounts not to be taken literally. — Discrepancies between them. — Months reckoned as Years. — Were ancient Annals forged? — Supposed astronomical Evidence. — Story of the Zodiac of Dendera. — Of the wooden Tablets. — HISTORIC TIMES. — Egyptian Chronology without Dates. — Manetho, his History and Character. — His Lists of the Egyptian Dynasties. — These Lists examined. — I. Their Sources unknown. — II. Have been corrupted. — III. Intrinsic Evidence of their Untrustworthiness. — IV. Contradicted by the "Old Chronicle." — By Eratosthenes. — By Josephus. — V. Not sustained by the Monuments. — Conclusion as to their Value.

WE propose to inquire, in the first place, of HISTORY, whether she has any evidence to afford us of the alleged remote antiquity of man on earth. And we will begin with what is confessedly one of the oldest of known nations — ancient Egypt.

Our knowledge of the antiquities of Egypt is derived partly from its temples and monuments, partly from the papyrus rolls and other literary remains still extant, and partly from the writings of historians and scholars of other lands, who have transmitted to us the facts and traditions known in their day, but which have otherwise been lost.

The first of these sources of information affords little help in determining the question before us. The work of deciphering the monumental inscriptions, since the discovery of the key to the system of hieroglyphics, as furnished by the Rosetta Stone, has been one of great interest, and some important results have been reached. Still it admits of a question whether, in the hands of those who but imperfectly understand them, they have not introduced much confusion into Egyptian history. However that may be, the data they furnish are too recent to be of much weight in the inquiry under consideration. It is the general admission of Egyptologers, that no monumental record can be dated back anterior to about B. C. 2500. Says Mr. Poole,[*] "The earliest record which all Egyptologers are agreed to regard

[*] Smith's Dictionary of the Bible, Art. *Egypt*.

as affording a date, is of the fifteenth century before Christ, and no one has alleged any such record to be of any earlier time than the twenty-fourth century before Christ."

The same thing is substantially true of the literary remains of ancient Egypt. It is generally admitted that the art of writing was known at a very early period, perhaps as early as the commencement of the empire under Menes, its first king. Clemens Alexandrinus mentions sacred Egyptian books to the number of forty-two; others, eleven hundred; others still, twenty thousand, and thirty-six thousand five hundred.* Some of these may still be extant in the numerous papyrus rolls now deposited in the museums of Egypt. It is, however, generally agreed that these books contain no history or chronology; and certain it is that, if they do, neither has, as yet, been brought to light. Bunsen (vol. ii. p. 16) expressly says, "We possess no Egyptian historical work."

For the history and chronology of ancient Egypt, then, we have to depend almost solely upon writers of other nations, mostly of the Greeks.

Diodorus Siculus (I. ii. 36) gives a list of the names of "illustrious Greeks," as he terms them, who had traveled in Egypt. He says that the

* Bunsen, vol. i. p. 7.

priests of that country read in their annals the names of these men whom they have seen among them, beginning with the semi-fabulous name of Orpheus. He then mentions Homer, Lycurgus, and others, down to his own time, giving more than half a score in all. Plutarch furnishes a similar list. Thus it appears that the principal of the Greek historians, philosophers, and poets visited Egypt for the express purpose of studying its customs, institutions, and whatever else was worthy to be known. And we find, in corroboration of these statements, very many things in Grecian mythology and science credited to that people. More than a dozen Grecian and Roman writers speak of Egypt in their works. Some, as Herodotus and Diodorus, go into details respecting the history of the country and its laws; others, as Plutarch, dwell more on matters pertaining to religion and the gods; others, still, speak of its language, pyramids, and other monuments. Now, when we consider the eminently practical character of the Greek mind, what those writers said of Egypt is of great importance in our discussion, although we may often be sorely vexed at the meagerness of the information they furnish on particular points, when they evidently had the means and the opportunity of giving us the very knowledge we seek.

In exhibiting the accounts which these writers have left us, it will be convenient to divide them into two classes — those which relate to prehistoric times, and those which relate to historic times. The time of separation between these has usually been placed at the reign of Menes, the first mortal king, though there is some evidence that Menes himself is a mythological personage.

I. The Prehistoric Times of Egypt.

The following are among the testimonies of ancient writers on this subject: —

From Diogenes Laertius (Int. § 2).

"The Egyptians say that Vulcan was the son of Nilus, and that he was the author of philosophy. . . . From his age to that of Alexander, king of the Macedonians, were forty-eight thousand eight hundred and sixty-three years, and, during this time, there were three hundred and seventy-three eclipses of the sun, and eight hundred and thirty-two eclipses of the moon."

From Diodorus Siculus (I. i. § 14).

"The priests of Egypt, summing up the time from the reign of Helius (the sun) to the passage of Alexander into Asia, find it more than twenty-three thousand years."

From Herodotus (II. 43).

"But there was a certain ancient god with the Egyptians, by name Hercules. Seventeen thousand years before the reign of Amasis, the twelve gods were, they affirm, produced from the eight, and, of these twelve, Hercules is one."

From Pomponius Mela (Cory's Anc. Fragments, p. 163).

"The Egyptians, according to their own accounts, are the most ancient of men, and they reckon, in their series of annals, three hundred and thirty kings, who reigned above thirteen thousand years."

From the "Old Chronicle." *

This venerable document is reported to us by George Syncellus, a Greek writer of the ninth century. It professes to give the duration of thirty dynasties of Egyptian kings, covering a period of thirty-six thousand five hundred and twenty-five years. The first fourteen of these belonged to prehistoric times, embracing thirty-four thousand two hundred and one years. According to this Chronicle, only the last sixteen of the thirty dynasties belong to historic times, which are made to commence about B. C. 2043.

From Eusebius.

This distinguished historian and chronologer devotes a chapter in his "Chronicon" (book i. ch. 20) to Egyp-

* See page 73.

tian chronology, expressly mentioning MANETHO * as his authority. He makes the reigns of the gods, from Vulcan (Hephaistus) to Bytis, to have been thirteen thousand nine hundred years, and those of demigods, manes, heroes, and other kings of the same age, eleven thousand years — in all, twenty-four thousand nine hundred years. He then gives an account of the so-called thirty-one dynasties, beginning with Menes, the first mortal king, who, according to the numbers mentioned, — if the dynasties are regarded as consecutive, — began his reign about B. C. 5500, thus carrying back the full antiquity of the Egyptian people to about 30,500 B. C.

From Julius Africanus.

This writer was a learned chronologer of the second century after Christ. He gives us a version of Manetho, which, so far as relates to the mythologic times of Egypt, differs, in essential particulars, from that of Eusebius. He states the reigns of the gods, beginning with Hephaistus, — whose sway was nine thousand years, — to have been eleven thousand nine hundred and eighty-five years, and those of the demigods, heroes, and manes, to have been eight hundred and fifty-three years.† Then follow

---

* The great differences that appear in the statements of the different writers who, in the matter of Egyptian history and chronology, have professed to take Manetho as authority, are an anomaly in literature.

† There is some doubt how far the details of this account are to be ascribed to Africanus, and how far to later historians and

the thirty-one dynasties, more nearly agreeing with the account of Eusebius. What is worthy of note in this connection is, that these two writers agree in putting the reigns of the gods, demigods, and manes *before* the so-called thirty-one dynasties, while other accounts, as that of the " Old Chronicle " and Castor, *include* them within the latter.

From Castor.

This was a heathen writer, who is believed to have flourished in the second century before Christ.* He also expressly mentions Manetho as his authority. According to him, the duration of the reigns of the gods was fifteen hundred and fifty years; then, of the demigods, heroes, and manes, twenty-one thousand years. Thus Egyptian prehistoric times, as measured by this writer, amount to but thirty-six hundred and fifty years, although the numbers he gives in the summing up do not agree with the details. The fragment of his work which has come down to us is, however, so corrupted that his statements are often self-contradictory. Like the preceding

chronologers, as Panodorus, Anianus, and Syncellus. The statements of Syncellus are not always definite, so that we can not determine whether he is giving his own language or that of another. There is scarcely room for doubt, however, that the numbers above given are, for the most part, correctly ascribed to Africanus.

* The chronological work of a Castor, supposed to be this author, is referred to by Apollodorus, who died about B. C. 140. — *Smith's Dict. Gr. and Rom. Biog.*, art. *Castor.*

authors, he makes Hephaistus, or Vulcan, the first of the gods, and Menes the first of the mortal kings. He enumerates only seventeen dynasties."

What, now, is the practical value of this testimony in determining the problem before us? How far does it go to prove the existence of man on earth, at a period antecedent to the date assigned to his creation in the Scriptures?

That these accounts are not to be taken *literally* is evident upon the face of them. It would be an insult to the understanding of my readers to assure them that gods, i. e., superhuman beings, demigods (persons half divine and half human), and *manes* (which are the spirits or ghosts of the dead), did, in fact, reign over men on the earth at any time, or during any period. Yet, strange as it may seem, there have been writers of eminence who have actually made these accounts the basis of their chronology, and taken them into their systems as having some substantial value. How true is the remark, that no persons manifest so much credulity in the acceptance of extravagant and impossible theories, as those who profess themselves incredulous of the statements of the Bible!

The worthlessness of these stories, as an element of chronology, is also shown by the *discrepancies* between them. The duration of the reign of the gods, &c., is variously stated to be all the way between thirty-six hundred and fifty and forty-eight thousand eight hundred and sixty-three years. There can be little doubt that these historians faithfully reported the accounts given them, either orally or in the sacred books. How evident it is, then, that those original authorities were utterly untrustworthy! — either that the earlier Egyptian records were not understood in the times of Herodotus, Diodorus, and Manetho,* or that the work of Manetho himself has been so abridged and corrupted by epitomizers, through whose writings alone it appears to have been known after the times of Josephus, that it is now of little or no value for purposes of accurate chronology.

There is, however, a mode of estimating these long prehistoric periods which should be adverted to in this place. "We know," says Palmer (Egyp.

---

* Dr. Samuel Birch, of the British Museum, in his translation of the "Book of the Dead," says, "The new exegetical researches into the hieratic papyri have contributed to throw additional light on many obscure passages; but there are others, the meaning of which will probably long remain ambiguous — a circumstance not to be wondered at when it is remembered that the correct or ancient reading was so to the Egyptians themselves at a very early period of their theology." — *Additional Notes*, p. 333.

Chron. vol. i. p. 30), "that under the Ptolemies and the Romans the idea existed that the vast periods of the Egyptians, of the Chronicle, and of Manetho in particular, had been swelled to their apparent bulk by counting, for the earlier spaces of time, months under the name of years." Herodotus and Plato, or Eudoxus, no less than later writers, had heard that the earliest Egyptian "years" were months of thirty days: "Εἰ δὲ καὶ ὅ φησιν Εὔδοξος ἀληθὲς, ὅτι Αἰγύπτιοι τὸν μῆνα ἐνιαυτὸν ἐκάλουν, οὐκ ἂν ἡ τῶν πολλῶν τούτων ἐνιαυτῶν ἀπαρίθμησις ἔχοι τι θαυμαστόν." * (Proclus. in Tim. p. 31, l. 50.) Diodorus Siculus adds more particularly that, according to some, the long reigns of the earlier gods, who had above 1200 years each, were composed of *months* of thirty days, not real years; and those of the later gods, who had over 300 years each, were composed of *seasons*,† of four months each, the native Egyptian year being divided into three seasons, of spring, summer, and winter, not four, like the Greek. On this ground, Eusebius reduced the whole period of the gods, demigods, and manes, to 2,206 years, which is *an approximation to the space from the creation to the deluge, according to the Septuagint chronology.*

---

* "And if Eudoxus reports correctly, that the Egyptians call a month a year, the reckoning of those many years would not contain anything wonderful."   † ὧραι.

The "Old Chronicle" allots 34,201 years to the ante-human reigns, which, reduced upon the same principle, amounts to 2765 solar years. Thus interpreted, we obtain a clew to the actual duration of the mythological period of the ancient Egyptians, viz., that there had been a space of between two and three thousand years from the creation to the commencement of the Egyptian monarchy.

This, certainly, is a possible explanation of the matter. I know, indeed, that Bunsen mentions it with a sneer, and dismisses it as not entitled to a moment's thought. He regards it as a mere expedient of Christian chronographers to bring the chronology of Egypt into harmony with that of the Jewish Scriptures. Wilkinson likewise says that this ground is untenable. But the explanation was not first made by Christian writers. When Herodotus, Diodorus, and others spoke of it as an ancient method of reckoning time, they doubtless had evidence of the fact, which may now be lost; and they manifestly give it as a fact, and not as a mere opinion of their own.

Such a mode of reckoning time would, at first, be the most natural and easy. It is, in fact, that of almost all uncultivated nations to this day. The revolutions of the moon are more obvious and definite than those of the earth, the diurnal excepted, and the supposition is more than plausible, that, in the earliest ages, the lunar measure of time would prevail.

Besides, if this mode of explaining the immense periods of Egyptian chronology be rejected, what is the true one? Let those who sneer at this tell us what those periods do mean. Do those thirteen thousand nine hundred years of the reign of the gods signify a real condition of men and things on earth? Did the twelve hundred and fifty-five years' sway of the demigods — beings whose fathers were gods and mothers women, or vice versa — cover an actual state of affairs in this world? So with the fifty-eight hundred and thirteen years attributed to the demigods and manes. What is the practical meaning of these? Perhaps our friends the "spiritualists" can explain them. I cannot. Perhaps they may find in these old Egyptian legends evidence of the actual participation of departed spirits in the affairs of men. Be it so. But a sober student of history and chronology, when confronted with myths like these, cannot help asking some questions in regard to them which are not so easily disposed of. And the only rational conclusion he can reach is, that as to determining the actual existence of man on earth, unless upon the supposition that they involve other than the usual modes of reckoning, they are utterly worthless.

It has been sometimes said that ancient nations have forged the large periods of their early annals for the express purpose of gratifying their pride of a high antiquity. But I doubt the assertion. Such a motive would imply an appreciation of the value of history in the true sense of the term. And when such an appreciation is reached by any people, it is too late to falsify it; or, if falsification were attempted, it could not be perpetuated. Still, if any one should maintain that, in remote prehistoric times, some bard or story-teller invented these large Egyptian numbers, and gave them currency *before* the true idea and value of history had been attained, I should have no controversy with him. But I have a controversy with those who accept these numbers as any part of authenticated history, and weave them into systems of chronology claiming our confidence or respect.

Before leaving the prehistoric times of Egypt, I should allude to certain evidence supposed to be derived from astronomical inscriptions upon the temples corroborative of the alleged extreme antiquity of that people. Among these was the famous Zodiac of Denderah, which attracted so much attention a few years ago.* The following narrative concern-

* Though the pretensions based upon this zodiac are now so completely exploded, yet it is still adduced by some as proving a

ing it is from the pen of a learned writer, who had a personal knowledge of some of the things of which he speaks, and was familiar with the whole subject: —

"Some time about the year 1798, General Bonaparte, with his host of French soldiery and a number of literary men, entered the small town of Denderah, in Central Egypt, and found there a large and small temple, in a good state of preservation, both of which were decorated with images of deities and hieroglyphics. The literary men copied the drawings as well as their time would permit, but they secured the whole ceiling of the smaller, flat temple, by cutting out the stone slab by means of a saw. They were also fortunate enough in getting the old, black, and smoky stone — which, by the way, had the length and breadth of the ceiling of a middle-sized room — safe to Paris. Arrived here, the literati went to work in deciphering the inscriptions and figures of both temples. And what did they make of them?

"Why, they thought, from the inscriptions, that both temples must be at least 17,000 years old, and tried to prove this by their astronomical calculations — in short, made it mathematically sure. Volume after volume was then published on this subject. But in this case, as in many others, the reckoning had been made without their

high date for the human occupancy of the Nile valley. Since these pages were written, a gentleman urged it to prove to me the incorrectness of the Mosaic chronology. For this reason I refer to it in this place.

host, for men of letters could not agree altogether. Some considered the stone older, and others of less age; but all united on one point, that both temples at Denderah must have stood before the great deluge, and even the creation. A certain professor of the University of Breslau edited, for instance, a pamphlet, entitled 'Invincible Proof that our Earth is at least ten times older than taught by the Bible.' More than fifty publications, of a similar purport, have treated of the temples of Denderah. Besides these, a host of newspaper writers trumpeted the great discovery of the nineteenth century, in innumerable sheets and periodicals all over Europe.

"The stone of Denderah was kept, at this time, in the National Library at Paris, and was visited by hundreds of thousands of the curious, all anxious to see the antediluvian monument. But King Charles X. was compelled, at last, to place it in a dark chamber, because the crowd became too large and unruly. This naturally caused a great deal of grumbling, because the king and priesthood had combined, as they said, to keep the people from becoming enlightened.

"This was a time of woe for a small band of Christians, and of great rejoicing for the infidels of all countries. 'You credulous fools,' railed they, 'don't you see how you have been imposed upon by the wily priesthood, with the chronology of your "Word of God"? There was never a deluge, nor a creation, at least not at the period stated by the Bible. Now you can see that the Old and New Testaments contain, from beginning to end, a series of lies!' Nobody was able, in those times, to gainsay so many books of learning, and many poor Christians were led astray."

The author then proceeds to explain the method by which so great an antiquity was deduced from the inscription. They found certain marks, from which they *inferred* that the vernal equinox, at the time the temple was erected, was between the signs Cancer and Leo, of the zodiac, and, as the equinoxes recede at the rate of about fifty seconds a year, or one degree in seventy-two years, a simple calculation showed that it must have been at the point supposed not less than 17,000 years ago. Hence the date of the temple, and hence, too, the demonstration that the Bible was false! But alas for pretensions so confident! When Champollion, having discovered the mode of deciphering the hieroglyphics, examined this famous zodiac, he read upon it the name and titles of *Augustus Cæsar*, showing that its origin was no more ancient than the Christian era. And this conclusion has been abundantly confirmed by others. Thus Letronne,* having recited some of the principal facts, particularly in relation to a zodiac found in a mummy-case, — precisely like that at Denderah, — on which was

---

* Recueil des Inscriptions, Grecques et Latines, de l'Egypt. Paris, 1842. Introd. p. 20.

traced a Greek inscription, giving the name of the deceased, and date of his death, which was the nineteenth year of Trajan, remarks, —

"Thus it was demonstrated that all the zodiacal representations which existed in Egypt are found only upon monuments of the Greek and Roman periods, and that none of those of Pharaonic times — temples, tombs, or mummies — offer the least trace of them; from which results the evident proof that the zodiac, so far from having originated in Egypt, as was generally believed, after the opinion of Dupuis, was a stranger in that country till after it had passed through the hands of the Greeks."

The same writer adds, in another work,* that, in his opinion, all the six Egyptian zodiacs which have been discovered were posterior to the reign of Tiberius, and were "executed in the space of less than one hundred years — between 57 and 150 of our era."

Similar results have been derived from an examination of four wooden *tablets* brought from Egypt by Rev. Henry Stobart in 1854.† These measured each four by two and a half inches, and were covered on both sides with quintuple columns of demotic characters, which proved to be a series of

---

* Sur l'Origine Grecque des zodiaques pretendus Egyptiennes. Paris, 1837.

† Dr. J. P. Thompson, in Bib. Sacra, vol. xiv. pp. 651–654.

observations upon the places of the five planets in the signs of the zodiac. The reading of these tablets by the eminent Egyptologists Brugsch and Lepsius affords a curious example of the different conclusions reached by the masters of Egyptian interpretation. In regard to four out of the five planets, the two are in entire disagreement, that of Mars alone being the same in both readings.

M. Brugsch submitted a careful translation of these tablets to some of the leading astronomers of Europe, and received a reply from M. Biot, of Paris, transmitting the calculations of Mr. Ellis, of the Greenwich Observatory, to the effect that "these are, without doubt, records of the places of the planets. Those which he has restored extend *from the year* 105 *to the year* 114 *of our era*. This last point corresponds with the close of the reign of Trajan in Egypt." Mr. Biot adds, "That these notations of planetary places were made after actual observations seems to me not at all probable. In fact, for this there must have been, in the time of Trajan, at Thebes or Memphis, a grand observatory, manned by accomplished observers, well appointed with instruments, and making constant note of the movements of the planets; all things of which there is no trace in Egypt at that epoch except at Alexandria, and there only to a limited extent.

I therefore incline to regard these tablets as having been the note-book (*calepin*) or the year-book of a Roman or Greek astrologer living in Egypt, who thus inscribed for his own use the places of the planets calculated in advance, according to the Greek astronomy, merely transforming the dates of the vague year into corresponding dates of the fixed year." *

Enough has now been said to show the fallacy of any conclusion respecting the antiquity of our race, drawn from the mythologic period of Egyptian chronolgy. We come next to consider, —

II. The Historic Times of Egypt.

It is almost universally admitted that historic times in Egypt began with Menes, although, for myself, I cannot, as heretofore remarked, but regard him more as a mythological than an historical personage. But, conceding for the present the common view, that he was the founder of the Egyptian empire, the inquiry before us is, When did he live?

And here it is important to remark that Egyptian chronology *has no dates*. There was no common era, like that of the Greek olympiads, or of the founding of Rome, or our own Christian era, to

* Ibidem.

which events were referred, and the time of their occurrence noted. Sometimes the year of the reigning monarch is mentioned, but neither this, nor the date of the dynasty of which this was a part, was recorded. The only mode, then, in which the foundation of the empire may be even approximately ascertained, is by summing up the whole number of reigns, and the duration of each, as given us in the lists of Manetho. The importance of these lists, as lying at the very foundation of Egyptian chronology, requires some particular notice, both of them and their author.

Manetho was a high priest of the temple of Isis at Sebennytus, a town in Lower Egypt, in the time of Ptolemy Philadelphus, about B. C. 276. He wrote a history of Egypt, in three books, which he professed to have derived from sacred writings preserved in the temples, which had been handed down from ancient times. His original work is now lost, but portions of it were incorporated by Julius Africanus, in a work on chronology, written in the third century, and transmitted to us in another work on the same subject by George Syncellus,* a writer at Constantinople, of the ninth century. Another version of Manetho is found in the writings of Eusebius, the church historian, of which some fragments

---

* See Appendix, D.

are also given by Syncellus, and a more perfect copy, in Armenian, found at Constantinople, and published in 1818. Some suppose that Eusebius copied from Africanus, but the differences between them make this improbable. It is more likely that both of them copied from epitomes of Manetho's work, and that these differences existed in those epitomes themselves. The charge of arbitrarily altering the numbers, etc., of his authorities, so often made against Eusebius, is not well sustained, at least to the extent alleged by Bunsen and some others.

The following is a summary of the dynasties, with the number of reigns in each, and their duration, as given by Manetho in the two versions above described.* Those marked * in the list of Eusebius are transcribed from Africanus: —

Dyn.	According to Africanus. Name.	No. of Kings.	Years	Dyn.	According to Eusebius. Name.	No. of Kings.	Years
I.	Thinite,	8	253	I.	Thinite,	8	*253
II.	Thinite,	9	302	II.	Thinite,	9	297
III.	Memphite,	9	214	III.	Memphite,	8	197
IV.	Memphite,	8	274	IV.	Memphite,	17	448
V.	Elephantine	9	248	V.	Elephantine,	31	*248
VI.	Memphite,	6	203	VI.	Memphite,*	*6	203
VII.	Memphite,	70	70 dy's	VII.	Memphite,	5	75
VIII.	Memphite,	27	146	VIII.	Memphite,	9	100
IX.	Heracleopolite,	19	409	IX.	Heracleopolite,	4	100
X.	Heracleopolite,	19	185	X.	Heracleopolite,	19	185
XI.	Diospolite,	16	43	XI.	Diospolite,	16	43
XII.	Diospolite,	7	160	XII.	Diospolite,	7	245
XIII.	Diospolite,	60	453	XIII.	Diospolite,	60	453

* See Appendix, E.

Dyn.	According to Africanus. Name.	No. of Kings.	Years.	Dyn.	According to Eusebius. Name.	No. of Kings.	Years.
XIV.	Xoite,	76	184	XIV.	Xoite,	76	484
XV.	Shepherds,	6	284	XV.	Diospolite,	6	250
XVI	Shepherds,	32	518	XVI.	Theban,	5	190
XVII.	Shepherds and Diospolites,	86	151	XVII.	Shepherds,	4	103
XVIII.	Diospolite,	16	263	XVIII.	Diospolite,	14	348
XIX.	Diospolite,	7	209	XIX.	Diospolite,	5	194
XX.	Diospolite.	12	135	XX.	Diospolite,	12	172
XXI.	Tanite,	7	130	XXI.	Tanite,	7	130
XXII.	Bubastite,	9	120	XXII.	Bubastite,	3	49
XXIII.	Tanite,	4	89	XXIII.	Tanite,	3	44
XXIV.	Saite,	1	44	XXIV.	Saite,	1	44
XXV.	Ethiopian,	3	40	XXV.	Ethiopian,	3	40
XXVI.	Saite,	9	150	XXVI.	Saite,	9	167
XXVII.	Persian,	8	124	XXVII.	Persian,	8	124
XXVIII.	Saite,	1	6	XXVIII.	Saite,	1	6
XXIX.	Mendesian,	4	20	XXIX.	Mendesian,	5	21
XXX.	Sebennyte,	3	38	XXX.	Sebennyte,	3	20
XXXI.	Persian,	3	9	XXXI.	Persian,	3	16
		554	5,404			367	5249

Without noticing now the discrepancies between these lists, and assuming, as is generally done, that that given by Africanus is to be preferred, we have only to ascertain the date of their termination at the close of the XXXIst dynasty, and add to this the whole number of years covered by them to arrive at the age of Menes. The XXXIst dynasty ended with the death of Nectanebus, fifteen years before the accession of Alexander of Macedon, B. C. 339.* The whole duration of the monarchy being 5404 years, we arrive at the conclusion that Menes began to reign 5743 years before the Christian era, which was at least sixty-two years before the creation, according to the Septuagint chronology. This date

* Smith's Dict. Gr. and Rom. Geog., art. *Ægyptus.*

is otherwise fixed, owing to different readings of the lists, by Rodier at B. C. 5853, by Boëckh at B. C. 5702, by Lenormant at B. C. 5004, by Brugsch at B. C. 4555, etc.

1. We know nothing as to the truthfulness of the *original sources* from which Manetho professed to derive his account. His authority was the priests, and the sacred books under their care. But we know from Herodotus what incredible stories the priests were wont to relate to inquisitive travelers, — tales of mingled fact and fable too gross even for those who were in quest of the marvelous and strange to believe. We know not whence the priests derived their information in the first place, how truthful they were in recording and transmitting it, or with what fidelity and accuracy Manetho himself transcribed it. The very first elements are wanting of a basis for an intelligent belief of the document.

2. Even if the account were originally true, it has evidently become so *corrupt* that it is now utterly impossible to determine what its genuine contents were. The copies we have, all come to us at second or third hand, and present the greatest

discrepancies with each other. Bunsen exhibits a tabular view of these in the three leading versions: first, of Africanus; second, of Eusebius, as quoted by Syncellus; and third, of Eusebius, as translated from the Armenian. These three contain about one hundred numbers, in less than twenty of which is there entire harmony in all the versions. Two of the three harmonize in some eight or ten more. The number of reigns varies from 366 — some say from 288 — to 554; their aggregate duration from 4922 to 5404 years. Granting, then, that what Manetho actually wrote is to be received, the question still remains undecided, What *did* he write? In the present multiplicity of versions and of readings, nobody can tell. Sober criticism can not employ them to fix a single date.

3. The lists themselves bear *internal evidence* of their untrustworthiness. They relate the reigns of the gods, and demigods, and ghosts as positively, and with the same exact report of the years embraced in them, as in the case of the human monarchs who succeeded them. Many whole dynasties, covering, together, nearly 2000 years, show not the name of a single king. It gravely records that the Nile flowed with honey for eleven days, that one dynasty of seventy kings reigned just seventy days, and that, under one reign, a lamb

spoke — stories evidently no better than old wives' fables. It is, besides, self-contradictory. The sum of the years assigned to the several kings of a dynasty often differs from the alleged duration of the dynasty itself, and the aggregate duration of all the dynasties it expressly declares was only 3555 years, which is 1849 less than the footing of the details.* A document exhibiting within itself such evidences of untruthfulness, is utterly unworthy of confidence. Only the most unbounded credulity can give to it any weight of authority.

4. The statements of Manetho are abundantly contradicted and refuted by other authority of far greater reliability than they.

(*a*.) The first is that of the *Old Chronicle*, so called. Syncellus, who transmitted to us the lists of Manetho, as above related (p. 68), states as follows (pp. 51, 52): "There is extant among the Egyptians a certain *Old Chronicle*, the source, as I suppose, which led Manetho astray, — ἐξ οὗ καὶ τὸν Μανεθῶ πεπλανῆσθαι νομίζω, — exhibiting thirty dynasties, and again one hundred and thirteen generations, with an infinite space of time, — not the same, either, as that of Manetho, — viz., three myriads six thousand five hundred and twenty-five years, first of the Æritæ, secondly of the Mestræans, and thirdly of

---

* See page 70.

Egyptians."* Of these 36,525 years, it proceeds to say the first fifteen dynasties are of gods (Æritæ) and demigods (Mestræans), who together reigned 34,644 years, leaving the human period to begin with the XVIth dynasty, and extending only 1881 years. This, Syncellus says, "is accounted the oldest Egyptian document," — αὕτη μὲν ἡ παλαιοτέρα νομιζομένη Αἰγυπτίων συγγραφή, — i. e., probably the oldest written in Greek. It was, according to this author, one of the documents consulted by Manetho in making up his lists, in regard to which he made the mistake of reckoning all the dynasties, instead of the last fifteen only, as mortal kings, and carrying up the beginning of the monarchy 3523 years above the date at which it was set by the Chronicle — a very grave mistake truly, and rendering the list, as usually read, entirely worthless. According to this venerable document, therefore, the true date of Menes is B. C. 2220.

(*b.*) Nearly contemporary with Manetho was the distinguished scholar, historian, and critic *Eratosthenes*, who wrote an important work on the history of Egypt, of which portions are preserved to us in the writings of Apollodorus, an equally eminent scholar of the succeeding century. Bunsen (vol. i. pp. 119–121) styles Eratosthenes "the father of chronology and geography," and says, —

* See Appendix, F.

"Everything relative to Egypt, emanating from a man of such rare talent and extensive learning, is deserving of the highest respect. Besides which, we must also reflect that for the history of Egypt, above that of all other countries, every attainable material was at his disposal. Born in the 126th Olympiad, about B. C. 276, in the early part, therefore, of the reign of Philadelphus, he succeeded, probably under Evergetes, to the honorable post of director of the Alexandrian Library, which he filled to the time of his death, in his eightieth or eighty-second year. The very researches to which our attention is here directed, were undertaken by the command of the king, consequently with every advantage that royal patronage could procure for the investigation from the Egyptian priests."

Of Apollodorus, also, Bunsen speaks in terms scarcely less eulogistic. The testimony of these eminent scholars is reported to us by Syncellus, as follows: —

"The chronographer Apollodorus has written of another kingdom (Egyptian) of thirty-eight Theban kings, so called, amounting to 1076 years, which began at the 2900th, and ended in the 3975th (3976th) year of the world, the knowledge of which he says Eratosthenes derived from Egyptian records and lists of names, and by royal command translated into Greek, thus." Then, after reciting the names, he adds, "The dominion ($ἀρχή$) of the thirty-eight kings, called, in Egypt, Theban, whose names Eratosthenes received from the sacred scribes in Diospolis, and translated from Egyptian into Greek, ended here, having begun at the 2900th year of the world, — 124 years after the confusion of tongues, — and terminating at this 3975th (3976th) year of the world. But the names of the fifty-three other Theban kings after these, I think it needless to give here, since they are nothing to my purpose, as, indeed, is true of those already given."

According to this eminent authority, therefore, the entire Egyptian monarchy extended through only ninety-one reigns, instead of the several hundred claimed for it by Manetho. It is true that Bunsen denies that the fifty-three unnamed kings reached down to the close of the empire, and insists that they belong to what he calls the " Middle Kingdom," extending from the XIIth to the XVIIIth dynasty. In this, however, he stands alone, so far as I am aware. He concedes, however, that the thirty-eight reigns cover the first twelve dynasties; and there is decisive evidence from the monuments, as we shall presently see, that the XVIIIth dynasty immediately succeeded the XIIth, the intermediate ones either not existing at all, or being scattered in fragments, contemporaneous with those preceding or following. In this view the so-called Middle Kingdom wholly disappears. The fifty-three unnamed kings of Eratosthenes, then, probably covered the remainder of the monarchy from the beginning of the XVIIIth dynasty, which may be the reason why Syncellus deemed it unnecessary to name them, as they agreed substantially with Manetho's lists (in Eusebius). At any rate, the fact is admitted by Lepsius,* one of the greatest Egyptologers, and can not well be disputed.

This period, according to Africanus, was 1377 years, which, added to the 1076 of the preceding thirty-eight reigns, makes the entire duration of the monarchy 2453 years, and, dating back from Alexander, B. C. 340, carries the age of Menes to B. C. 2793, or 362 years after the flood, which sufficiently harmonizes with the Scripture chronology.†

(*c.*) Our next authority on the point before us is *Josephus*, the eminent Jewish historian, who, for the elegance and vigor of his style, has been named the Greek Livy. His work, entitled "Against Apion," is a vindication of the antiquity of his nation from

---

* He points out the important fact that, according to Syncellus,. there were just fifty-three kings from Amosis I., who expelled the Shepherds, to Amosis II., the contemporary of Cambyses.

† Bunsen himself places the beginning of the XVIIIth dynasty at B. C. 1633, which all admit to be near the truth. Thus, instead of carrying up the era of Menes, as he does, to B. C. 3623, or 3059, we bring it down by the list of Eratosthenes to (1633 + 1076) B. C. 2709. See Appendix, G.

the charge that it had not been mentioned by Greek historians. In this work he refers to Manetho by name, and gives, professedly verbatim, long extracts from him.* In comparing these with what we have of that author, we find very little resemblance between them. Of the narrative portion cited by Josephus there is absolutely nothing. His list of kings, twenty-five in all, begins with the XVth dynasty of Africanus, and ends with the early part of the XXth — a period to which Manetho assigns ninety-eight kings. In Eusebius it begins with the XVIIth dynasty, and includes a period of but nineteen kings. The whole duration of these reigns in Josephus is 492 years, in Africanus 1216, in Eusebius 451. Nothing more, surely, is needed to show how utterly unworthy of confidence are the lists of Manetho. There is no reason to believe that Josephus did not give, literally, his extracts, as he professed to do, or that his works, which have been otherwise so well preserved, have been corrupted. He evidently had what he regarded as the original work before him. We see not how to avoid the conclusion, that Africanus and Eusebius, or Syncellus, who reported them, used some abridgment or epitome made by some other person, either a bungling transcriber, a willful falsifier, or an impos-

* See Appendix, II.

tor, who put forth his own work under the stolen name of Manetho.

(*d.*) The lists before us are not sustained by the evidence furnished by the *monuments*. We have no space to exhibit this fact in detail, and must be content with some general statements. The first is, that but a small portion of the names given by Manetho can be identified. Of the 554 in Africanus, or 367 in Eusebius, occurring in the first seventeen dynasties, Bunsen, with his utmost ingenuity, does not pretend to have identified more than 110, Lepsius about as many, Poole only 76, etc. No trace whatever is found of dynasties VII., VIII., IX., X., XIII., XIV., XV. Euseb., XVI., XVII. Afric. A period of Egyptian history, midway in its splendid career of art and arms, as long as the interval from Alfred the Great to Victoria, has left not a single fact or monument, nor even a *grave*, to attest its existence. Even Bunsen admits that it is "improbable and unexampled that a foreign people (the so-called "Shepherds") should maintain themselves in Egypt for nine, or even five centuries, and have lived so like barbarians that not a single monument of theirs can be pointed out." "But this," adds Canon Trevor,[*] "is far from stating the entire marvel. Not only is no Hyksos monument remaining,

[*] Ancient Egypt, p. 262.

but none belonging to the native princes, their tributaries. Not one pyramid, obelisk, temple, palace, or tomb, nor the fragment of one, can be found for the whole period. Not that Egyptian art had as yet no existence, for the works of the IVth and XIIth dynasties attest its progress up to the time in question. Not that it was then suddenly and permanently quenched under the inroad of the barbarians, for Bunsen himself observes that, 'at the end of this period, which is longer, perhaps, than the duration of the historical life of most modern people, the old Egyptian empire comes forth again in renovated youth, and in fact, as the monuments prove, with its national peculiarities, its religion, its language, its writing, its art, in precisely the same condition as if no interruption had occurred, or, at most, nothing beyond the temporary inroad of some Bedouin robbers!'" Nay, more; the tablet of Abydos clearly shows that such a period never existed. The escutcheon or cartouche, bearing the name and titles of Amosis, the first sovereign of the XVIIIth dynasty, stands there immediately after that of Ammenemes, the last of the XIIth. Not a single monument remains which can positively be assigned a date earlier than Sesonchosis, or Sheshonk, of the XXIId dynasty — the Shishak of the Scriptures, who was contemporary with Rehoboam, about B. C. 972.

Doubtless the pyramids and many other structures are much older, but they bear no independent data of their own by which their real age can be determined, much less that carry us back within 500 years of the flood.

But, while these lists of Manetho are thus, by numerous proofs, shown to be utterly unreliable, as establishing a positive chronology of Egypt, we do not think it necessary, on the other hand, to discard them altogether. The truth seems to be that, originally, they were a collection of names of sovereigns, handed down by tradition, with such exaggerations and additions as would naturally be made in the progress of time, who were believed to have reigned somewhere and at some time in that country. That portion which is earlier than the XVIIIth dynasty may be related to true history, much as the names transmitted from the semi-fabulous periods of England, the Briton, Welsh, and Saxon chieftains, who for a thousand years before the Norman conquest exercised a sway more or less extensive in that island, are related to the authentic records of later times. But what historian would gravely undertake, by grouping these names into "dynasties," and counting up their number, and the alleged years of their reign, to arrive at the foundation of monarchy in England, or the exact date at which its first inhabitants came thither!

There is another consideration of much importance in this connection. Even if we concede that the persons embraced in the lists really existed and reigned in Egypt, it does not follow that their reigns were all *consecutive*. The contrary supposition seems every way probable. "Egypt," says Osborn (Mon. Hist. vol. i. p. 183), "on its first settlement, was divided into nomes or provinces. The boundaries of these nomes, and the customs and usages of each of them, were component parts of the common law of Egypt at all periods of its history. What, therefore, is more probable, — we had almost said more certain, — than that, in the first place, the founder of each new city would be accounted the king of it, and of the nome or district that surrounded it? This was the case on the settlement of all other countries in the ancient world,* and that Egypt would not depart from this universal rule is the highest of all conceivable probabilities." It has been claimed, however, that Manetho has made due allowance for this state of things, and excluded from his list all merely contemporary reigns. Says M. Mariette, "It would certainly be contrary to established facts to pretend that, from the days of Menes to the Greek conquest, Egypt always formed one united kingdom, and it is possible that unexpected

---

* Gen. chaps. 10, 14, 36, etc.

discoveries may one day prove that throughout nearly the whole duration of this vast empire, there were even more collateral dynasties than the partisans of that system now contend for. But everything shows us that the work of elimination has been already performed on the lists of Manetho, in the state in which they have reached us. If, in fact, these lists contained the collateral dynasties, we should find in them, either before or after the XXIst, the dynasty of high priests who reigned at Thebes, while the XXIst occupied Tanis. In the same way we should have to count, either before or after the XXIIId, the seven or eight independent kings who were contemporary with it, and who, if Manetho had not rejected them, would have added as many successive royal families to the lists of the Egyptian priest, the dodecarchy for one, at least, between the XXVth and XXVIth dynasties, and, finally, the Theban kings, rivals of the Shepherds, would have taken rank before or after the XVIIth. There were, therefore, incontestably contemporaneous dynasties in Egypt; but Manetho has thrown them out, and admitted those only whom he regarded as legitimate, and his lists contain no others. If it were not so, it would not be thirty-one dynasties that we should have to reckon in the list of royal families previous to Alexander, but probably nearer sixty."

We submit that this reasoning is not conclusive. If the unsettled state of the monarchy, during its long existence, was such as to make necessary the cutting down of its royal annals one half,—from sixty to thirty-one dynasties,—what evidence is there that it did not require a further curtailment? That such is the fact, is agreed by the great body of Egyptologers, though they may differ as to how much and where it should be made.

Our conclusion, then, is very certain. We look in vain into the history and antiquities of Egypt for any evidence whatever of the existence of man earlier than the time of Noah. According to the Septuagint chronology, we may allow full thirty centuries between that time and the Christian era, a period amply sufficient to account for every known trace of man in the valley of the Nile.

CHAPTER III.

THE ARGUMENT FROM HISTORY (*continued*).

II. GREECE AND ROME.

Identity of Origin between the Greeks and Romans. — Practical Character of the Greek Mind. — Greek Literature comprehended all known Science. — Date of the First Olympiad. — Mythological Character of Times preceding. — The Trojan War. — Its Value in History and Chronology. — No Claim to an Antiquity exceeding Eighteen Centuries before Christ. — Date of the Foundation of Rome.

THE Greeks and Romans were so connected in their origin, as is indicated by their language, religion, and mythology, that a separate consideration of their respective antiquities is not required by my present object. Indeed, the mythologic or prehistoric traditions of the two peoples are so interwoven and so nearly identical, that a separate consideration of them would scarcely be possible. It will be necessary, therefore, to exhibit only the fuller and older traditions embodied in the Greek literature, to show all that has a bearing on our subject.

The evidence drawn from this source, in relation to the antiquity of our race, is of great importance, in some respects more important than that afforded us by the literature of any other ancient nation. For the Greeks were eminently practical. History and philosophy, as well as poetry, were cultivated by them, and their writings embody nearly all that was known in their times. A literature which has preserved in its poetry the most ancient traditions of the race, in its philosophical speculations the researches of the wisest men in antiquity as to the origin of things, and in its history all that the most learned men and travelers knew of other nations and people as well as their own, can scarcely fail to afford much valuable evidence in relation to the inquiry before us. We have already seen that we are indebted to it for nearly all the information we have of Egyptian antiquities, and its testimony can not be less trustworthy concerning those of Greece and Rome.

Omitting, for the present, what is purely mythological, the highest date in Grecian history, which is accurately fixed, is the first Olympiad, usually called the Olympiad of Chorœbus, B. C. 776. There was history before that time, but no accurate chronology. Many things are recorded, and many actual events described, but there was no era to which to refer them, so that their true times can not be ascertained. Nor is this all. In Greece, as elsewhere, historic times emerge out of the dim ages of fable and legend, in which fact and fiction were indistinguishably blended. The period preceding the Olympic era can do little more than furnish a kind of background for the true historical picture of later times; and if it can not afford us accurate chronology, it may furnish some materials to aid in fixing its outlines and limits.

The most conspicuous event of which we have any account in that remote age, was the siege and destruction of Troy. It can hardly be called an historical event at all. A war in which the gods take sides, and enter into combat with each other and with men, whose heroes are demigods, and who fight in armor forged by divinities, can not be set down as sober fact. We are told that the beautiful Helen, the immediate occasion of the war, was the daughter of Jupiter or Zeus. Achilles, the most illustrious chieftain of the Greeks, was the son of Thetis, an ocean nymph. Æneas, one of the Trojan heroes, was a son of Venus. The very occasion of the war originated in a dispute between the goddesses Juno, Venus, and Minerva, as to which was the most beautiful. And so on to the end of the chapter. Now, such a story belongs to mythology, rather than to history. And yet there can be no doubt that there was some historical fact at the foundation. There must have been an ancient city called Troy, which was besieged and taken by the Greeks. But that there ever were such personages, divine and human, as Homer describes, or such exploits as he attributes to them, may certainly more than admit of a doubt.

Though the narrative of the Trojan war can not, therefore, be set down as veritable history, yet enough of fact was embraced under it to give it a real value, both in history and chronology. The Greek writers made it *an era*, to which they referred the events and supposed events of their early ages. The highest assigned date for the fall of Troy was that of Herodotus, about B. C. 1263. The Parian marble places it at B. C. 1209. Eratosthenes fixed it at B. C. 1183, or about 156 years prior to the building of the temple by Solomon. The lowest date I have found in any author is B. C. 1120.* The date of Eratosthenes was adopted by Eusebius, and seems to be the most generally received. This era was a convenient one for the Greek historians. For instance, the "dynasty of Pelasgic chiefs which ex-

---

* Clinton's Fasti Hellenici. The dates now given are taken from that author's Epitome of Grecian Chronology (ed. Oxford, 1851), compiled from the larger work. pp. 61, 63.

isted in Greece before any other dynasty is heard of in Greek traditions," can be traced back only eighteen generations before the Trojan war. "Inachus, the father of Phoroneus, was the highest term in Grecian history."* The latter was of the eighteenth generation before the war, in the fifty-fifth year of whose reign the flood of Ogyges is said to have occurred, B. C. 1796. "Excepting this line," says Clinton, " none of the genealogies ascend higher than the ninth, eighth, or seventh generation before the Trojan war." †

The foundation of the Grecian states, then, was placed, by their own traditions, at a comparatively low antiquity, not exceeding, in any case, eighteen centuries before Christ. At that time the generations of men were accounted the immediate descendants of the gods. Inachus was a deity, and his sons were said to be *autochthonous*, i. e., sprung from the soil, or aborigines of the country.‡ The Greeks did not claim, in their traditions, to be the oldest of nations, as did the Egyptians, Phrygians, and Scythians.§ Danaus, Cadmus, Cecrops, and Pelops, the reputed founders of as many of their states, were immigrants from abroad, and brought with them arts and institutions already known in their native lands.

* Clinton's Fasti Hellenici. † Ibid. ‡ Ibid. § Ibid.

The origin of Rome is as uncertain as that of Greece. No fewer than twenty-five different legends have come down to us out of the mists of antiquity relating to the foundation of that city. They may, however, be reduced to three principal theories: first, that it was founded by Evander in the age preceding the Trojan war; second, by Æneas and his associates shortly after that war; and third, by Romulus and Remus, the twins, in the year B. C. 753. For our present purpose, it matters not which of these is preferred. In point of fact, neither of them is of undoubted authenticity, and most modern historians do not pretend to carry back the beginnings of Roman history more than two or three hundred years before Christ, regarding all before this as fabulous.

Nothing, then, can be derived from either Greek or Roman history invalidating in the slightest degree the sacred chronology as to the age of man on the earth. The beginning of that history is confessedly far within the date of the time of Noah.

CHAPTER IV.

THE ARGUMENT FROM HISTORY (*continued*).

III. THE CHALDEANS.

Extravagant Claims. — BEROSUS and his Writings. — His Annals of an Antediluvian Kingdom. — These evidently mythical. — His Measures of Time. — Elements of true History in them. — Negatively, they contain Nothing inconsistent with Bible Chronology. — Positively, they tend to its Confirmation. — Earliest Historic Dynasty, B. C. 2458.

THE ancient Chaldeans, according to the usual interpretation of their records, claimed for their nation a higher antiquity than any other people, the Hindus, perhaps, excepted. As usual, however, in statements of this kind, there is great discrepancy in the numbers. I believe the largest number of years claimed by them, antecedent to historic times, is *two million one hundred and fifty thousand*. Other estimates claim 720,000, 490,000, 473,000, 470,000, 432,000, 270,000, 31,000,* etc. Sometimes

---

* Sir G. C. Lewis's Survey of the Astronomy of the Ancients, pp. 263, 286.

these numbers profess to give the duration of Chaldean history previous to the time of Alexander. Thus, according to Porphyry, a writer of the third century, "Callisthenes sent from Babylon to Aristotle a series of astronomical observations, reaching back from the time of Alexander over a space of 31,000 years."

The authority most generally quoted in reference to Chaldean antiquities is BEROSUS, a priest of Belus at Babylon, and an historian who lived in the time of Alexander. He wrote the Chaldean history in three books. This work is now lost, except some few extracts preserved mostly in Josephus, Eusebius, and Syncellus, which again, especially those found in the last two authors named, were taken from the original work of Berosus by three heathen writers, — Apollodorus, Abydenus, and Alexander Polyhistor, — all of whom flourished between the time of Alexander the Great and the Christian era. According to them, Berosus "narrates that there were at Babylon the writings of many authors, preserved with the greatest care, which comprised a history through a period of 215 myriads (2,150,000) of years,* in which was an account of the computa-

---

* Thus in Euseb. Chron. (in Armen.), chap. ii. col. 109; but in Syncellus, p. 28, it is "fifteen myriads (150,000) years;" ὑπὲρ μυριάδων δεκαπέντε.

tions of time, a history of the heaven, the earth, and the sea, of the birth of mankind, of kings, and of their memorable deeds."

The portion of these extracts which relates particularly to our present object, is that which professes to give the annals of an antediluvian Chaldean kingdom, of the flood, and of a long succession of the kings following through a period amounting in aggregate to 462,080 years. After this are enumerated five or six dynasties of Median, Chaldean, Assyrian, and Arabian monarchs, through a period of 1550 years, to Pul, the Assyrian king mentioned in 2 Kings xv. 19, 1 Chron. v. 26, B. C. 770. It devolves upon us, then, to inquire what historical value is to be attached to these supposed records.

The antediluvian kingdom of ten reigns is said to have extended through a duration of 120 *sari*. "The first king," says Eusebius, quoting Berosus,* "was Alorus, a Chaldean from Babylon. He reigned ten *sari*. Now, a sarus is 3600 years; he adds, "I know not how many *neri* and *sossi*." A *nerus*, he says, is 600 years, and a *sossus* 60 years.† Thus he reckons years in connection with the affairs of the ancients.

* Chron. Armen. I. chap. i.
† Syncellus says (p. 17), "Berosus wrote in *sari*, *neri*, and *sossi*, of which a *sarus* is 3600 years, a *nerus* is 600, and a *sossus* 60 years."

"Having said these things, he goes on and enumerates the Assyrian kings, giving their names in order. There were ten kings from Alorus, the first, to Xisuthrus, in whose time happened that first great flood of which Moses speaks. Now, the sum of the years which these kings reigned is 120 *sari*, that is, forty-three myriads, and two thousand (432,000) years. He then writes in these express words. He says, 'Alorus being dead, his son Alaparus reigned three *sari;* after Alaparus, Almelon, from the city of Pantibiblis, a Chaldean, thirteen *sari;* Ammenon, also from Pantibiblis, a Chaldean, succeeded Almenon, thirteen *sari;* then Amegalarus, of Pantibiblis, reigned eighteen *sari;* then Daonus, a Shepherd, from Pantibiblis, reigned ten *sari;* afterwards Edoranchus, a Pantibiblian, reigned eighteen *sari;* then Amempsimus, from Lancharis, a Chaldean, reigned ten *sari;* then Otiartes, from Lancharis, a Chaldean, took the kingdom, eight *sari;* Otiartes being dead, Xisuthrus ruled the kingdom eighteen *sari*. In his time happened the great flood. The sum is ten kings, and one hundred and twenty *sari*.' Now, they say that these one hundred and twenty *sari* amount to forty-three myriads and two thousand years (432,000), since a *sarus* is 3600 years. These things Alexander Polyhistor narrates in his books. Now, if any one yields confidence to these books, boasting of so many myriads of years, he must likewise believe many other manifestly incredible things which they contain."

It is very evident that this account, as it stands, is mythical. It is not history, and can afford us, therefore, no reliable chronology. No advocate of the extreme antiquity of the race, however sanguine, would, on the credit of this statement, pretend to date man's actual creation at 720,000, or 432,000 years B. C. These immense periods must be classed with those that meet us in the earliest Egyptian chronology, which were appropriately remitted to the reigns of the gods and manes.

But if not historical, have they not historical *elements* in them? If they are not to be taken literally, do they not at least warrant the general conclusion that man has lived during a *very long* period; thus, in some sense, justifying such authors as Bunsen, and Rodier, and Lyell, in their assumptions, and countenancing the tendency of the age to set aside the Mosaic narrative of the creation as unsupported and unworthy of acceptance? To answer these inquiries satisfactorily, let us examine, with some care, the statement itself.

Various opinions have been held as to the measures of time named in it. Suidas regards the *sarus* as equal to 222 lunar months, or nearly $18\frac{1}{2}$

years,* so that the 120 *sari*, assigned to the antediluvian kings, amount, according to him, to 2222 years. This number he doubtless intended for 2242, the space of time between the creation and flood, as given in the Alexandrian Septuagint, thus making the Chaldean antediluvian period coextensive with that related by Moses. Latham,† a distinguished chronologer, regards the sarus equal to 4 years and 340 days; Raske, a space of 23 months; and Ideler,‡ a lunar period which he can not define. But the most probable opinion is that of Alexander Polyhistor,§ that the sarus was a period of *ten* years, of 360 days each, which was the year of the most ancient times — an opinion held by the two learned monks Anianus and Polydorus (who flourished about A. D. 400); also by Africanus,‖ although regarded by many as a mere expedient to get rid of a difficulty. This interpretation is strongly

* *Sari*, a measure and number among the Chaldeans. They make 120 sari equal to 2222 years, since a sarus is 222 lunar months, which amount to eighteen years and six months. Lex. sub voce Σάροι.

† Latham's Chronographical Essays, pp. 81, 84.

‡ Ideler on the era of the Chaldeans, in "Recherche Historique sur les Observationes astronomiques des Anciens," in Halma's Almageste, vol. iv. p. 62.

§ Syncellus, p. 32, B.

‖ See Jackson's Chron. Ant. vol. i. pp. 200-202.

corroborated by the probable etymology of the terms. *Saros*, or *sar*, as it is very properly Anglicized, seems to have been allied to the Hebrew word עָשָׂר, *asar*, ten, and *sossus*, from שֵׁשׁ *shesh*,* six, so that a *sar* would be 10 years or 3600 days, a *soss* a sixth of a year, or 60 days, and a *nerus*, or *ner*, of which the etymology is not apparent, a sixth of a *sar*, or 600 days. This view is further confirmed by the fact that in the Semitic languages the word to designate days was sometimes employed to signify years. Jackson asserts directly that in the Chaldee the word *yōmim*, as in Hebrew the corresponding *yāmim*, was employed to signify both days and years.† Indeed, the words denoting periods of time, in most ancient languages, etymologically mean a completed *course* or *circuit*, such as *annus* in Latin, ἔτος, ἔνος, ἐνιαυτός, in Greek, שָׁנָה in Hebrew, etc., and hence are sometimes applied to any revolution, whether of the sun or moon, so that the same word might denote the solar year, the lunar month, or the solar day. Hence it would be both easy and natural for Berosus, or any one translating ancient records, to make the mistake of calling days years, especially when influenced by the desire, so common among historians, of enhancing, as much as possible, the antiquity of their own nations.

* Latham's Essays, p. 84. † Chron. Ant. vol. i. p. 200.

As a further evidence of the correctness of this interpretation, it should be mentioned that this ancient manner of reckoning was continued after the flood of Xisuthrus through 9 sari, 2 neri, and 8 sossi, when these terms are suddenly dropped, and the reigns given in solar years. It is true that the break is after a succession of 86 kings, but the kingdom continues with a simple change of dynasties; there is no passing from the reign of gods or demigods to that of mortal men, such as would be not only natural, but necessary, in order to account for the immense difference in the duration of the reigns. While the pretended antediluvian reigns varied from 10,000 to 64,800 years in length, and those immediately following averaged full 400 years each, the eight Median kings that succeeded extended only over 224 years, or an average of about 28 years; after which came other dynasties (Chaldean, Arabian, and Assyrian), all of ordinary historical lengths. These discrepancies can only be explained by the supposition that, in the prehistoric periods, days and months were magnified into years, as we have already seen was the case in the mythologic chronology of Egypt.*

I have dwelt the longer on these measures of time in Chaldea, because the subject has not met

* Ante, p. 67 seq.

with justice from some writers of high standing. For example, Sir George Cornwall Lewis, in his Survey of the Astronomy of the Ancients, in speaking of Chaldean antiquities, gives all the high numbers which he found scattered through ancient authors, as expressing the antiquity of that nation, as 720,000, 432,000, etc., years; but he adds not a word as to the peculiar manner in which time was computed by that people, and which would render an interpretation more nearly consistent with history both plausible and probable. And Philip Smith, in his History of the World, — a very valuable work, — mentions the Chaldean antediluvian period of 432,000 years, and the postdiluvian period of 34,080 years, as computed by *sars*, and explains that a sar is 3600 years, without a word to intimate that any other value has ever been given to the term, or is even possible.* He then exhibits a chronological table of Babylonian history, of eight postdi-

* He adds a note in the following unqualified language: "In the Babylonian system of notation, the numbers 6 and 10 were employed alternately. Time was measured ordinarily by the *soss*, the *ner*, and the *sar* — the *soss* being $10 \times 6 = 60$ years, the *ner* $60 \times 10 = 600$ years, and the sar $600 \times 6 = 3600$ years. The next term in this series would evidently be $3600 \times 10 = 36,000$ years, and the term following $36,000 \times 6 = 216,000$ years. Berosus' antediluvian cycle consists of 432,000, or two such periods." Vol. i. p. 195.

luvian dynasties, extending down to B. C. 538, the first of which comprised eighty-six kings during the aforesaid period of 34,080 years. He simply styles this "mythic;" yet when we consider how natural is the reckoning which makes the sarus 3600 days instead of years, — i. e., 10 years of 360 days each, — how simple and consistent with the rude and elementary knowledge of those early times, and how harmonious also with the facts of history as learned from other sources, we cannot but wonder that eminent scholars should have disregarded it, and preferred theories so much more complicated instead. Such preferences wholly mistake the character of those remote ages when knowledge, especially astronomical knowledge, was very simple, and embraced only the most obvious facts. At that time nothing was known of what in later times were called "lunar periods." The whole meaning was on the surface, and not involved in a mass of recondite facts, which required an intricate calculation to discover, and an intricate theory to explain them.

Our conclusion, then, is this: that while the immense periods of Chaldean antediluvian reigns are not historical, neither are they wholly mythical. In this respect they differ from the corresponding periods of Egyptian chronology. They contain historical elements which have a twofold value — negative and positive. The negative is that, interpreted as they have now been, they contain nothing inconsistent with the Mosaic account of the creation. The very longest duration assigned to the antediluvian period may easily be brought within the 2256 years assigned to it in the Septuagint. The positive value is, that so far as they go, they confirm the sacred record. As in the latter, they assert that there was an antediluvian period. The ten generations of kings correspond with the line of ten patriarchs from Adam to Noah. The details of Chaldean tradition are but dim and distorted, but easily recognizable, copies of the events mentioned in the Scriptures. Chaldean and Jewish antiquities cover precisely the same ground. Moses and Berosus speak of the same times, and, in general, of the same facts; not, indeed, always with the same fullness, — some particulars being recorded by one and some by the other, — but the ground covered by each is the same, and the two narratives, instead of being set in antagonism, should be taken as mutually confirmatory.

The date of the earliest historical dynasty after the flood is thought to be established thus: The list of astronomical observations, sent by Callisthenes to Aristotle, in the time of Alexander the Great, extended backward in an uninterrupted series 1903 years, i. e., till B. C. 2234. This is supposed to have been at the beginning of the IIId dynasty of Berosus, which was Chaldean, and under which the worship of the heavenly bodies began. Previous to this, a Median dynasty, who were probably of the Turanian or Scythian race, had reigned 224 years, carrying up the monarchy to B. C. 2458. Still further back was the before-mentioned "mythic" dynasty of 86 kings, whose duration was said to have been 34,080 years, so that the earliest *historical* date is that of the beginning of the second dynasty, B. C. 2458.* The existence, however, of this Median dynasty, much more its assigned duration, is very uncertain, lying, as it does, in the very border land between fable and history, and with both, probably, in varying proportions, intermingling in it.

* Smith's History of the World, vol. i. p. 196.

CHAPTER V.

THE ARGUMENT FROM HISTORY (*continued*).

III. THE HINDUS.

Importance of the Discovery of the Sanskrit. — View of the Sanskrit Literature. — The VEDAS. — The UPAVEDAS. — The VEDANGAS. — The UPANGAS. — These contain no History. — Severe Judgment upon the Sanskrit Literature by Missionaries. — Reason for this. — Comparison between the Hindus and Greeks. — Origin of the Vedas. — Their Contents. — Their Antiquity. — They contain Nothing inconsistent with the Bible Chronology.

THE discovery of the Sanskrit language and literature may almost be said to have constituted an era in the world. As the discovery of the continent of India — for it may appropriately be termed such — by the Portuguese, at the close of the fifteenth century, was an era in the history of commerce, so the introduction of its sacred language, and the treasures it contains, to the knowledge of Europeans, was an event of signal importance in the history of literature, philology, and ethnology. This event occurred about one hundred years ago, at which time the language began to be successfully unfolded by Sir William Jones and other Oriental scholars. At the present time, the Sanskrit literature has been pretty fully explored, though much remains to be done in reference to portions of it. Within the last ten years, several important works have been published upon it, and much discussion, active, if not violent, has been had both among European and American investigators.

I shall endeavor, first, to give a summary idea of the nature of the Sanskrit literature, and, secondly, inquire what it contains, as bearing upon the question of the antiquity of man on the earth.

I. The whole circle of Hindu knowledge and science is divided into eighteen parts. The first four of these are the VEDAS proper, so called from *ved*, the law, which are named respectively the Rig-Veda, the Yajur-Veda, the Sama-Veda, and the Atharva-Veda. These are regarded as having come immediately from God, and as containing the true knowledge of the Deity, of his religion, and of his worship. Each Veda consists of two parts, the first called *Sanhita*, comprising hymns, prayers, and ceremonies to be used in sacrifices and oblations; the second, *Brahmana*, describing the First Cause, and the creation of the world, also moral precepts, duties, rewards, punishments, purifications, etc. Next to these rank the UPAVEDAS, or supplementary Vedas, of which there are four, treating of disease and medicine, of music, of the fabrication and use of arms, and of the mechanic arts. Next are six VEDANGAS, i. e., members of the Vedas, which are also supplementary to them, relating to the sacred sciences, pronunciation, meter, grammar, explanation of words, astronomy, and ceremonials. Lastly, four UPANGAS, called *Purana*, or history, *Nyaya*, or logic, *Mimansa*, or moral philosophy, and *Dharmshastra*, or jurisprudence. Several of these departments of literature contain numerous treatises. For example, there are six systems of philosophy, eighteen puranas, eighteen siddhanta, or treatises on astronomy, besides works on grammar, logic, etc. In addition to these, there are the Institutes of Manu, a code of civil and religious laws, and the two great epic poems, the Ramayana and the Mahabharata, which are sometimes called a fifth Veda.

Our purpose does not call for any detailed account of the contents of these sacred books. It would indeed require a large volume, perhaps many volumes, to do this. The single inquiry before us is, What do they contain that affords any light as to the past duration of our race on earth?

The following estimate of the Sanskrit literature, from the pen of one who had thoroughly studied it, given in the Calcutta Review, will be, perhaps, our best answer to this inquiry: —

"The Sanskrit language contains *nothing of genuine importance*, no national annals, no biography of eminent patriots, statesmen, warriors, philosophers, poets, or others, who have figured on the theater of Indian life, public or private. Not a single page of pure historical matter, unmixed with monstrous and absurd fable, is extant, or probably was ever written in it. It supplies us with no assistance whatever in rescuing from eternal oblivion the worthies or the curses of past ages. It affords no certain clew to the discovery or even the origin of the races who first spoke or adopted it. Fabulous and extravagant legends are all that in this class it furnishes. European ingenuity, penetration, and perseverance, may indeed, by dint of hard and continued labor, elicit a few isolated facts here and there, and by comparison of dates and circumstances, rejecting the crudities and absurdities that have gathered round them, bring them to bear upon some point of ancient story yet in the depths of obscurity. But nothing is certain; all is only a happy guess, or probable inference, at best. The very principle of historic narration appears either to have never entered into the minds of early writers in this language, or else a base and selfish policy led them to falsify, obscure, and mysticize all events, in order to conceal their own usurpations, violence, and injustice."

The writer then proceeds to specify particulars in exemplification of these remarks, such as relate to geography, astronomy, music, medicine, the fine arts, etc., and making a partial exception in favor of logic, geometry, and arithmetic, finds little in these treatises worthy of commendation, or as having any value. Or if they contain some truth and real science, it is still mixed with a great deal that is crude, and fanciful, and puerile. He adds, "The real domain of Sanskrit literature is in the departments of grammar, rhetoric, and poetry." (p. 18.) In this estimate this author is doubtless, in general, correct, though possibly, in some respects, he may be too severe. Missionaries — to which class he belongs — have often been accused of unfair judgments respecting the heathen, especially the Hindus. The explanation is natural and easy, and does not compromise either their ability or disposition to judge fairly. In their every-day work they come into contact with heathenism in all its corruptions, degradation, and sin, and know these to be the legitimate fruit of the doctrines embodied in their literature. With this knowledge they are not in a state of mind to be carried into ecstasies over a fine piece of poetry, or an exhibition of refined skill in the niceties of grammar and logic, and are not likely to speak of them in terms of high commendation. When they draw a picture of any of these systems, there will of necessity be a dark background of practical heathen life that will impart more or less of its shade to the whole. On the other hand, our western philosopher and learned Orientalist, in the seclusion of his study, from which he steps into the most refined circles of Christian society, examines at his leisure a few of the masterpieces of the heathen poets and philosophers, and is rapt into admiration of them. It is not necessary to weigh one of these judgments against the other. Both may be right from the point of view in which the estimates are made.

It is doubtless unjust to judge the Sanskrit literature by that of later and more enlightened times. Grant that science is found in it intermixed with fable; the same was true of that of all the ancient nations. Excepting perhaps the Greeks, as much credit is due for the successful cultivation of science and art to the Hindus as to any people of that age; and if we go back of the times of Herodotus, they stand without a rival in any department of ancient learning. Professor Max Müller, in his history of Sanskrit literature, gives an interesting comparison between the characters of the Hindus and the Greeks, a single paragraph from which I will quote.

" Greece and India are indeed the two opposite poles in the historical development of the Aryan man. To the Greek, existence is full of life and reality; to the Hindu, it is a dream and illusion. The Greek is at home where he is born. All his energies belong to his country: he stands or falls with his party, and is ready to sacrifice even his life to the glory and independence of Hellas. The Hindu enters this world as a stranger; all his thoughts are directed to another world; he takes no part even where he is driven to act, and when he sacrifices his life it is but to be delivered from it." (p. 18.)

This is strikingly true. The Greeks were eminently a practical people. This characteristic stands out prominently from the very beginning of their national existence. The opposite is true of the Hindus. Their speculations in philosophy and religion are almost all connected with a preëxistent state in the past, or an equally shadowy one in the future, or with topics of pure imagination; and it is very remarkable how seldom their literature in any department has to do with the realities of this worldly life. Hence that most singular fact noticed by the writer before quoted, that from the first hymn of the first Veda to the last chapter in the last of the Puranas, there is not in all that literature, extending over a period of three thousand years, a single page of plain matter-of-fact history unmixed with fable, or a single truthful biographical account of any poet, statesman, or philosopher, such as constitutes so valuable a portion of Grecian literature. Nor has the Sanskrit any chronology. It does not in all its extent furnish a single reliable date by which any event, or series of events, of which it treats, may be assigned its proper chronological place in the world's history. We are actually indebted to the Greek historians for the only trustworthy date that can be used as a starting-point in Hindu chronology. It is the fortunate occurrence of the name of an Indian prince in connection with the name of one of Alexander's successors that enables us to fix the date of that prince's reign, and from thence determine approximately that of other events, either before or after it, in the annals of that people.

While, however, we look in vain *in* the Sanskrit for any history or chronology asserting an earlier history of our race than we have been taught to believe, it may be asked whether the Sanscrit *itself* is not such evidence. There can be no doubt that the Vedas are among the oldest of the extant writings of antiquity, perhaps the very oldest. It is an important inquiry, as bearing upon the subject in hand, What were their origin and their probable date?

In respect to their origin, the Hindus put forth various conflicting statements; and even in the later portions of the writings which are regarded as parts of the Vedas, it is ascribed to different sources. Thus it is alleged that they are eternal; that they issued from the mouth of Brahma at the creation; that they are the breath of Brahma, etc. It is said that the Rig-Veda was produced from fire, the Yajur-Veda from air, and the Sama-Veda from the sun; again, that the goddess Saraswati is the mother of the Vedas; still again, that they are derived from the mystical victim Purusha, or from the Gayatri, a sacred verse personified as a goddess, the wife of Brahma;* or once more, that they

---

* The GAYATRI, or holiest verse in the Vedas. This is merely a prayer, as follows: "Let us adore the supremacy of that divine sun, the godhead, who illuminates all, who recreates all, from whom all proceed, to whom all must return, whom we invoke to direct our understandings aright in our progress towards his holy seat." — *Rammohun Roy*, p. 117.

This verse is preceded by a mysterious monosyllable (Om), a type of the three divinities Brahma, Vishnu, Siva, and the essence of the Vedas, and by the three scarcely less sacred

are the offspring of Time. This enumeration is not designed to be exhaustive.

These assertions show that there was much speculation among the Hindus regarding the origin of their sacred books; not, however, as implying any question as to their divine inspiration, which was never denied except by a single one of their schools of philosophy, and the heretical sect of the Buddhists. Nor did these statements, so far as I am aware, indicate speculations or discussions analogous to those held respecting the origin and inspiration of the Hebrew and Christian Scriptures, but rather as to the divine character and authority of these writings, in what the Hindus would call a higher sense.

Each *sukta*, or hymn, has for its reputed author

---

words, *bhur*, *bhuwar*, and *swar*, denoting earth, atmosphere, and heaven."

It is said, "Whoever shall repeat these lines, day by day, for three years, without negligence, shall approach the most high God, become free as air, and acquire after death an ethereal essence." — *Rammohun Roy*, pp. 110, 117.

"The Veda begins," says Rammohun Roy, "and concludes with three peculiar and mysterious epithets of God: first, OM; second, TAT; third, SUT. The first of these signifies 'that being which preserves, destroys, creates.' The second implies 'that only being which is neither male nor female.' The third announces 'the true being.' These collective terms simply affirm, ONE UNKNOWN TRUE BEING IS THE CREATOR, PRESERVER, AND DESTROYER OF THE UNIVERSE." — *Trans. of the Vedas*, p. 22.

a *rishi*, or teacher, by whom, in Brahmanical phraseology, it was "seen," that is, to whom it was revealed. For the names of these rishis we are indebted, except when incidentally mentioned in the hymns themselves, to an index of the contents of the Vedas, which also specifies the meter and the number of stanzas in each hymn. The Rig-Veda has 1017 hymns, and 10,417 stanzas (there is a difference of six or eight stanzas in different enumerations), the authorship of which is attributed to nearly 100 different rishis. Many of these hymns and parts of hymns appear in the three other Vedas, which are of a later date; indeed, the whole of the second or Sama-Veda has been found to have been taken from the first. The same is true of large portions of the contents of the Yajur and Atharva Vedas, so that these 1017 hymns of the Rig-Veda are regarded as constituting almost all of the original Vedic hymns. Some of their reputed authors are the subjects of legends in the later mythology, but many are not mentioned in other parts of Sanskrit literature.

In regard to the antiquity of these ancient writings, scholars are by no means agreed. Baron Bunsen thinks that some of the hymns were composed as long ago as B. C. 3000. Professor Whitney, who is probably the first Sanskrit scholar in America, has expressed the opinion that they were written during the first half of the second millennium before Christ (B. C. 2000–1500). Professor Max Müller, who has nearly completed his most valuable edition of the Rig-Veda, thinks that their collection and arrangement in their present form took place at least as early as from the 12th to the 10th century before Christ, but that their composition occupied quite an indefinite period of some centuries before. The late Professor Wilson, who was, I believe, regarded as the best Sanskrit scholar in England, thought Müller's date too recent by some two or three centuries. Ritter supposes they were composed or collected from 1600 to 1400 B. C. The most modern date I recollect to have seen is from 1000 to 1200 B. C. In each case, some centuries previous are allowed for their composition.

My own opinion, if I may be allowed to express one, after the eminent scholars just named, is, that the collection and arrangement of these hymns, as we now have them in the Rig-Veda Sanhita, was made as early as the 15th or 16th century before Christ, and that the composition of the earliest of them may have been some five centuries previous, carrying it back to about the time of Abraham. This opinion is based partly on the style of the language, which is simple and archaic, and had become in a measure obsolete when the next portion of the Vedic literature (the Brahmanas) were written. The meters also are archaic, and unknown in later versification, and in the later of the hymns reference is made to the earlier ones as already ancient. Now, since the period of the Brahmana must, on separate grounds, be made to begin at least as early as B. C. 1000, it seems necessary to date the collection and arrangement of the hymns two or three centuries earlier, and their composition at least as many more.

Again, there is appended to these collections of hymns a tract on astronomy — the *Jyotisha*, — the object of which is to prescribe rules for regulating the time of the sacrifices prescribed in the hymns. In this treatise there is a record of the places of the solstitial points at the time. These places are about twenty-four degrees east of those they occupied at the time when the modern Hindu sphere was fixed, viz., *Mesha*, in the 1st of Aries, which was about A. D. 500. Calculating from the known rate of the precession of the equinoxes, we are carried back to the early part of the twelfth century before Christ as the time when the recorded observation was made. And we are safe in assuming that so much knowledge of astronomy as is disclosed in this observation and record, and in the complicated rules derived from them for regulating the times of the sacrifices, requires at least a period of several centuries for its growth. Such a system of rites, so regulated, with its corresponding literature, is not the product of one century, or of two or three. And this view is strengthened by the fact that there are, in connection with Hindu astronomical works, intimations that at the time the modern Hindu sphere was fixed at the 1st degree of Aries, A. D. 500, the equinoxes had fallen back twenty-seven degrees from the places they occupied when first observed by their ancient astronomers. This brings the time of those first observations into the middle of the fifteenth century before the Christian era. It should, however, in fairness, be added, that some Sanskrit scholars do not attach so much importance to this Iyotisha record as is implied in the foregoing remarks, since it is assumed that in the absence of suitable astronomical instruments, it was not possible for the Hindus to make their observations with a sufficient degree of accuracy to warrant these definite results.

Our conclusion, then, from a careful survey of the Sanskrit language and literature, is the same as from that of the other ancient peoples of the East. The oldest Hindu writings, and the earliest astronomical observation on record, can not be *proved* to have had an earlier date than the fourteenth or fifteenth century before Christ, though a few hundred more may be conceded as probable. The oldest astronomical treatise, which has been regarded as an important witness against the Bible, is proved incontrovertibly to have been composed some four or five centuries after Christ. And as the work of bringing to light the ancient literature of the Brahmas proceeds, the tendency among European scholars is to bring it within more and more modern limits. This tendency to modernize is sometimes, doubtless, suffered to proceed too far. But however this may be, this fact may be regarded as established, viz., that the ancient literature of India affords no materials for disproving the truthfulness of the Bible; on the contrary, it contains much that corroborates the claims of the sacred volume to a divine authenticity.

CHAPTER VI.

THE ARGUMENT FROM HISTORY (*continued*).

V. THE CHINESE.

First explorers of Chinese Literature. — Jesuit and Protestant Missionaries. — View of the Chinese Chronology. — Pauthier's System. — The Ante-historic Period. — The Semi-historic. — The Historic. — How far is this Chronology reliable? — Views of Pauthier. — Of Amiot. — Of Williams. — Examination of the Elements of Computation. — Testimony of the Shu-king. — The Cycle of Sixty Years. — Statements of Rev. J. Chambers. — Of Dr. Legge. — Elements of the Chinese Chronology borrowed. — Its present Form dates only to about the Christian Era. — Materials for the History of the earliest Dynasties unreliable. — The Shu-king, how compiled. — Its Destruction and Recovery. — Conclusion.

THE first European explorers of the literature and antiquities of China were the Jesuit missionaries, who labored in that country in the early part of the eighteenth century, among the most prominent of whom were Fathers Amiot, Souciet, and Gaubil. The latter of these appears to have been distinguished for his investigations in the department of science for which his mathematical education had specially prepared him. M. Gaubil went to China in 1723, at the age of thirty-four, and died there, after a laborious life, in 1759. His dissertations on various subjects — particularly on the astronomy of the Chinese, which he sent to his friends at home — awakened an interest in Oriental studies, and, with the contributions of other missionaries, greatly aided the study of Chinese literature in France. At the close of the last century and the beginning of the present, Europe, especially France, could boast of many eminent Sinologues, as M. Stanislaus Julien, M. G. Pauthier, MM. Biot, father and son.

It is worthy of notice that the principal writers on Chinese astronomy, as Delambre and Biot, rely mostly on the works of Gaubil as authority. His writings and opinions are always mentioned with respect, though they have been subjected to severe criticism. His translations have been revised, and in some passages modified. This was to have been expected, while as a pioneer in Chinese studies his labors have been very valuable. The position of the Jesuit missionaries in connection with, and at the head of, the Tribunal of Mathematics, afforded them rare opportunities for becoming acquainted with the science of that country; and the results of their labors furnished a good foundation for those who should come after them in the same field of research.

In the present century, Protestant missionaries, English and American, have pursued these studies with success, and, in connection with other European scholars, have brought the treasures of Chinese literature, such as they are, within reach of all. The last, if not the greatest contribution to this end, is a work by the Rev. James Legge, D. D., of the London Missionary Society, entitled *The Chinese Classics: with a Translation, Critical and Exegetical Notes, Prolegomena, and Copious Indexes.* The work consists of seven volumes, and contains the Confucian Analects, an account of Mencius, his disciples and doctrines, the Shu-king, the annals of the Bamboo books, so called, etc. These are specially valuable as bearing upon our present discussion, the Shu-king being the most important of the Chinese classics, in exhibiting the ancient science of that country.

Two points of inquiry here claim our attention: 1. What is the ancient Chinese chronology? and 2. What are the reasons for regarding it as reliable, or otherwise?

In regard to the first, I give the elements of the system as found in M. G. Pauthier's History of China, in the *Univers*, which is, I believe, the commonly received chronology of China.*

Pauthier divides his chronology into three periods — *ante-historic, semi-historic,* and *historic.*

The first period begins with Pan-kou, the primeval man, who is placed by the native historians at from 2,000,000 to 96,000,000 years before the death of Confucius, B. C. 479. During this interval flourished the three sovereignties of Heaven, Earth, and Man, followed by the ten periods, the last of which began with the Emperor Hoang-ti. In reference to those mythic times, I need only remark that there is much in the details to remind us of the corresponding era among the Hindus. Indeed, Pauthier says, if the tradition in respect to Pan-kou is not borrowed from India, it comes from the same source as the Hindu traditions; "for," he continues, "it is impossible not to recognize in the name and attributes of the Chinese *Pan-kou*, or, softening the pronunciation, *Man-hou*, — a transcription as exact as the former for a certain latitude, — the Indian *Manou*, who acts the same

---

* It is followed by Drs. Gutzlaff and Williams, in their works on China, except in relation to ante-historic times. After the emperor Hoang-ti, they agree. Before this, Gutzlaff gives no dates, and Williams goes back to Fuh-hi, making his reign to begin B. C. 2852.

part in the mythological tradition of India." (Chine, vol. ii. p. 22.) Both the Hindu and Chinese traditions, as we shall show hereafter, are derived originally from the events related in the Mosaic records. The ten periods are, doubtless, the ten generations from Adam to Noah.

Semi-historic times began with Fuh-hi, B. C. 3468,* who is said to have reigned 150 years. He was succeeded by Chin-noung (Shinnung) and others, the last of whom was Hoang-ti, whose reign began in B. C. 2698. Williams, however, enumerates these emperors thus: Fuh-hi, 115 years; Shinnung, 140 years; Hoang-ti, 100 years, who began to reign B. C. 2697. He regards historic times as commencing with Fuh-hi.

Historic times begin in the reign of Hoang-ti. The first cycle of sixty years, so famous in Chinese chronology, dates from the sixty-first year of this emperor, B. C. 2637. After him, Shan-hau reigned 84 years; Chiuen-hiuh, 78; Kuh, 78; Yau, 102; Shun, 50. Then follow 26 dynasties of monarchs, beginning with the Hia, B. C. 2205, and ending with the present (the Tau-kwang), embracing 235 sovereigns. Or, if we begin with Fuh-hi, the num-

* Williams puts the beginning of Fuh-hi's reign at B. C. 2852. — *Mid. Kingdom*, ii. p. 203.

ber is 243, embracing a period of 4721 years, to A. D. 1869.*

Minute chronological detail does not fall within my present purpose. We are now concerned only with the earliest portion of the system, and in this only with the principal dates.

The author informs us that this chronological record was forwarded from Peking, in 1767, by the Catholic missionary P. Amiot, who says of it, "It is a chronological table of all the sovereigns who have reigned in China, ranged in the order of the cycles, and exactly calculated from authentic monuments, from the sixty-first year of the Emperor Hoang-ti . . . to the present reigning monarch (1769), . . . and printed at Peking, in the imperial palace, after having been subjected to the close examination of the different academies or literary tribunals of this capital, in the 32d year of Kien-loung, — i. e., in 1767 of our era, — to serve ever after as a rule for the historians and other public writers of the empire." †

The inquiry now arises, Is this chronology reliable? It comes to us, with high claims, in a scientific dress, and challenges our confidence. How far is this confidence deserved?

---

* Williams (Summary, ii. p. 229), whom I have followed in the number of the dynasties, being more definite and complete than Pauthier. † Pauthier's Chine, ii. p. 268.

In answering this inquiry, I will first allude to some of the opinions which have been expressed in its favor, and then adduce what may be said on the other side.

M. Pauthier evidently accepts this chronology, even in its earliest dates. In summing up what he has to say regarding it, he remarks, "This confidence granted to the Chinese historians can not be condemned, for we can boldly affirm that no people ever possessed bodies of history so complete and so authentic as the Chinese. This should not surprise us, when we recollect that through all time, history, or the intelligent registering of human events, has been honored and favored in China; that since the Emperor Hoang-ti, 2637 years before our era, there has existed an historical tribunal in the capital of the empire, the members of which, chosen from the most distinguished of the literati, have, in many respects, the prerogatives and permanency of our magistrates."

He then cites, at length, the opinion of Amiot, one of the most laborious and learned of the French missionaries in China, to the following import: —

"The Chinese annals are preferable to the historic monuments of all other nations because they are the most free from fables, the most ancient, the most consecutive, and the most abounding in facts.. . . . They have epochs, demonstrated by astronomical observations, joined to the monuments of every kind, in which the annals abound; they furnish to each other reciprocal proofs, mutually sustain each other, and together concur to show the good faith of the writers who have transmitted them to us. . . . They can aid us to mount up surely, even to the first centuries after the renewal of the world, as they furnish, for that purpose, the necessary guides and assistants, such as the cycle of sixty years, . . . the radical epoch of which is B. C. 2637; . . . genealogies of the first sovereigns which bear the stamp of verity in the lacunæ which are found in them, and which no one has attempted to fill, though it would have been easy to do so had any one wished to add anything of his own; chronological tables which mark with exactitude the uninterrupted succession of all the emperors that have reigned for more than four thousand years.

"And, finally, those annals are in themselves the most authentic literary work there is in the world, because there is not in the world (*tout l'univers*) a work which has been so elaborated during the space of nearly eighteen hundred years, that has been revised, corrected, and augmented as new material was discovered, by so great a number of learned men united, provided with all possible assistance, etc." And Pauthier indorses all this, as he closes the argument, by saying, "Chinese history, therefore, possesses all the characters of certitude which historical criticism has a right to demand." *

* Pauthier's Chine, vol. ii. pp. 32, 33.

This opinion of Amiot, and of his biographer Pauthier, has been very extensively received. Williams, in his "Middle Kingdom" (vol. ii. p. 201), says of it, "The earliest records of the Chinese correspond rather too closely with their present character to receive full belief; but while they may be considered as unworthy of entire confidence, it will be allowed that they present an appearance of probability and naturalness hardly possessed by the early annals of Greece."

Let us now turn to the other side, and see what grounds there are for calling in question the reliableness of that chronology, at least in regard to its earlier dates.

Pauthier gives the following as "the chronological elements that serve as a basis to the certainty of the Chinese history : " —

"These elements are very simple and very regular. They are, 1. The *civil or equinoctial year*, composed of three hundred and sixty-five and a quarter sidereal days, recognized and followed in China from the highest antiquity, as we shall see hereafter, and which corresponds perfectly to our Julian year; 2. The *cycle of sixty years*, the series of which has been continued, without interruption, from the 61st year of the reign of Hoang-ti (B. C. 2637), and with as much regularity as the centuries in European computation. Our common year 1834 thus corresponds to the 31st of the 75th sexagenary Chinese cycle. There is no other chronology which offers so much certainty for so long a space of time." (Vol. ii. p. 27.)

1. These assumptions respecting the Chinese calendar, with its alleged Julian year of $365\frac{1}{4}$ days, are based upon a passage occurring in the Shu-king, which Pauthier renders in French, thus: —

"L'Empereur dit, ' Hi et Ho ; une periode solaire est de trois cent soixante-six jours ; en intercalant une lune et en déterminant ainsi quatre saisons, l'année se trouve exactement complétée. Cela étant parfaitement réglé, chaque functionnaire s'acquittera, selon le temps et la saison de son emploi ; et tout sera dans le bon ordre.' " *

Dr. Legge's translation is as follows : " The emperor said, ' Ah, you! Hi and Ho ; a round year consists of three hundred sixty and six days. By means of an intercalary month do you fix the four seasons, and complete the determination of the year. Thereafter, in exact accordance with this, regulating the various officers, all the works of the year will be fully performed." †

* Translation of Le Chou-king in Les Livres Sacrés de l'Orient, p. 47, par. 8.
† Chin. Classics, vol. iii. part 1, p. 23. Appendix, I.

There is some difference in these versions, though perhaps it is not greatly important as bearing on the present subject. That of Dr. Legge makes the emperor to command the astronomers by intercalating a month to fix the four seasons, and complete the determination of the year, saying that the round year consists of 366 days. The other version represents the work of adjustment as already made. The two points of interest apparently contained in it are a knowledge of the year as consisting of 366 days, and of the principle of intercalation to bring the seasons into their proper places. As to the first, the French missionaries all assume that it means only that *each fourth year* has 366 days, the three intervening ones having but 365. But the passage itself, in either version, has not a word to warrant this assumption. As to the second, the intercalation was not to be of one day each fourth year, but of *one month*. Whether this was to be done at stated intervals, in order to *retain* the seasons in their proper places, or once for all, does not appear. What were the principles of intercalation observed at that early period, if any, Dr. Legge says "we cannot tell." He adds, "Previous to the Han dynasty, Chinese history does not furnish us with the details on the subject of intercalation. In the time of that dynasty (B. C. 202–A. D. 221), we find what is called the Metonic cycle,* well known. It is not mentioned as any discovery of that age. . . . No doubt it came down to the Han from the Chan, and was probably known in China long before Meton reformed the Athenian calendar according to its principles, B. C. 432."

Dr. Legge also quotes from a native commentator of the Shu-king this remark: "When it is said that the year consists of 366 days, we are to understand that Yaou was speaking only in round numbers."

While, therefore, we must concede no small praise to the ancient Chinese, on account of their calendar, we can not admit that there is any evidence of the accuracy that is claimed for it. The inference, that in the 24th century before Christ they were acquainted with the Julian year of $365\frac{1}{4}$ days, is an unwarrantable straining of the text.

2. The other chronological element embraced in the Chinese system, according to Pauthier, is the cycle of sixty years. We have seen that this claims to have been introduced into use in the year B. C. 2637. If it could be proved that it was actually so employed from that early date, it

* Note, p. 134.

would be a fact of great importance. Williams says of it,* "The uniform adherence to this peculiar mode of reckoning time, certainly since the days of Confucius, and the high probability that it was generally adopted long before his time, the remembrance of the individual Nau the Great, who invented it, and the odd date of its adoption in the middle of a reign, are all strong testimonies in favor of the date and antiquity ascribed to it." This very claim, however, in its qualifying phrase, "certainly since the days of Confucius," is a virtual admission that there is no *proof* of its use prior to that time. But the claim itself is not borne out by facts. Other authorities of equal credit assert that the sexagenary cycle was not used to chronicle *years* till within about a century of the Christian era; some say till even after that era. Dr. Legge, in his Prolegomena to the translation of the Shu-king, has inserted an essay by the Rev. John Chalmers, "On the Astronomy of the ancient Chinese," in which this point, among others relevant to our subject, is ably discussed. I quote a few paragraphs: —

"The invention of the cycle of sixty is ascribed to Hoang-ti (B. C. 2637), and in particular its application to years is affirmed to have commenced in his

---

* Mid. Kingdom, ii. p. 201.

reign; but this is a mere fiction. It was not applied to years even in the time of Confucius." The writer then describes the structure of the cycle, showing that its original application was to days, for which purpose he admits it was "of very ancient practice." The first instance of its use in this manner, so far as known, dates back to B. C. 1752, in the commonly received chronology, which, however, he pronounces worthless. He then continues: —

"The state of confusion in which Chinese chronology is found to be, down to the time of the Eastern Chan,* and the fact that not a single instance of the application of the cycle to years can be found till after the classical period, are sufficient to satisfy us that this invaluable method of dating years was never used in ancient times. The first attempt to arrange the years in cycles of 60 is found in Szema-Ts'een's Historical Records, in a table constructed for the purpose of intercalation, and extending over a period of seventy-six years, the first year being B. C. 103. But instead of using the Chinese cyclical characters, he employs words of two and three syllables, which, considered from a Chinese stand-point, must be pronounced barbarous."

Mr. Chalmers closes his discussion of this point

* The Chan dynasty began to reign B. C. 1121.
† The Tsin dynasty began B. C. 249; the Han B. C. 202.

in these words: "So, then, the cycle of sixty years can not have commenced earlier than the Han, and owes its present form to the scholars of the Tsin, although the Chinese, for the most part, still glory in the delusion that it was invented by Hoang-ti (60 × 75 =) 4500 years ago."

Dr. Legge's own testimony is to the same effect. Having advanced the opinion that Hoang-ti, to whom the invention of the cycle is ascribed, is a fabulous person, he adds, —

"What is of more importance to observe is, that the cycle, as it is now universally recited and written, was not employed before the end of the former Han dynasty, i. e., until after the commencement of the Christian era, to chronicle *years* at all; its exclusive use was to chronicle *days*. Koo-yen-woo, one of the ablest scholars of the present dynasty, says expressly on this point, 'The twenty-two cycle characters (i. e., the ten stem characters from *këā* to *kwei*, and the twelve branch characters from *tsze* to *hae*) were used by the ancients to chronicle *days*, not *years*. For recording years, there were the ten names of *oh-fung*, etc., down to *twan-mung*, and the twelve branch names, *shĕ-t'e-kih*, etc., down to *juy-han*. The way of later times, to say that a year was *këā-tsze*, and so on, was not the ancient way.' Yen-woo then quotes from the preface of the *Wae-ke*, or 'Additional Records,' a supplement to the 'General Survey' of history by *Sze-ma-kwang*, with whom Lew-shu, its author, was associated, the following testimony: 'The years of the sovereigns before and after Fu-hi down to King Le, are, I apprehend, dark, and hardly to be ascertained,* and we borrow the names of the keā-tsze cycle to chronicle them,' adding himself, ' When did this practice of using the cycle names to chronicle *years* commence? It commenced in the time of the usurper Mang.' (A. D. 9–22)." †

Mr. Chalmers is of the opinion that the Chinese borrowed the elements of their chronological system. He remarks, "In the second century before the Christian era, the Chinese made extraordinary efforts to open communication with the west. They explored due west as far as the borders of Persia. At the same time they became acquainted with the northern parts of India. Sze-ma-Ts'een, who gives

---

* The first king, Le, in the list of Chinese sovereigns, is the tenth of the Chan dynasty, beginning to reign B. C. 878.

† Legge's Chinese Classics, vol. iii. prol. p. 82. "Sze-ma-kwang gets the credit of fixing the standard chronology; but let me call the attention of the student to Choo-he's (died A. D. 1200) account of the matter. He tells us, 'When Kwang first made a chronological scheme, his earliest date was the first year of Wei-lĕĕ (B. C. 424). Afterward he extended his dates to the time of Kung and Ho (B. C. 840). After this again, he made his " Examination of Antiquity," beginning with the highest period; but he could give no dates earlier than that time of Kung and Ho. It was Shaou-K'ang-tsĕĕ who pushed the calculations up to the first year of Yaou,'"—i. e., to B. C. 2357.—*Ib.*

I am unable to state the precise time when Sze-ma-kwang lived.

a full history of these discoveries, does not, indeed, tell us that they became acquainted with the period of Calippus,* either through the Bactrians or the Hindus; but there is scarcely a shadow of doubt that this was the case. In no other way can we account for the sudden appearance in Ts'een's history of a method so far in advance of anything known before in China, and one which had already been employed in the west for more than two centuries.†

This opinion, while probably correct in the main, is, I think, erroneous as to the derivation of the cycle of sixty from a foreign source. There seems to be good evidence that it was employed in comparatively ancient times, though its application was to days only. This supposition may explain some seeming contradictions and inconsistencies in the Chinese records, while it admits the antiquity of the cycle itself.

From what has now been advanced, it appears that the received Chinese chronological system, in its present form, owes its origin to scholars of the Han

---

* A correction of the Metonic cycle of 19 solar years, at which time the new moons return to the same days of the year. This period exceeding 235 lunations by 7½ hours, Calippus proposed to drop a day at the end of four cycles, or 76 years, by changing one of the months of 30 days to 29 days. — *Brande's Dict.*

† Chin. Classics, vol. iii. prol. pp. 96, 99.

dynasties (B. C. 202–A. D. 220.) That was the Augustan age in Chinese literature. Those scholars, doubtless, made the best use of the materials at their command in constructing an accurate chronology of their national history. The question then remains, Were those materials reliable? Did they have sufficient data for constructing an accurate chronology for times very long anterior to their own?

On this point, Dr. Legge remarks (vol. iii. prol. p. 83), "There can be no doubt that, before the Han dynasty, a list of sovereigns, and the lengths of their several reigns, was the only means which the Chinese had of determining the duration of their national history. And it would still be a sufficiently satisfactory method if we had a list of sovereigns, and of the years each reigned, that was complete and reliable. We do not have this, however. Even in the earlier part of the Han dynasty, Sze-ma-Ts'een's father and himself were obliged to content themselves with giving simply the names and order of most of the rulers of Shang and Hia.* The lengths of the several reigns in the standard chronology have been determined mainly, I believe, to make the whole line stretch out to the years which had been fixed, on astronomical considerations, for

* The IIId and IId dynasties, B. C. 2205-1122.

the periods of Chung-k'ang of the Hia dynasty, and of Yaou."

From this opinion of Dr. Legge I see no good reason for dissenting. It finds abundant support in the facts and arguments which he has furnished. He seems to regard the chronology from the commencement of the Chan dynasty (B. C. 1122) as reliable; that of the Shang dynasty (B. C. 1766–1122) as doubtful in regard to the details of reigns and dates; while that of the first or Hia dynasty is still more unreliable.

The founder of this dynasty was Yu the Great. The accounts given of him show that he was a mythological personage. His birth was preternatural. The record says, " His mother saw a falling star, which went through the constellation *Maou*, and in a dream her thoughts were moved till she became pregnant; after which she swallowed a spirit's pearl. Her back opened in due time, and she gave birth to Yu in Shih-neu. He had a tiger nose and a large mouth. . . . When he grew up, he had the virtue of a sage, and was nine cubits and six inches long." * The story of his great deeds, especially in draining off the waters of the inundation, is evidently mythical. One is reminded,

* Translation of the Annals of the Bamboo Books, in Dr. Legge's Chin. Classics, vol. iii. part 1, p. 117.

in reading it, of the labors of Hercules. So with his predecessors just named. Their births were as marvelous as that of Yu. Things are related of some of them which suggest a suspicion that they are confused traditions of events described in the Mosaic records. What more plausible supposition than that the inventor of the famous cycle of sixty, Nau (or Nao) the Great is no other than the Jewish patriarch himself, with but the slightest change or corruption of the name? One certainly can not but be surprised that such a writer as Pauthier should say, as before quoted, "Chinese history possesses all the characters of certitude which historic criticism has a right to demand." (Vol. ii. p. 33.)

And here the question naturally arises, whether the Chinese historians had the materials for writing authentic annals of the early ages of that country. The most valued of the Chinese classics, as already intimated, is the Shu-king, or Book of Records, of which Confucius is the reputed author or compiler (born B. C. 549). It is a series of dialogues designed to give a brief history of China from the time of Yaou down to Ping Wang, of the Chan dynasty, B. C. 770. "The internal evidence," says Williams (Mid. King. i. p. 504), "leads to the conclusion that Confucius acted principally as editor of documents existing in his day; but the changes that this ancient work underwent in his hands can not now be ascertained." One of his commentators gives the following description of the manner in which he used his materials: —

"He examined and arranged the grand monuments and records, deciding to commence with Yaou and Shun, and to come down to the times of Chan. When there was perplexity and confusion he removed them. Expressions frothy and unallowable he cut away. What embraced great principles he retained and developed. What were more minute, and yet of importance, he carefully selected. Of those deserving to be handed down to other ages, and to supply permanent lessons, he made in all one hundred books, consisting of canons, counsels, instructions, announcements, speeches, and charges."*

How much, therefore, in this venerable work are the genuine remains of remote antiquity, and how much originated with the compiler, we can not know. That the materials which came to his hand were more or less modified by him, is apparent. The whole cast of the work shows its author to have been more of a philosopher than historian. In reading these fragments in their translation, one can not but exclaim, How very different from the writ-

* Chin. Classics, vol. iii. prol. p. 4.

ings of Herodotus, who wrote at nearly the same time!

There is another fact of some importance. Whatever the Shu-king may have been originally, as to faithfully transmitting the early history and chronology of that nation, we now have that work only in mutilated form; and the mutilation is so extensive, and of such a character, as seriously to impair its authority in every particular. All readers of Chinese history are familiar with the burning of the books by the Emperor Chi Hoang-ti, B. C. 213, famed also as being the builder of the Great Wall: —

" The vanity of this monarch led him to endeavor to destroy all records written anterior to his own reign, that he might be by posterity regarded as the first emperor of the Chinese race. Orders were issued that every book should be burned, and especially the writings of Confucius and Mencius upon the feudal states of Chan, whose remembrance he wished to blot out. This strange command was executed to such an extent that many of the Chinese literati believe that not a perfect copy of the classical works escaped destruction, and the texts were only recovered by rewriting them from the memories of old scholars — a mode of reproduction that does not appear so singular to a Chinese as it does to us. . . . The destruction was, no doubt, as nearly complete as possible; and not only were many works entirely destroyed, but a shade of doubt thereby thrown over the accuracy of others, and the records of the ancient dynasties rendered suspicious as well as incomplete. Not only were the books sought after to be destroyed, but nearly five hundred literati were buried alive, in order that no one might remain to reproach, in their writings, the first emperor with having committed so barbarous and insane an act." *

As to the mode in which the Shu-king was recovered, accounts somewhat differ. One story is, that about thirty-seven years after the burning, some twenty-eight or twenty-nine chapters were partially restored from the memory of Fuh-Shang, a man then ninety years old. When the Ch'aou Ts'o, or imperial messenger, went to him, Fuh-Shang, being so aged, was unable to speak plainly, and made use of a daughter to repeat what he said; and her dialect being different from Ts'o's, he lost two or three in every ten words, supplying them, as he best could, according to his conception of the meaning. This account, as being more marvelous, has become the accepted history of the manner in which so many books of the Shu were recovered.

Another story relates that, when the orders were issued for the destruction of the books, the old man hid his copy in a wall. During the struggle that

---

* Williams's Mid. Kingdom, vol. ii. pp. 212, 213.

ensued, he was a fugitive in various parts; but when the rule of the Han was established, he went to look for his treasure, but many of the tablets had perished. He recovered only twenty-nine of the books. Forthwith he commenced teaching, making these the basis of his instructions, and from all parts of Shan-tung scholars resorted to him, and sat at his feet.

In all this time no copy had reached the court. The Emperor Wan (B. C. 178–156), after ineffectual attempts to find some scholar who could reproduce it, heard at last of Fuh-Shang, and sent to call him. Fuh was then more than ninety years old, and could not travel, and an officer called Ch'aou Ts'o was sent to receive from him what he had of the Shu. These books appear to have been transcribed in the new form of character introduced under the Tsin dynasty, as they were designated ever after "the modern text."

About forty years later, i. e., seventy-three after the burning, another mutilated copy of the Shu was discovered in the ruined house of Confucius, by one of his descendants. In this copy were found the twenty-nine books already recovered, and some twenty-five or thirty more, making in all fifty-eight of the one hundred of which the work originally consisted.

We come, then, to the conclusion that there is nothing in the literature or antiquities of China which contravenes or is inconsistent with the Mosaic history. Its most venerable classics, even conceding their genuineness in their present form, afford us no *reliable* chronology prior to the Chan dynasty (B. C. 1121). Their highest historical date, from which the cycle of sixty is reputed to be reckoned, is B. C. 2637, which is more than five hundred years subsequent to the flood of Noah, according to the Septuagint chronology. Fuh-hi himself lived only B. C. 2852. (Williams.) We have shown, besides, that exactness of dates in that earlier period can not be affirmed, since neither the Chinese calendar nor the cycle of sixty, which are professedly " the elements of Chinese chronology," can be relied on as accurate.

Dr. Legge's conclusion on this subject is as follows: " The accession of Yu, the first sovereign of the nation, was probably at some time in the nineteenth century before Christ; and previous to him there were the chiefs Shun and Yaou. Twenty centuries before our era, the Chinese nation appears beginning to be. To attempt to carry its early history to a higher antiquity is without any historical justification. There may have been such personages as Chinese writers talk of under the appellations of Chiuen-hiuh, Hoang-ti, Shinnung, Fuh-hi, etc., but they can not have been rulers of China. They are children of the mist of tradition, if we should not rather place them in the land of phantasy."

CHAPTER VII.

THE ARGUMENT FROM ETHNOLOGY.

Descent of all known Nations from Noah. — The Tenth Chapter of Genesis. — Importance of this Statement. — The Posterity of Shem; of Japheth; of Ham. — Agreement of this Account with History. — The so-called Aboriginal Races. — Scripture Language not to be pressed too literally. — Earlier and later Departures from the original Seats of Population. — Opinion of Rawlinson. — Alleged Aborigines of Egypt; of India; of Western Europe.

IN the preceding chapters we have shown at length that there is nothing in the known history or antiquities of the most ancient nations that is inconsistent with the Mosaic records. No authentic date goes back so far as the Noachian deluge; no event of which any memorial has been preserved in written annals or monumental inscriptions can be assigned to a period so remote.

We are now prepared to show, on the other hand, that all human history, so far as it speaks on the subject, confirms those sacred records. It testifies both that all the nations of the earth whose history is known, or can be traced back to their origin, are descended from the family of Noah, and that this has taken place since the period at which, according to the Septuagint chronology, he and his sons went forth from the ark to be the new heads of the human race. At the same time it may be shown that there is nothing in the condition or known facts of any nation inconsistent with the same origin. In other words, it may be proved beyond reasonable doubt, from the traces which man himself has left in the world, that all the known races and families which have peopled the earth sprung from a common source, on the continent of Asia, at a period not exceeding 5000 years ago, while there is no evidence as to any other race or people that is not reconcilable with that conclusion.

The Scripture account of the origin and descent of the various nations of men is given in the tenth chapter of Genesis. This chapter has always been considered a document of great interest to students of ethnology, and that, too, to whatever school of biblical interpretation they may belong, whether they accept or reject the Mosaic authorship of the Pentateuch, whether they assign the date of its composition to the reputed time of Moses, or a thousand years later. This is justly due to its subject-matter, and the place it occupies in the sacred narrative. It occurs just at that point where the account ceases to be general, and is thenceforth devoted more especially to a single branch of the human family. The first five chapters are occupied with the creation and the history of the antediluvian generations, the next three to the deluge, the ninth to the new laws and instructions given to Noah as the second founder of the race, and to the birth and conduct of his sons. Then follows, in the tenth chapter, a more detailed account of "the generations of the sons of Noah," giving the descendants of each, in some instances, to the third or fourth generation, and, in other cases, pointing out the geographical localities occupied by particular families.

This account is as follows, beginning with SHEM, who was probably the oldest of the three sons: —

1. "The children of Shem, Elam, and Asshur, and Arphaxad, and Lud, and Aram." (Ver. 22.)

Elam was the father of the *Elamites*, who dwelt around the northern shore of the Persian Gulf, in the province of Susiana, a part of ancient Babylonia.

Asshur is identical with the Assyrians in the upper valleys of the Tigris. After the Cushite invasion under Nimrod, this became a great Shemitic monarchy, whose capital, Nineveh, was one of the most splendid cities of ancient times.

Arphaxad, the eldest son of Shem, born two years after the flood, is believed to have settled the southern part of the Armenian highlands, near the sources of the Tigris. He was the ancestor of the Hebrews, so named from Eber, his grandson. Through Joktan, one of the sons of Eber, he is also the ancestor of numerous tribes of Semitic Arabs, the heads of whose families are given in ver. 26–30, and whose abode was "from Mesha as thou goest unto Sephar, a mount of the east," the modern Zafari or Dhafar, in the southern part of the Arabian peninsula.

Lud was the progenitor of the Lydians, in Asia Minor.

Aram, from a word signifying *high*, was the ancestor of the people occupying the highlands of Syria, and spreading thence into the vast plains of Mesopotamia. One of his sons, Uz, seems to have given his name to a district in the latter region, distinguished as the residence of the patriarch Job.

2. The second son of Noah was JAPHETH, a name signifying "enlargement," and denoting the wide extent of country which was to be occupied by his descendants. It is intimated, also, that this was to be the dominant race among the families of mankind (chap. ix. 27), both of which predictions have been signally verified in their subsequent history.

"The sons of Japheth: Gomer, and Magog, and Madai, and Javan, and Tubal, and Meshech, and Tiras." (Ver. 2.)

Gomer is regarded as the founder of the tribes which first settled on the shores of the Black Sea, and from thence, under the names of *Cimmerians*, *Cimbri*, or *Kymry*, ultimately spread throughout Northern Europe. His sons were Ashkenaz, Riphath, and Togarmah. The first is supposed by some to have given its name to *Asia*;[*] others regard it as equivalent to the Gothic *As-chunis*, the race of Ases, representing "the Germanic and Scandinavian nations not yet separated, and inhabiting a limited district to the north-east of the Black Sea."[†] Riphath is "the group of Celts, or Gauls, then established in their first European settlements on the *Riphæan* Mountains, — the present Carpathians, — before entering on their last migration toward the France of our days."[‡] Togarmah is universally regarded as *Armenia*.

Magog was the progenitor of an extensive race of wild people, north of the Caucasus, called by the Greeks Scythians. The ultimate subdivisions of this race, and their migrations in Europe and Asia, are little known. Many suppose them to constitute

---

[*] Philip Smith's Hist. of the World, p. 41.
[†] Anc. Hist. of the East, vol. ii. p. 61.   [‡] Ibid.

what is called the *Turanian* races, including the Hungarians and Sarmatians of the west, the Turks, Finns, Tatars of the north, and the original tribes of Central and Southern India on the south.

Madai represents the *Medes*, or the great Iranian family of Persia.

Javan was the father of the *Ionians* and Greeks. Of his four sons, Elishah is supposed to be the same as *Hellas;* Tarshish is thought to be *Tartessus*, in Spain, or, as others suggest, "the Tyrrhenian Pelasgians, who formed the primitive population of a great part of Italy;* Kittim, the inhabitants of Cyprus, where was the ancient town of *Citium;* and Dodanim, the *Dardanians* of Asia Minor, or the Epirotes, among whom was the famous town and oracle of *Dodona*.

Tubal is identified with the *Tibareni* of Pontus.

Meshech is probably the *Moschi* mentioned by Herodotus, as living in the same vicinity.

Tiras was the ancestor of the Thracians.

3. HAM was the youngest son of Noah. (Chap. ix. 24.) The word means "black," or "sunburned," and is especially applicable to the dark-skinned families of mankind, although individuals of other families, living in hot countries, acquire also dark complexions.

* Anc. Hist. of the East, vol. ii. p. 61.

"The sons of Ham: Cush, and Mizraim, and Phut, and Canaan." (Ver. 6.)

Cush was the ancestor of the Ethiopians. His eldest son, Seba, gave his name to the capital of the ancient kingdom of Meroe, and perhaps to the Sabeans, who dwelt partly in Arabia and partly in Abyssinia. His remaining sons, Havilah, Sabtah, Raamah, and Sabtechah, occupied the Arabian peninsula, and regions adjacent. From some one of these was descended Nimrod, the founder of the Babylonian empire, embracing the cities of Babel, Erech, Accad, and Calneh, in the land of Shinar, and possibly also the Assyrian kingdom, including the cities of Nineveh, Rehoboth, Caleh, and Resen.* Traces of this dynasty are seen in the names Cuthah, Cossaei, Chuzistan (Susiana), as also in the Hindu Koosh, the name still borne by the mountain regions of the Upper Indus.

Mizraim, a word in the dual form, meaning the two Egypts, i. e., the Upper and Lower. The Arabs still apply the name Misr both to the country itself and to its capital. The Ludim,

---

* The reading of Gen. x. 11, now generally preferred, is, "Out of that land he (i. e., Cush) went into Assyria." But it is not certain that the authorized version is not correct. Asshur, the son of Shem, may have been driven from the country before by this fierce Cushite invader, and founded the more northern monarchy called from him Assyria.

Anamim, Lehabim, Naphtuhim, Pathrusim, and Caphtorim are not personal names, but the appellations of tribes descended from Mizraim, which settled the country west of Egypt, the Delta, the maritime coast of Philistia, and perhaps Crete, and some of the neighboring islands. The Caphtorim may have given their name to the Copts, which, in turn, originated the Greek designation of the country, viz., *Ai-guptos*, Egypt, the land of the Copt.

Phut was probably the ancestor of the Libyans, inhabiting the country lying west of Egypt, along the northern shore of Africa.

Canaan was the father of the tribes which originally occupied Palestine, and which for the most part were exterminated by the Hebrews after their exodus from Egypt.

Such is a concise view of the origin and affinities of the various nations of mankind, as given in the Scriptures. That it is in entire harmony with secular history, so far as the latter is known, is evident to all intelligent readers. Now, this general fact, even if we can go no further, is very remarkable. We need not suggest how utterly unlike this inspired genealogy is to those which are found in the literature of any other people. Confessedly one of the oldest documents in the world, written in an age when as yet historical science had not begun to be, it maps out the existing families of mankind, and the localities they occupied, so minutely and accurately that the very latest investigations of modern science, with all the helps which have accumulated through thousands of years, serve only to verify and illustrate it. The very names contained in these patriarchal lists, entering into the numerous and intermingling channels of history, and floating down through the most diverse languages and dialects, are still, for the most part, recognizable as the distinctive appellations of the leading nationalities and peoples of this day. We know not how to resist the demonstration thus afforded both of the unity of all the known branches of the human race, and their origin at a date no more remote than the family of Noah.

But there are, or have been, nations and tribes of men whose descent from Noah can not be traced through any line of actual history. When his descendants migrated from the primitive seats in which, after the flood, they settled, to the countries which were to be their future homes, they found everywhere, it is said, *aboriginal races* already occupants of the soil. "We have," says Agassiz, "nowhere a positive record of a people having migrated far, and found countries entirely destitute of inhabitants." * These aboriginal races, often designated the pre-historic, but whom I would rather name the *un-historic nations*, prove, it is claimed, " the primitive ubiquity of mankind upon earth," and refute both the unity and the recent origin of the human family.

We think this statement, as is usual with objections of this kind, exaggerated. We know of no evidence to show the fact so universal as is alleged. Where is the " positive record of a people having migrated far," and not having " found countries entirely destitute of inhabitants "? The Pelasgians claimed to have been autochthons in Greece, though certainly having emigrated from Asia. We have never seen any evidence, or even allegation, that the ancient Egyptians did not consider themselves autochthons in the valley of the Nile. But without insisting on this, we may freely concede the reality of these so called aboriginal races without any detriment to the authority of the sacred record.

For, first, Scripture language in general statements is not always to be pressed to a rigidly literal meaning. Such a general statement is that of Gen. ix. 19 : " These are the three sons of Noah, and of them was *the whole earth* overspread." This may be taken literally, as, until recently, has always

* Christian Examiner, March, 1850.

been done, or its application may be limited to the "Adamite race," whose creation had just been recorded, and whose history is given in the subsequent portions of the sacred writings, without either affirming or denying the existence of another race not descended from Adam. The latter interpretation, though less obvious than the former, is certainly consistent with usage in other parts of the Bible. For example, the statement in Luke ii. 1, that "there went out a decree from Cæsar Augustus, that *all the world* should be taxed." Also, Matt. iii. 5, that there " went out to him [John] Jerusalem and *all* Judæa, and *all* the region round about Jordan." These statements are certainly to be understood in a sense more restricted than the literal one. Numerous other passages of a similar kind might be cited. Such being the case, the truthfulness of the Mosaic account, in the tenth chapter of Genesis, would not necessarily be impaired should it be proved that there has existed a race or races of men descended neither from Noah nor Adam. There are distinguished scholars who maintain the polygenetic origin of mankind, and endeavor to prove it from the Bible, believing that such an interpretation is consistent with the truthfulness of the sacred narrative.*

But without resorting to this possible view of the

* Page 170.

matter, — one in which I must, by no means, be understood to concur, — it is sufficient to say that if history does not, in the case of these nations now under consideration, establish their descent from Noah, neither, on the other hand, does it disprove it. The argument is at best a negative one, and determines nothing. If the Scripture narrative lacks confirmation as respects them, it is because there are no sufficient historical data in the case. At the same time these facts create a strong *probability* in favor of including these nations within the comprehension of the sacred record. If this be found to be literally true as respects all the nations whose history is known, the presumption is irresistible that it must be true respecting those whose history is unknown.

There is still another view which I deem more satisfactory; indeed, I see not why it does not meet all the exigencies of the case. It is conceded by all that the ancestors of the Semitic and Indo-European races remained together in their primitive seats longer than did those of the Turanian families; and some of the greatest scholars in comparative philology explain the diversity of language between these races by the supposition of *an earlier departure* of the latter from those seats. It has, indeed, been the common opinion that the whole race remained together in the region around Babylon till the confounding of their language, as described in the eleventh chapter of Genesis; and this, certainly, is the most obvious import of the record. But as I have already said, such is the use of general, comprehensive terms in the Bible, that there is nothing to forbid the idea of repeated *earlier separations* of colonies from the primitive seat, and their migration to different parts of the earth. The following extract gives the views of one of the most accomplished ethnographers, Sir Henry Rawlinson, on this point: —

"It must have been during this interval," referring to what he denominates the "Ante-Semitic Period," "that the nationalities must have been established, and that the original Scyths or Hamites appear to have been the principal movers in this great work of social organization. They would seem, indeed, simultaneously or progressively to have passed, in one direction, by Southern Persia into India; in another, through Southern Arabia to Ethiopia, Egypt, and Numidia. They must have spread themselves, at the same time, over Syria and Asia Minor, sending out colonies from one country to Mauritania, Sicily, and Iberia; from the other, to the southern coasts of Greece and Italy. They further, probably, occupied the whole area of modern Persia, and, thence proceeding to the north of Chalcis and the Caucasus, they penetrated to the extreme northern point of the European and Asiatic continents. It is well known to ethnographers that the passage of the Scyths is to be traced along these lines either by direct historical tradition or by the cognate dialects spoken by their descendants at the present day; and it is further pleasing to remark, that if we were to be guided by the mere linguistic paths, and independently of all reference to the scriptural record, we should still be led to fix upon the plains of Shinar as the focus from which the various lines had radiated.

"When I propose to class the multitude of nations here indicated in a common category, I do not pretend that a connection can be established between them by direct historical evidence, or by any positive test of philology. All that I maintain is, that certain special ethnic names have everywhere prevailed amongst them, and that either from ancient monuments, or from tradition, or from the dialects now spoken by their descendants, we are authorized to infer that, at some very remote period before the rise of the Semitic and Aryan nations, *a great Scythic population must have overspread Europe, Asia, and Africa*, speaking languages all more or less dissimilar in their vocabulary, but possessing similarity in certain common organic characteristics of grammar and construction." *

I have quoted this opinion of Rawlinson — which more strictly belongs to the argument from Philology — because it so clearly enunciates the fact of

* Notes on the early history of the Babylonians. — *Journal Roy. Asiatic Soc.*, vól. xv. p. 232.

an earlier immigration from the primitive seats of the race, than that which originated the nations of history, which fact, as it seems to me, is sufficient to account for the existence of the un-historic nations, without resorting to the supposition that they belonged to a pre-Adamite or a non-Adamite race.

But let us consider these so-called pre-historic races more in detail. Those of most importance are the alleged aborigines of Egypt, of India, and of Western Europe.*

I have already, in Chapter II., shown at length the entire want of evidence that any such primeval race ever occupied the valley of the Nile, or that Menes, the reputed founder of the nation, lived at a period at all inconsistent with the chronology of Moses, according to the Septuagint. Doubtless Egypt was one of the earliest nations, dating back, according to the best authority we have, — that of Eratosthenes, — as far as the 27th or 28th century B. C.† But this will allow some four or five hundred years after the flood in which that earliest Hamitic emigration from the first abode of Noah's family to the Nile valley may have taken place — a

---

* Mr. J. D. Baldwin makes these three cases corner-stones of his theory, which would attribute to the human race an antiquity of some 10,000 or 20,000 years. See his "Pre-historic Nations."

† Ante, p. 77.

period amply sufficient to meet all the exigencies of the case.

While there is, therefore, no proof of an alleged pre-historic people and civilization in Egypt, there is, on the other hand, much evidence confirmatory of the Mosaic account of the origin of that nation in the family of Ham.

We have, first, its name. This, in the language of its earliest inhabitants, was HAM, written in the hieroglyphics KEM, and in Coptic variously *Chame*, *Chemi*, and *Cheme*. The word even was applied to the soil itself, and thus, from its rich, dark color, came to signify "black," or rather "sunburned." Among the Hebrews, the name of the country was MISRAIM, the dual form of which seems to have denoted the two provinces of Upper and Lower Egypt — equivalent to the "two Egypts." This name is retained by the Arabs at the present day, who call the country Misr.

Traces of the names of the sub-families are also found in Egypt and the vicinity. "The Ludim were the true and dominant Egyptian race, called, in their language, Rut, or Lut, i. e., 'men' par excellence. Next, the Pathrusim, or 'people of the southern country,' that is, of the Thebaid, in Egyptian, P-TO-RES. The Naphtuhim, or people of Memphis, the sacerdotal name of which was Na

Phtah (the 'Part of Phtah'), and lastly, the Anamim, the Anu of the Egyptian monuments, who seem originally to have been dispersed throughout the whole Nile valley, and who have left traces of their name in the cities of Heliopolis (in Egyptian, An), Tentyris or Denderah (also sometimes called An), and Hermonthis (An-res, Southern An). A branch of this race maintained, for a long time, a separate existence in a part of the Sinaitic peninsula."* The Caphtorim, from whom were descended the Philistines,† are believed to have originated the name Coptos, as applied to the district or nome which they first settled, which, in its turn, suggested the Greek designation now borne by the entire country, viz., *Ai-guptos*, Egypt, i. e., the land of Copt. The Casluhim are supposed to have been the aborigines of Casiotis, a region lying on the borders of Egypt, toward Arabia Petræa, where is the modern town of El-kas. The Lehabim were undoubtedly the Libyans, who dwelt in the country west of Egypt, stretching across the desert to the Atlantic.

Second, The physical characteristics and language

---

* Anc. Hist. of the East, Lenormant, p. 202.

† In Gen. x. 14, they are said to have proceeded from the Casluhim. But this is probably an error, the clause having been transposed from Caphtorim. Compare Jer. xlvii. 4, Amos ix. 7.

of the people. The "Coptic skull and facial outline" are of "the Caucasian type." "We may allow, too, for considerable admixture with the cognate races to the south and east; and hence, on the one hand, the fullness of lips, and, on the other, the elongated Nubian eye, need not compel us to define the inhabitants of the Nile valley as an African rather than an Asiatic race. The Egyptians may be said to be intermediate between the Syro-Arabian and the Ethiopic type." *

Osburn is still more emphatic in expressing the same opinion. "There is yet another historic trait whereby this most ancient of languages and of modes of writing discourses of its origin. A large class of words in it are Semitic, or (to drop the terminology of a system which modern discovery has shown to be erroneous) are identical with the Hebrew of the Bible. The personal pronoun, the numerals, as well as many names and verbs, expressing actions or objects of very common occurrence, were the same in the Hebrew and Egyptian languages. . . . The words of the ancient Egyptian language, derived from the Hebrew, seem to be those which are of the very essence of human intercommunication. Such are pronouns, numerals, appellations for heat, cold, sitting, standing, moving,

* Smith's Dict. of Geog., art. *Ægyptus.*

11

dividing, etc., etc. We believe there exists, either in the Coptic or hieroglyphic texts, words identical with the Hebrew for these and other objects and ideas, all of which, so far as we can collect, are of this primitive and essential character in the structure of speech. Without them, it would be impossible for human beings to interchange thoughts or hold communication by speech at all." *

The testimony of the monuments is to the same effect, proving that the first settlement of the country was in Lower Egypt, precisely where the theory of an Asiatic origin would place it. Mr. Osburn shows this at length, quoting also the opinions of that eminent scholar Lepsius, that " the antiquity of Egyptian monuments, considered in relation to the larger masses of their remains, becomes less remote the higher we ascend the valley, in direct opposition to that which might have been anticipated according to the very eminently received theory, which assumes that the Egyptian civilization in the valley of the Nile originated in the south, and extended itself northward." He then continues, " Thus are we able to indicate, with absolute certainty, the point in the valley of the Nile in which are found the monuments of the remotest antiquity, and therefore, by the unerring analogy of the cus-

* Monumental History of Egypt, vol. i. pp. 209, 210.

toms of all ancient nations, the spot in which the first settlement in Egypt took place. Everything, both to the northward and southward of this point, is more modern. It will also be seen, by a reference to the map, that this point lies exactly parallel to the Isthmus of Suez, and is precisely the place at which immigrants over that thoroughfare between Asia and Africa, would first find a locality suited to their purpose, after traversing the sands of the desert, and attempting in vain to penetrate the swamps of the Delta."

The second of the supposed pre-historic nations, which, it is thought, could not have been of the Noachian family, are the aborigines of India. The Sanskrit, as is well known, belongs to the Aryan, or, as it is sometimes called, the Japetic family of languages, and is a sufficient proof that the people of India, who spoke that tongue, were of the Japetic stock. But it is claimed that when the Aryans came into India, they found there a primitive people of another race. Mr. Baldwin regards these as Cushites from Arabia, who were themselves preceded by a nation of Malays. He speaks of the "Cyclopean works of the Cushites" as found in the rock-cut temples, pagodas, etc., which Orientalists have generally regarded as not antedating the time of Buddha, say from five to six centuries B. C.

Now, we fully admit that the earliest writings of the Sanskrit-speaking people afford evidence that when that people reached the Punjaub, in Northern India, they found the country already occupied by inhabitants; but the same writings also as clearly seem to intimate that these were *not* a distinct race from the new comers. This evidence may be regarded as conclusive, at least in reference to those tribes called in the Vedas and elsewhere *Dasyas*,* and, in fact, all the original tribes of Northern India. This is shown, at some length, by Muir, in his "Sanskrit Texts," one of the most valuable works we have on Indian archæology.† He says, in conclusion, "I have gone over the names of the Dasyas, or Asuras, mentioned in the Rig-Veda, with the view of discovering whether any of them would be regarded as of non-Aryan or indigenous origin, but I have not observed any that appear to be of this character." ‡ He also quotes Professors Müller

---

* This, and not Dasyu (sing.), as Muir writes it, is the proper orthography, according to the usual way of Anglicizing Sanskrit words. The vowel in the last syllable is the same as in the first, viz., short ă, pronounced like *u* in *but* — Dăsyă.

† Original Sanskrit Texts, on the Origin and Progress of the Religion and Institutions of India, Part I. and History of the People of India, their Religion and Institutions, Part II. By J. Muir, Esq., D. C. L., late of the Bengal civil service. London, 1858 and 1860. ‡ Ibid p. 403.

and Lassen, to the same effect. "Dasyu simply means enemy; for instance, where Indra is praised 'because he destroyed the Dasyus, and protected the Aryan Color.' The Dasyus, in the Veda, may mean non-Aryan races in many hymns, yet the mere fact of tribes being called the enemies of certain kings or priests can hardly be said to prove their barbarian origin."* "Though in individual passages of the Mahabharata hatred and contempt are expressed in reference to the tribes living on the Indus and its five great tributaries, yet there is no trace of these tribes being ever regarded as of non-Indian origin. That there was no essential difference in their language is proved, as regards a later period, by the testimony of Panini."†

It is more probable that the primitive inhabitants of Southern India were of a non-Aryan stock, though I do not regard it as proved. Muir supposes them to have been allied to the Finnish or Tatar races, and Baldwin, as we have seen, to the Cushites. But in reality the question, both as it relates to them and to the more northern tribes, is of little comparative importance in the present discussion. It may be conceded that neither were Aryans without any danger of im-

---

* Müller, "Last Results of the Turanian Researches," p. 344.
† Lassen, Zeitsch. fur die Kunde des Morgenl, iii. 206.

pugning their descent from Noah. All the data we have from the Sanskrit, or elsewhere, show that the Aryans did not arrive in the upper valleys of the Indus and the Ganges much before the 13th century before Christ. Professor Müller, indeed, places it as early as the 15th century.* Even if we take this date, we have a period of some 1600 or 1700 years between it and the deluge, according to the Septuagint chronology, — a period amply sufficient to admit of repeated migrations from the original seats of the race. It is perfectly consistent with all the known facts respecting the original inhabitants of India, to assume that six, eight, or ten centuries after the deluge, straggling colonies of unlettered men wandered from their primitive home into this country, where they were found by the lettered Aryans perhaps as many centuries later. The supposition meets every exigency of the case, without resorting to the theory of a non-Adamite race, or a condition of human population at all inconsistent with the Bible chronology.

The remaining nations, termed pre-historic, which are claimed to have had an antiquity exceeding that of the deluge, are those whose remains are found in Europe, in association with the bones of antediluvian animals, accompanied by rude implements of

* Last Results, etc., p. 432.

flint and stone; also in ancient peat-beds, and at the bottom of various lakes. The character and probable origin of these remains will be considered at length in a subsequent chapter.*

It will be sufficient here to observe that the fact that all historical traces of these people are lost, — in other words, that they are pre-historic, — is, in the circumstances, no proof of a remote antiquity. Historic times in France, Germany, and Britain go but a little way back of Julius Cæsar. Even if we carry them as far as to the founding of Rome, B. C. 753, we have left a period of some twenty-five hundred years subsequent to the flood — a period amply sufficient for the rise, decay, and extinction of numerous nations, without having left even a name to indicate their origin or affinities.

It will be shown further that the most diligent explorers into the subject of these ancient remains are clearly of opinion that the people to whom they belonged were of Celtic origin, a branch of the great Aryan or Indo-European family, which confessedly were among the latest to leave the primeval seats of emigration in Asia.

The conclusion, then, to which Ethnology brings us, is in accordance with that derived from her sister sciences. So far as she can trace the origin and

* Infra, p. 320.

affinities of all, whether historic or unhistoric nations, she refers them to Central Asia and the family of Noah, and of course brings them into harmony with the chronology of that event. Where she can not trace that origin, she still leaves all the probabilities pointing the same way. She allows ample time, in the period since the flood, for all the migrations and developments required by the hypothesis of such a common descent, and, what is equally significant, she affords not one fact, nor even one reasonable probability, which is in the least inconsistent with it.

CHAPTER VIII.

THE ARGUMENT FROM PHYSIOLOGY.

Differences in existing Races of Men urged to prove a Plurality of Origin. — This Doctrine first advanced by La Peyrère. — Espoused by Infidel Writers. — Its supposed Bearings on Slavery. — Agassiz's Theory of Natural Provinces. — And of Unity of Species. — Estimate of this Theory. — I. It is a mere Theory. — II. No Inconsistency of known Facts with the Bible Narrative. — The Case of Cain and his Wife. — The Diversities among Races. — 1. Man is of a single Species, having same Physical and Mental Characteristics. — The single Head of the Animal Kingdom. — Intermixture of Races futile. — Unity of Species proves Unity of Origin. — 2. Similar Changes now taking place. — 3. Similar Changes among other Animals. — III. The Theory contrary to Analogy in other Departments of Creation. — IV. Opposed by Theological and Moral Science. — Conclusion.

THE preceding chapter was devoted to the argument from Ethnology, in what may be denominated its *historical* department. It is necessary, in view of objections which have been raised, to consider the same subject further under its *physiological* aspect.

We have argued the recent origin of man on earth from the fact that all known nations and families have descended from Noah, and therefore must come within the range of the Noachian chronology. But, apart from the historical evidence of such descent, it is urged, from a study of man as he now is, the diversities of his form, size, color, physiognomy, etc., that existing races could not have had a common origin. It is claimed that this diversity requires, and that the Scriptures themselves virtually warrant, the belief that beside Adam and his descendants, there has been at least one, perhaps several, other original stocks of the human family, older than that of Adam; that the Scripture account of the creation does not include these, being designed to refer only to that branch to which the Jews, and the white races generally, belonged; and therefore that we are at liberty to assign to this elder branch or branches any supposable antiquity which modern scientific discoveries may require.

This doctrine of the plurality of the human species was first advanced by La Peyrère, a French writer, in a work published in 1655. The ground on which he professed to base it was the Bible itself, which, he maintained, gave clear intimations of a non-Adamite race. The principal passage he adduced in support of this theory was that which speaks of

Cain, after he received sentence for his crime, going out from the presence of the Lord, and dwelling in the land of Nod, marrying a wife there, and building a city. (Gen. iv. 16, 17.) In the preceding verses, also, when complaining of his sentence, he says, " I shall be a fugitive and a vagabond in the earth, and it shall come to pass that every one that findeth me shall slay me ; " in consequence of which " the Lord set a mark upon Cain, lest any finding him should kill him." La Peyrère argued from these passages that there were, at that time, other men beside the family of Adam, which then consisted of only three persons ; and that these other men, or this other race, must have been previously created. They were, he thought, the ancestors of the Gentiles, while Adam was the ancestor of the Jewish race, with whose creation and history the Bible is mainly occupied.

The distinguished writer * from whom I derive this account says that La Peyrère was in no sense a free thinker (n'est nullement un libre penseur). " He was a theologian, a believer, who admits as true all that is in the Bible, and miracles in particular. . . . He always finds in the book which serves him as a guide some reason to support his interpretation. In a word, we find throughout, in

---

* Quatrefages, Introduction, pp. 7, 8.

La Peyrère, a mixture of complete faith and free criticism. This book convinced no one, and the doctrine of the author soon fell into forgetfulness, until within a few years since it has been reproduced and welcomed with a favor sufficiently unexpected."

It is not surprising that a theory so repugnant to the general teachings of Christianity should have met with favor from the apostles of French infidelity. Voltaire and Rousseau reproduced this argument in their attempts to shake the authority of the Scriptures.* But, according to Quatrefages, it was reserved for America to bring this doctrine into notice, and give it any considerable currency. His account of the matter is substantially this: In 1846 Professor L. Agassiz, in a visit to Charleston, S. C., broached the theory of the plurality of origin for the human race in the "Literary Conversations Club," of that city. The expression of these views aroused a decided antagonism in that meeting. The professor found two able opponents in the persons of the Rev. Drs. Bachman and Smyth, who both spoke and wrote in opposition to him. Professor A. published his views *in extenso* in the "Christian Examiner" for March and July, 1850; and afterward, in 1854, in an essay entitled "The Natural Provinces

* Smyth's Unity of the Human Species, p. 163, Eng. ed.

of the Animal World, and their Relation to the Different Types of Man," inserted in Nott and Gliddon's "Types of Mankind." In 1849 Dr. Nott published his work entitled "Biblical and Physical History of Man," being the substance of two lectures delivered by him in New Orleans the previous year. In 1854 Nott and Gliddon issued the book just mentioned on the "Types of Mankind."

It was in this manner that the discussion of the question as to the unity of the human race was renewed, after a silence of two hundred years. The agitation of it on this side of the Atlantic drew attention to it on the other, and brought into the field a considerable number of able writers, most of whom, so far as I am aware, took ground in favor of the unity of the race as descended from the family of Noah.

According to Quatrefages, the chief interest of the discussion in this country grew out of its supposed bearings upon the institution of slavery. "Thus in America," he says, "the anthropological question is complicated with that of slavery; and from reading the greater part of the writings that have come to us from beyond the sea, it is clear that there they are, before all, advocates or opponents of that institution. But in the United States it is necessary always to be biblical; and hence came the particular shades which distinguish certain anthropological works in that country. The anti-slavists are generally outspoken monogenists, and accept the dogma of Adam as it is commonly understood. Such is, also, professedly the faith of a certain number of slavists. These latter, to justify their conduct toward their *black brethren*, refer to the history of Noah and his sons. Ham, say they, was cursed by his father, and condemned to be the servant of his brethren. The negroes descended from Ham; therefore, in reducing them to slavery, we are obeying Holy Writ. But America reckons some beside slavists who are polygenists. These latter have again placed in honor, under different forms and in support of modern knowledge, the doctrine of La Peyrère, of which otherwise they say but little. All, speaking highly of the inspiration of the Old and New Testaments, endeavor to demonstrate, by linguistic, geographical, and historical researches, that the biblical accounts relative to the origin and affiliation of men apply only to the white races. Thus put at ease, they have regarded the different groups as so many distinct species." *

By far the most distinguished of this latter class of writers is Professor Agassiz. His opinions I will cite at length from the essay before referred to,

* Quatrefages, p. 11.

published in the "Christian Examiner" for July, 1850.

"The circumstance that, wherever we find a human race naturally circumscribed, it is connected in its limitation with what we call, in natural history, a zoölogical and botanical province, — that is to say, with a natural limitation of a particular association of animals and plants, — shows most unequivocally the intimate relation existing between mankind and the animal kingdom in their adaptation to the physical world. The Arctic race of men, covering the treeless region near the Arctics, in Europe, Asia, and America, is circumscribed, in the three continents, within limits very similar to those occupied by that particular combination of animals which are peculiar to the same tracts of land and sea.

"The region inhabited by the Mongolian race is also a natural zoölogical province, covered by a combination of animals naturally circumscribed within the same regions. The Malay race covers also a natural zoölogical province. New Holland again constitutes a very peculiar zoölogical province, in which we have another particular race of men. And it is further remarkable, in this connection, that the plants and animals now living on the continent of Africa, south of the Atlas, within the same range within which the Negroes are naturally circumscribed, have a character differing widely from that of the plants and animals of the northern shores of Africa and the valley of Egypt; while the Cape of Good Hope, within the limits inhabited by Hottentots, is characterized by a vegetation and a fauna equally peculiar, and differing in its features from that over which the African race is spread.

"Such identical circumscriptions between the limits of two series of organized beings, so widely differing as man, and animals, and plants, and so entirely unconnected in point of descent, would, to the mind of a naturalist, amount to a demonstration that they originated together within the districts which they now inhabit. We say that such an accumulation of evidence would amount to demonstration; for how could it, on the contrary, be supposed that man alone would assume peculiarities and features so different from his primitive characteristics, while the animals and plants circumscribed within the same limits, would continue to preserve their natural relations to the fauna and flora of other parts of the world?

"If the Creator of one set of these living beings had not been also the Creator of the other, and if we did not trace the same general laws throughout nature, there might be room for the supposition that, while men inhabiting different parts of the world originated from a common center, the plants and animals now associated with them in the same countries originated on the spot. But such inconsistencies do not occur in the laws of nature.

"The coincidences of the geographical distribution of the human races with that of animals, the disconnection of the climatic conditions where we have similar races, and the connection of climatic conditions where we have different human races, show, further, that the adaptation of the different races of men to different parts of the world must be intentional, as well as that of other beings; that men were primitively located in the various parts they inhabit; and that they arose everywhere in those harmonious numeric proportions with other living beings, which would at once secure their preservation, and contribute to their welfare. To suppose that all men originated from Adam and Eve is to assume that the order of creation has been changed in the course of historical times, and to give to the Mosaic record a meaning that it was never intended to have. On that ground we would particularly insist upon the propriety of considering Genesis as chiefly relating to the history of the white race, with special reference to the history of the Jews."

Notwithstanding that the learned professor thus denies the common descent of mankind from Adam and Eve, he still insists that the race is but of one species. He remarks, —

"There are two distinct questions involved in the subject which we have under discussion — the Unity of Mankind, and the Diversity of Origin of the Human Races. These are two distinct questions, having almost no connection with each other; but they are constantly confounded, as if they were but one."* And again, "We began by stating that the subject of unity and plurality of races involves two distinct questions — the question of the essential unity of mankind, and the question of the origin

* Christ. Exam. July, 1850, p. 110.

of men upon our globe. There is another view involved in this second question, which we would not dismiss without a few remarks.

"Are men, even if diversity of origin is established, to be considered as belonging to one species? or are we to conclude that there are several different species among them? The writer has been in this respect strangely misrepresented. Because he has at one time said that mankind constitutes one species, and at another time has said that men did not originate from one common stock, he has been represented as contradicting himself, as stating at one time one thing and at another time another. He would, therefore, insist upon this distinction — that the unity of species does not involve a unity of origin, and that a diversity of origin does not involve a plurality of species. Moreover, what we should now consider as the characteristic of species is something very different from what has formerly been so considered. As soon as it was ascertained that animals differ so widely, it was found that what constitutes a species in certain types is something very different from what constitutes a species in other types, and that facts which prove an identity of species in some animals do not prove an identity or plurality in another group." (p. 113.)

Thus we see this distinguished naturalist holds to the doctrine of the unity of mankind, but with this he likewise maintains the plurality of origin; a position which, according to the manner in which certain matters in natural science have heretofore been viewed, is a strange one. But some others have adopted it; and they maintain the unity of the human races in such a way as to be consistent, in their own view, with the declaration of Paul, when he says, " He [God] hath made of one blood all nations of men for to dwell on all the face of the earth." (Acts xvii. 26.) There is the actual relationship of consanguinity — all are made of one blood, although the different races are descended from different, distinct, primitive pairs, which were created at different times in different parts of the earth. And Prof. Agassiz is particular to state that he regards all the races, though descended from different primeval pairs, as having the same relations to the moral government of God, as constituting, spiritually and intellectually, one brotherhood, and as having one destiny. He claims, moreover, that all this is consistent with the sacred Scriptures, and feels it keenly that he has been represented as holding doctrines at variance with the teachings of the Bible.

Let us now inquire what estimate should be placed upon the theory thus set forth.

I. In the first place, let it be remembered that it is a *mere theory*. No one, so far as we know, has attempted to *prove* it, or even claimed that it is susceptible of proof. It is an hypothesis resorted to for the purpose of escaping the difficulties supposed to arise from the inconsistency of certain facts revealed by modern science with the ordinary view of the chronology and unity of the race. It is not pretended that any clear traces can be discerned along the track of man's history of a plural origin of the race. There is certainly, as we go back in time, a convergence of lineage, of language, and of tradition toward *one* parental center; there is not toward any other. The streams of migration during the ages have apparently come from *one* common fountain in Central Asia; there is no other such fountain from which they came. If there are or have been any nations whose origin can not be traced to Adam or Noah, it is sufficient to say that neither can they be traced to any other source. All positive evidence that there was more than one parental stock, from whom the various races and families have descended, is absolutely wanting.

II. The alleged inconsistency of any known facts of science with the Scripture doctrine, to obviate which resort is had to the theory of plurality, has *never yet been demonstrated*.

Take, first, the case of Cain. It is said that he was afraid that somebody would slay him for his crime of murdering Abel; and as there were then but three living persons of the family of Adam, he must have referred to people of another race. But how is it ascertained that there were then but three persons living? Who knows how many children may have been born to our first parents between these two brothers, or how many after the birth of Abel? Who can tell what the age of either of the brothers was at the time of the homicide? Certainly, even Abel had grown to something like man's estate, and Cain was older than he. Besides, why limit the murderer's fears to persons then living? There were generations to come, among whom he knew that the story would be told; and he might well apprehend that some avenger of blood would arise long years after that, to redress the wrong done to his kinsman, and inflict justice upon his slayer.

In the matter of Cain's wife, also, the difficulty is greatly exaggerated. It is conceded that the first marriage among Adam's descendants must have been between a brother and sister. But it by no means follows that such a marriage, in those circumstances, was incestuous, in the later signification of that term. He who appointed marriage for the welfare of the race could have sanctioned it, in this necessary instance, as readily as he forbade the repetition of it afterward. Besides, the difficulty is not obviated by the supposition of another race, among whom Cain may have found a wife. For she must, again, have been descended from some primeval pair, in whose family the same difficulty must have existed — a marriage equally incestuous. Or if, to avoid this, you suppose still another race, whence the needed wife or husband might have come, you only shift the difficulty again to this. You must, therefore, resort to the absurd supposition of an infinite number of distinct human races, or you must confront the marriage itself, and justify it in its own nature, which you can as well do in the case of Cain and his sister-wife as in any other.

But the chief difficulties which have caused a resort to the theory under examination grow out of the diversities in color, physiognomy, and other personal characteristics existing among different branches of the race. It is claimed that these diversities are too great, and have been of too long standing to be consistent with the idea of a common descent, especially within the circumscribed period between their actual appearance and the time of Noah. In the proof and illustration of these diversities, great research and learning have been exhibited, and many able works have been written. To treat this topic according to its importance will require a somewhat lengthened consideration.

The subject really involves two questions: first, Can the known diversities existing in the various branches of the human race have come, in the way of gradual variation, from one original type? and second, If intrinsically possible, can it have been done within the limited space of *time* which, with the most pliant Scripture chronology, we are able to allow for it? These questions, however, though properly separate, so run into each other, that it will be more easy to consider them together.

The affirmative of both of them is argued, 1. From the superficial character of these diversities; 2. The actual changes which have been observed as taking place in particular circumstances of the race; 3. From the analogy of similar changes which have occurred in other animals, particularly in those most nearly associated with man, and subject to the same general influences that have operated on him.

1. Naturalists are not agreed as to the number of sub-races into which the human family should be divided. Some make two only, the white and the black. Morton reckons twenty-two, and Burke sixty-three. Agassiz makes eight principal centers of creation, which he calls "zoölogical provinces," viz., the Arctic, the Mongolian, the European, the American, the Negro, the Hottentot, the Malay, and the Australian. But whatever be the number, it is now regarded as settled that the differences between them are not *specific* — that the entire genus *homo* consists of but a single *species*.

In this position all the best authorities are agreed. "Linnæus, Blumenbach, Cuvier, Lawrence, Camper, Dr. Prichard, Humboldt, Zimmerman, Pickering, and many other distinguished naturalists, consider the species as sufficiently proved; and the French Academy of Science, in one of its reports, speaking of Blumenbach, remarks that 'a profound gulf, without connection or passage, separates the human species from every other. There is no other species that is akin to the human, nor any genus whatever. The human race stands alone.'" *

This is proved, first, from the fact that "there is an essential identity among men of all races in physical and mental characteristics." † Our space will not allow us to go over the whole field, and show this fact in detail. Dr. Bachman, in his "Doctrine of the Unity of the Human Race," adduces a large number of particulars in the osteological structure of man in which the various races are identical. Professor Godron, the distinguished French naturalist, in the second chapter of his great work, ‡ treats

* Dr. John Hall, in Pickering's Races of Men, Introd. p. 27.
† Professor J. D. Dana, Geology, p. 584.
‡ De l'Espèce et des Races dans les êtres Organisés, et specialement de l'Unité de l'Espèce Humaine. Par D. A. Godron, Docteur en Médecine, Docteur ès Sciences, Doyen de la Faculté des Sciences de Nancy, Professeur d'Histoire Naturelle à la même Faculté, Directeur du Jardin des Plantes, etc. 2 vols., 8vo.

of the organic, physiological, and psychological differences which were present among themselves, and compares them with those which are shown among domestic animals. He takes into view all the variations in the form of the skull, and bones in other parts of the body, the size, color of the skin, color and quality of the hair, etc., etc., and draws from the whole the following conclusion: "The organic and physiological differences seen in the different varieties of mankind are analogous to those which are known to exist among the domestic animals, and the psychological differences of the different peoples of the earth are neither original nor permanent." And Professor Owen, than whom there is no greater authority on topics of this kind, says, "With regard to the value to be assigned to the distinctions of race, in consequence of not any of these differences being equivalent to those characteristics of the skeleton or other parts of the frame upon which specific differences are founded by naturalists in reference to the rest of the animal creation, I have come to the conclusion that man forms one species, and that *differences are but indicative of varieties.* . . . These varieties merge into each other by easy gradations. The Malay and the Polynesian link the Mongolian and the Indian [Indo-European] varieties, and the Indian is linked by the Esquimaux again to the Mongolian. The inhabitants of the Andaman Islands, New Guinea, New Caledonia, and Australia, in a minor degree, seem to fill up the hiatus between the Malay and the Ethiopian varieties; and in no case can a well-marked, definite line be drawn between the physical characteristics of allied varieties, these merging more or less gradationally the one into the other." * "The unity of the human species is demonstrated by the constancy of those osteological and dental characters to which the attention is more particularly directed in the investigation of the corresponding characters in the higher quadrumana." †

2. In the ascending scale of animals the number of species in any genus diminishes as we rise, and should, by analogy, be the smallest at the head of the series. Professor Dana states this rule thus: "Among the mammals the higher genera have few species, and the highest group next to man — that of the orang outang — contains only eight, and these eight belong to two genera. . . . Analogy requires that man should here have the preëminence. If more than one species be admitted, there is scarcely a limit to the number that may be made." ‡ The different varieties shade off into each other by

---

* Lect. before Cambridge University, May 10, 1859, p. 98.
† Ibid. p. 103.   ‡ Geology, p. 584.

insensible gradations. "Some," says Bachman,* " have divided man into two species, some into three, some into five, one into eight separate creations, and one, more enthusiastic than all the rest, can see no reason why 'there were not originally a hundred species.' (Nott's Bib. Hist. p. 33.)" A position which thus violates one of the great principles that rule through the whole animal world can not be admitted without the most stringent necessity.

3. All the varieties of the race are capable of intermixture, and the mixed breeds have the power of self-perpetuation to any extent, which is not true of hybrids between two distinct species. It is a law both of the animal and vegetable kingdoms, that the union of different species can never produce a perpetually fertile offspring. In other words, the distinction of species through the whole realm of life is fixed and permanent; it is never obliterated by intermixtures; it is extinguished only by the extinction of the race itself. This law is set forth so clearly and forcibly by Professor Dana,† that we take leave to quote it in full.

"PERMANENCE OF SPECIES.

" What now may we infer with regard to the permanence or fixedness of species from a general survey of nature?

* Examination of the Character of Genera and Species, p. 18.
† In the Bib. Sacra for October, 1857, pp. 862-866.

"Let us turn again to the inorganic world. Do we there find oxygen blending by indefinite shadings with hydrogen, or with any other element? Is its combining number, its potential equivalent, a varying number — usually 8, but at times 8 and a fraction, 9, and so on? Far from this; the number is as fixed as the universe. There are no indefinite blendings of elements. There are combinations by multiples or sub-multiples, but these prove the dominance and fixedness of the combining numbers.

"But further than this, fixed numbers, definite in value and defiant of all destroying powers, are well known to characterize nature from its basement to its top-stone. We find them in combinations by volume as well as weight, that is, in all the relations of chemical attraction; in the mathematical forms of crystals and the simple ratios in their modifications — evidence of a numerical basis to cohesive attraction; in the laws of light, heat, and sound. Indeed, as we have elsewhere said, the whole constitution of inorganic nature, and of our minds with reference to nature, involves fixed numbers; and the universe is not only based on mathematics, but on finite determinate numbers, in the very natures of all its elemental forces. Thus the temple of nature is made, we may say, of hewn and measured stones, so that, although reaching to the heavens, we may measure, and thus use the finite to rise toward the infinite.

"This being true for inorganic nature, it is necessarily the law for all nature; for the ideas that pervade the universe are not ideas of contrariety, but of unity and universality beneath and through diversity.

. . . . . .

"Looking to facts in nature, we see, accordingly, everywhere, that the purity of species has been guarded with great precision. It strikes us naturally with wonder, that even in senseless plants, without the emotional repugnance of instinct, and with reproductive organs that are all outside, the free winds being often the means of transmission, there should be rigid law sustained against intermixture. The supposed cases of perpetuated fertile hybridity are so exceedingly few as almost to condemn themselves, as no true examples of an abnormity so abhorrent to the system. They violate a principle so essential to the integrity of the plant-kingdom, and so opposed to nature's whole plan, that we rightly demand long and careful study before admitting the exceptions.

"A few words will explain what is meant by perpetuated fertile hybridity. The following are the supposable grades of results from intermixture between two species: —

" 1. No issue whatever — the usual case in nature.

" 2. Mules (naming thus the issue) that are wholly infertile, whether among themselves or in case of connection with the pure or original stock.

" 3. Mules that are wholly infertile among themselves, but may have issue for a generation or two by connection with one of the original stock.

" 4. Mules that are wholly infertile among themselves,

but may have issue through indefinite generations by connection for each with an individual of the original stock.

"5. Mules that are fertile among themselves through one or two generations.

"6. Mules that are fertile among themselves through many generations.

"7. Mules that are fertile among themselves through an indefinite number of generations.

"The cases 1 to 5 are known to be established facts in nature, and each bears its testimony to the grand law of purity and permanence. The examples under the heads 2 to 5 become severally less and less numerous, and art must generally use an unnatural play of forces or arrangements to bring them about.

"Again, in the animal kingdom there is the same aversion in nature to intermixture, and it is emotional as well as physical. The supposed cases of fertile hybridity are fewer than among plants.

"Moreover, in both kingdoms, if hybridity be begun, nature commences at once to purify herself as of an ulcer on the system. It is treated like a disease, and the energies of the species combine to throw it off. The short run of hybridity between the horse and the ass, — species very closely related, — reaching its end *in one single generation*, instead of favoring the idea that the perpetuated fertile hybridity is possible, is a speaking protest against a principle that would ruin the system, if allowed free scope.

" The finiteness of nature in all her proportions, and the necessity of finiteness and fixedness for the very existence of a kingdom of life, or of human science its impress on finite mind, are hence strong arguments for the belief that hybridity can not seriously trifle with the true units of nature, and, at the best, can only make temporary variations.

" It is fair to make the supposition that, in case of a very close proximity of species, there might be a degree of fertile hybridity allowed, and that a closer and closer affinity *might* give a longer and longer range of fertility. But the case just now alluded to, seems to cut the hypothesis short; and, moreover, it is not reasonable to attribute such indefiniteness to nature's outlines, for it is at variance with the spirit of her system.

" Were such a case demonstrated by well-established facts, it would necessarily be admitted; and we would add, that investigations directed to this point are the most important that modern science can undertake. But until proved by arguments better than those drawn from domesticated animals, we may plead the general principle against the *possibilities* on the other side. If there is a law to be discovered, it is a wide and comprehensive law, for such are all nature's principles. Nature will teach it, not in one corner of her system only, but more or less in every part. We have, therefore, a right to ask for well-defined facts, taken from the study of successive generations of the interbreeding of species known to be distinct.

" Least of all should we expect that a law which is so

rigid among plants and the lower animals should have its main exceptions in the highest class of the animal kingdom, and its most extravagant violations in the genus Homo; for if there are more than one species of Man, they have become, in the main, indefinite by intermixture. The very crown of the kingdom has been despoiled; for a kingdom in nature is perfect only as it retains all its original parts in their full symmetry, undefaced and unblurred. Man, by receiving a plastic body, in accordance with a law that species most capable of domestication should necessarily be most pliant, was fitted to take the whole earth as his dominion, and live under every zone. And surely it would have been a very clumsy method of accomplishing the same result, to have made him of many species, all admitting of indefinite or nearly indefinite hybridization, in direct opposition to a grand principle elsewhere recognized in the organic kingdoms. It would have been using a process that produces impotence or nothing among animals for the perpetuation and progress of the human race. . . .

"We have, therefore, reason to believe, from man's fertile intermixture, that he is one in species; and that all organic species are divine appointments, which cannot be obliterated unless by annihilating the individuals representing the species."

We regard it, then, as a settled truth, no longer capable of being controverted, that the human family, throughout all its varieties, constitutes *one species*.

And if so, then they *may*, at least, have all descended from a single parental pair. However great the diversities between them, or of however long standing, there is nothing in this fact to disprove the Bible doctrine of the unity of the race, or to make necessary the hypothesis of one, or any number of races, different from and perhaps older than that which descended from Adam.

We have said that they *may* have all descended from one pair; and this is all that my argument requires in this place. But we might go further, and insist that the unity of species *requires* the idea of such a descent; that it is given, indeed, in the very nature of a species. "We unite," says Candolle, "under the designation of a *species* all those individuals who mutually bear to each other so close a resemblance as to allow of our supposing that *they may have proceeded originally from a single being or a single pair*."* Professor Dana's definition appears to amount to the same thing. He says, "A species corresponds to a specific amount or condition of concentrated force, defined in the act or law of creation. . . . The species in any particular case began its existence when the first germ-cell or individual was created. . . . But the germ-cell is but an incipient state in a cycle of changes,

---

* Physiologie Végétale, ii. p. 689.

and is not the same for two successive instants; and this cycle is such that it includes, in its flow, a reproduction after an interval of a precise equivalent of the parent germ-cell. Thus an indefinite perpetuation of the germ-cell is in fact effected, yet it is not mere endless being, but like evolving like in an unlimited round. Hence, when individuals multiply from generation to generation, it is but a repetition of the primordial type-idea; and the true notion of the species is not in the resulting group, but in the idea or potential element which is at the basis of every individual of the group; that is, the specific law of force, alike in all, upon which the power of each, as an existence and agent in nature, depends." * This is but saying, in exact, scientific language, that all the individuals of a species are developed by this law of force from one " parent germ-cell." If, then, all the individuals of the human family are of one species, their descent from one pair is, by that very fact, established.

But we are aware that this idea of a species, as including the element of descent from a single pair or individual, is not conceded by polygenists. Agassiz, as we have seen, though asserting the specific unity of mankind, holds such an idea of species as to permit their descent from eight origi-

* Bib. Sac. October, 1857, p. 861.

nal centers. We will not, therefore, insist on the argument here, though we still claim that, on this point, he and all pluralists depart from the established usage of science, inventing definitions of their own for the sole purpose of maintaining preconceived theories.*

2. Not only are the diversities in the human family consistent with the unity of the species, but changes are even now constantly taking place, analogous, both in kind and degree, to those which originated those diversities. Nor are these changes confined to any race or country. They are seen in all cases where there is any considerable change in the condition and circumstances under which they live.

Says the writer of the article "Man," in the "Cyclopædia of Natural History," "What may be the precise influences which have caused so much difference to exist between the individuals of the human race, we are unable to say; but instances are constantly occurring which seem to show us how possible it is that all the varieties in human beings have occurred in a common family. Even amongst the races of our own island, when exposed to circumstances which deprive them of their usual nutriment and means of developing the civilized

* See Bachman's "Examination," etc.

instincts of mankind, we find that they sink in character, and become physically degraded to a level with races whose features, at first sight, are very far removed. We need but to travel across the Irish Channel to see many groups of our Celtic fellow-subjects, who have been reduced by famine and disease to a degraded condition closely bordering on that of these savages." To the same effect remarks Professor Whitney,* "Physical science is as yet far from having determined the kind, the rate, and the amount of modification which external conditions, as climate and mode of life, can introduce into a race-type; but that within certain undefined limits their influence is very powerful, is fully acknowledged. There is, to be sure, a party among zoölogists and ethnologists who insist much upon the dogma of 'fixity of type,' and assert that all human races are original; but the general tendency of scientific opinion is in the other direction, toward the fuller admission of the variability of species. The first naturalists are still, and more than ever, willing to admit that all the differences now existing among human races may be the effects of variation from a single type, and that it is at least not necessary to resort to the hypothesis of different origins in order to explain them."

* Language, and the Study of Language, p. 376.

Two or three instances of change in the physical characteristics of a people are all that our space will permit us to cite. One is that of the Jews. "For 1800 years," says Owen,* "that race has been dispersed in different latitudes and climates, and they have preserved themselves distinct from intermixture with other races of mankind. There are some Jews still lingering in the valley of the Jordan, having been oppressed by the successive conquerors of Syria for ages — a low race of people, and described, by trustworthy travelers, as being black as any of the Ethiopian races. Others of the Jewish people, participating in European civilization, and dwelling in the northern nations, show instances of the light complexion, the blue eyes, and the fair hair of the Scandinavian families. The condition of the Hebrews since their dispersion has not been such as to admit of much admixture by the proselytism of household slaves. We are thus led to account for the differences in color by the influence of climate, without having to refer them to original or specific distinctions."

Another case is that of the Portuguese, who settled in the East Indies in the beginning of the sixteenth century. They have now become as dark in their complexions as the native Hindus.

---

* Lecture before Camb. University, 1859, p. 96.

Latham * thus speaks of changes which have taken place in the Mantchu population of Tartary: "Well clothed, warmly lodged, and with an environment of civilization, many of the Mantchus of China have changed their physiognomy no less than their habits. Sir John Barrow saw both men and women of Mantchu blood who were extremely fair, and of a florid complexion. Some had light blue eyes, straight or aquiline noses, brown hair, immense bushy beards, and had more the appearance of Greeks than of Tatars. Whatever intermixtures may account for this description, it will not explain the beards. The Chinese have nothing of the kind; still less have the Mongols."

Mr. Reade, the writer quoted so largely in the Appendix, J, p. 396, after mentioning the various sub-classes of the African population, describes at length the changes which take place among them as they remove from their native districts toward the Atlantic coast, the proper locality of the typical negro.

"That the red races change to black when they descend into the lowlands can not, I think, be easily disputed. I was told by the Senegal residents, that some years ago it was very rarely that one saw a black Fula or Puelh. It is now almost impossible to find a Fula without travel-

* Descriptive Ethnology, i. p. 264.

ing some distance into the interior. With the Mandingos it is much the same. These two tribes are driving out the negroes that they may command certain positions on the river; the result of which is, that they are becoming negroes themselves.

"In the same manner the Fans, of the Sierra del Crystal, are taking possession of the lower Gaboon. There are now no black Fans. But they will be found there by future travelers.

"Sangnier, in his 'Voyage au Sénégal,' writes, 'The Satinguets (African), people of Podor, toward the Senegal, are not as black as the other negroes, but copper-colored and red; their children, who come to the Senegal and dwell there for some time, have a skin much blacker than it was.'

"It frequently occurs, too, that families or tribes with negro characters are found under circumstances which render an intermixture of race impossible; the cause, therefore, can only be ascribed to physical influence. . . .

"It has been frequently asserted that the Ethiopian can not change his skin; that Nature has placed, like a curse, an indelible stamp upon his form and features, which will never change, to whatever climate he may be borne.

"But proverbs are not arguments, nor assertions facts. That the type is stubborn I will allow, but I can not admit that it is permanent."

But it may be said that though certain changes in physical characteristics may have taken place in the lapse of time, yet all the existing races had reached their present types at the very beginning of the historic period, within a very few centuries, at most, of the flood — a space much too short to have developed the differences between them. Representations both of men and animals are found on the oldest monuments of Egypt and Assyria, which show all the diversities now existing among different nations. Even then, if we concede the common origin of men, we are compelled to throw it so far back in time as to be wholly inconsistent with the Mosaic chronology.

To this allegation Dr. Bachman well replies that the monumental figures referred to are too rude and imperfect to have any real value in the argument.

" The reduced figures in Nott and Gliddon we have not compared with the originals. Taking them, however, just as they are presented to the reader, and presuming them to be faithful copies, we have no hesitation in saying that, for all the purposes of the naturalist in the designation of species or varieties, the figures of animals on the monuments are entirely valueless, and can not advance him a single step in a science which requires the closest accuracy. . . . Let us only look at the figures on a single page, the 388th of 'Nott and Gliddon's Types,' and then inquire what lights these would afford us in the designation of species or varieties. If the upper figure is a greyhound, as is stated, it must be not only a new species, but a new genus, since we have evidently nothing in nature at the present day to correspond to it. If this is an accurate representation of the greyhound, as it then existed (with a short tail turned upward like that of the rabbit), it affords one of the strongest evidences of the changes which time has effected, since no such variety of greyhound exists in our day. . . . We feel convinced that the ancient artists were no naturalists, and are inclined to the belief that they had no specimens before them to aid in their delineations — that with them a dog was a dog; and it now requires the aid of the imagination to decide on the variety. We feel no disposition in this place to enter on an investigation of those caricatures of dogs, as we are fully aware that the book of nature is a much safer guide to the naturalist in the investigation of species than the very imperfect and unsatisfactory figures on the monuments. . . . We may here observe that the figures of dogs and men (the latter only are of any scientific value) on the Eastern monuments have been carefully studied and delineated by master minds — men at whose feet Gliddon has sat as a humble copyist. They have commenced giving to the world the result of their scientific researches. Both Lepsius and Bunsen have already proclaimed their belief in the doctrine of the unity of the human race. . . . Thus these monumental records, which caused Gliddon to pronounce, in the language of scorn and obloquy,* a tirade against the Scriptures, convinced the minds of Lepsius and Bunsen of their truth, and filled them with humility, reverence, and awe. Their scientific researches satisfied them of the doctrines proclaimed by Moses and confirmed by Paul. 'And [God] hath made of one blood all nations of men for to dwell on all the face of the earth.' . . .

"These distinguished naturalists both arrived at the conclusion from these very monuments, that the negro race had only been developed, in the course of ages, within the African tropics, and were derived from Egypt."

3. The possibility of the development of the existing races of men from a common origin, within the period since the time of Noah, is strongly confirmed by the analogous changes which have taken place in the various species of domestic animals — the horse, the ox, the swine, the sheep, the dog; also fowls, geese, ducks, etc. For an able exhibition of this argument, and of the facts which substantiate it, see Appendix, K.

III. The theory of the plural origin of the human species, in different localities and at different times, is contrary to the analogy afforded by all other departments of the animal kingdom. It is a law of universal creation, so far as known, that every

---

* A true charge. See Types of Mankind.

species of animals had a single origin. Says Professor Dana, —

"Among the higher mammals no species is known to have existed originally within the tropics or temperate zones on *both* the oriental and occidental continents. . . . And more than this, species have a limited range on that particular continent to which they are confined.

"The same species among monkeys — the tribe at the head of the brute mammals — in no instance occurs on both, nor even the same genus, nor even the same family, for the American type is that of the inferior *Platyrrhines*, while the African is that of the *Catarrhines*, which most approach man in their features and structure. This is only the highest of an extensive range of facts in zoölogy, sustaining the principle in view. If, therefore, man is of one species, he should be restricted also to one continent in his origin.

"Moreover, man's capability of spreading to all lands, and of adaptation to all climates, renders creation in different localities over the globe eminently unnecessary, and directly opposed to his own good. It would be doing for man what man could do of himself. It would be contracting the field of conquest before him in nature, thereby lessening his means and opportunities of development." *

Says Dr. Bachman, —

* Geology, p. 585.

"All our quadrupeds, birds, reptiles, and even our plants, in the temperate regions of America, are found to differ from those in every other part of the world.* The fauna of Europe so much resembles our own in its genera, that the American traveler feels in that country as if he was among neighbors, but not quite in his own family, inasmuch as the species, though nearly allied, all differ, with the exception of those that have been transported and become naturalized. Of birds, we are at present acquainted with 520 species that exist in America, north of the Tropic of Cancer. Of these, twenty-six land birds and seventy-six water birds are identical with those of Europe. The land birds here enumerated resort to the polar regions in summer, for the purpose of rearing their young, and in autumn find their way to the temperate regions of both continents. A few of the water birds, such as the wandering shear-water (*Puffinus Anglorum*), and the petrels, possess such powers of flight that they cross the Atlantic in any latitude. The geese, ducks, gulls, terns, common gannet, etc., proceed far north during summer, and, by their aquatic habits and great powers of flight, migrate southerly along the shores of the Atlantic, both in Northern Europe and America. Of the remaining 418 species, they are restricted within certain latitudes in America, and are found in no other country.

"We have within the parallels of latitude referred to

---

* Except, of course, those which have been introduced by man. — B.

above, in North America, two hundred and seven species of quadrupeds. Of these, only eight, all of which are polar animals, are found in the north of Europe, or the adjoining continent of Asia; these are the polar bear, arctic fox, wolverine, ermine, pine martin, wolf, beaver, and the polar hare. The remainder are restricted to certain geographical ranges, and are found nowhere else."

Professor B. advances similar statements respecting fishes and plants, and concludes as follows: " Reasoning then from analogy, we are led to conclude that, since no species of quadruped, bird, or reptile, and, we may add, insect or plant, has been created in two or more localities; therefore we are not warranted in adopting the improbable idea that God would create the same species of man in five, ten, or fifty localities, and thereby not only violate the order of creation, but even act contrary to the very laws of probability." (p. 266.)

It should be added, in this connection, that Professor Agassiz himself concedes that his view of the plural origin of man is *an exception* to the general rule in the animal creation. " While [the lower] animals are of distinct species in the different zoölogical provinces to which they belong, man, notwithstanding the diversity of his races, constitutes one only and the same species over all the surface of the globe. In this respect, as in many others, man seems to us to form *an exception to the general rule* in this creation, of which he is, at the same time, the object and the end." *

IV. The polygenetic theory of the origin of mankind meets with a formidable objection from theological and moral science. I know that many naturalists repudiate all reference to theology in the discussion of such a question as this. But are they consistent in so doing? They endeavor, as much as possible, to gather weapons from every department of natural science against theology; but when the batteries are turned in reply, they exclaim, " This is a question of science, and theology has nothing to do with it." But, we may ask, is not theology a science? And though professed theologians differ in regard to many essential doctrines of theology, yet do they differ more than do the naturalists — even the masters — in regard to some of the natural sciences, say, e. g., that of theology?

It is a maxim with scientific men that all the sciences harmonize with each other, and it is always customary to bring facts and illustrations from one to elucidate and confirm another. And it would be strange, indeed, if theology could shed no light on a

---

* An account of the geographical distribution of animals, by L. Agassiz, in the Swiss Review, Neufchatel. Quoted by Dr. Bachman, p. 248.

question so directly concerning a religious being. We admit that man is an animal, but he is a moral and religious animal. And having discussed the subject, as we properly may, in its purely natural aspects, by whose dictum shall we be debarred from considering it also in its supernatural, its religious aspects? Such an objection finds no warrant in true science, which looks for truth wherever it is to be found.

Two points here merit our attention. Whatever be the characteristics that make man a moral and religious being, they are possessed in common *by all races of men*. These characteristics are the power of speech, the moral sense, the æsthetic faculty, etc. I do not say that all races, in their rude condition, have these in a like degree, but that they all possess them. Not a people on the globe has been found so degraded that these qualities, under the influence of Christian missions, have not been developed among them. Of course teaching does not *create* them. It merely calls into exercise qualities which previously existed, though, in some cases, in almost a dormant state. In the fact that man thus possesses a moral nature, he stands apart from the entire animal creation besides, and constitutes a single distinct species.

The other fact is, that all men sustain a like relation to God and his government. All are in a fallen and morally debased state, and need redemption and salvation. And it is a doctrine of Christian theology, that Jesus Christ is a divine Redeemer for all. Now, this fact can not be adjusted to the theory of a plurality of origin without doing violence to the plainest teachings of the New Testament. By one man sin entered into the world, and the race became a fallen race; by one man also salvation is provided, and its blessings are opened to all. The very fact of the common relation of all men to Adam, their parental head, is made the type and the ground of their similar common relation to Christ, the second Adam, the Saviour of the world.*

We conclude, then, that Ethnology, in its physiological aspects, concurs with history as respects the unity of the race. She presents to us no facts which are inconsistent with that unity; she finds nothing in the analogies from the lower races of animals which does not illustrate and confirm it.

* Rom. v. 12-19; 1 Cor. xv. 21, 22, 45.

CHAPTER IX.

THE ARGUMENT FROM LANGUAGE.

The Hebrew formerly believed to have been the Primitive Language. — Discovery of the Sanskrit, and its Effects. — Views of Stewart and Lord Monboddo. — Labors of Sanskrit Scholars. — Key to the Classification of Indo-European Languages. — Three great Families. — I. The Aryan. — II. The Semitic. — III. The Turanian. — Classification according to Structure. — Monosyllabic, Agglutinative, and Inflectional. — Bearing of the Diversity of Languages on the Argument. — 1. The Miraculous "Confusion of Tongues." — 2. Languages have much in common between them. — 3. Differences diminish as our Knowledge increases. — 4. Languages undergo rapid Changes. — Conclusion.

SCARCELY three fourths of a century have elapsed since the belief prevailed almost universally that the Hebrew was the primitive language of mankind, and that all other languages have been derived from it. If we go back one or two centuries more, we arrive at a time when this opinion was quite universal. According to Professor Müller, Leibnitz was "the first who really conquered the prejudice that Hebrew was the source of all language."* "It is astonishing," he remarks, "what an immense amount of real learning and ingenuity was wasted on this question during the seventeenth and eighteenth centuries. It finds, perhaps, but one parallel — in the laborious calculations and constructions of early astronomers, who had to account for the movements of the heavenly bodies, always taking it for granted that the earth must be the fixed center of the planetary system.†

"These labors continued till near the close of the last century, when the discovery and opening up of the Sanskrit literature wrought an entire revolution in regard to the whole subject of the classification of languages. So great was the excitement caused by this discovery, so radical and important were the results which it was perceived must flow from it, that some of the first scholars and philosophers of Europe doubted its genuineness. For example, Dugald Stewart denied the reality of such a language as the Sanskrit altogether, and wrote his famous essay to prove that it had been put together after the model of the Greek and Latin by those arch forgers and liars the Brahmans, and that the whole of the Sanskrit literature was an imposition." ‡

---

* Science of Lang., first series, p. 134.
† Ibid. p. 133.   ‡ Ibid. p. 164.

Lord Monboddo treated the subject more philosophically, though scarcely more consistently. "He had," says Müller, "just finished his great work 'On the Origin and Progress of Languages,' in which he derives all mankind from a couple of apes, and all the dialects of the world from a language originally framed by some Egyptian gods, when the discovery of the Sanskrit came on him like a thunderbolt. It must be said, however, to his credit, that he at once perceived the immense importance of the discovery. He could not be expected to sacrifice his primeval monkeys or his Egyptian idols, but with that reservation the conclusions which he drew . . . are highly creditable to his acuteness. He says (1792), 'I have got such certain information from India, that if I live to finish my history of man, which I have begun in my third volume of "Ancient Metaphysics," I shall be able clearly to prove that the Greek is derived from the Sanskrit, which was the ancient language of Egypt, and was carried by the Egyptians into India with their other arts, and into Greece with the colonies which settled there.'

"A few years later (1795) he had arrived at more definite views on the relation of Sanskrit to Greek; and he writes, 'Mr. Wilkins has proved to my conviction such a resemblance between the Greek and the Sanskrit, that the one must be a dialect of the other, or both of some original language. Now, the Greek is certainly not a dialect of the Sanskrit, any more than the Sanskrit is of the Greek. They must, therefore, be both dialects of the same language; and that language could be no other than the language of Egypt brought into India by Osiris, of which undoubtedly the Greek was a dialect.'" *

But I must give another quotation from this distinguished nobleman and philosopher, to show his idea of the origin of human speech.

"I have supposed that language could not be invented without supernatural assistance, and accordingly I have maintained that it was the invention of the dæmon kings of Egypt, who, being more than men, first taught themselves to articulate, and then taught others. But even among them, I am persuaded there was a progress in the art, and that such a language as the Sanskrit was not at once invented." †

This passage constrains me to remark that, so far as I am aware, his lordship was the first to make any practical account of the dæmon dynasties — the *Manes* — of Egypt. It is true that others had allowed them a place in chronology, with a period of many

---

* Science of Lang., First Series, p. 140.
† Ibid. p. 160. Monboddo's Anc. Metaphysics, vol. iv. p. 357.

thousand years' duration, but it was reserved for our Scotch philosopher to tell us what those *ghost* monarchs did in the practical affairs of men. They invented the Sanskrit language!

These notices of two great scholars of the last century have a substantial value in relation to our subject. They should teach us the uselessness, the danger, of premature generalizations, when as yet we have but a partial view of the facts involved. Lord Monboddo died in 1799, and Dugald Stewart in 1828; yet in the brief space of time since elapsed, what an entire revolution, both in knowledge and opinion, has taken place in regard to things on which they pronounced with so much authority! And how often do we still see repetitions of the same haste in the conclusions which are drawn from imperfect data, especially as bearing on the divine origin and authority of the Bible!

The history of what may be called European Sanskrit philology dates from the foundation of the Asiatic Society at Calcutta, in 1784. It was through the efforts of Sir William Jones, the missionary Carey, and other English scholars, as Foster, Wilkins, Colebrooke, etc., members of that society, that the language and literature of the Brahmans first became accessible to Europeans. In 1808 Frederick Schlegel published his little work on "The Language and Wisdom of the Indians," which, says Professor Müller, "was like the wand of a magician." It pointed out the place where a new mine of knowledge should be opened, and it was not long before the most distinguished scholars of the day were sinking their shafts and raising the ore. The savants of the continent — as Bopp, Schlegel, Lassen, Rosen, and Burnouf — resorted to England for the purpose of copying manuscripts at the East India House, and receiving assistance from Wilkins, Colebrooke, Wilson, and other distinguished members of the old Indian civil service. The first elaborate comparison of the Sanskrit with the Greek and Latin was by Francis Bopp, in an essay published in 1816. Other works of his soon followed, and in 1833 appeared the first volume of his "Comparative Grammar of the Sanskrit, Zend, Greek, Latin, Lithuanian, Sclavonic, Gothic, and German languages." This work was not completed till 1852, nearly twenty years later. Other scholars entered the same rich field, and gathered from it very important and valuable fruits.

But why, it may naturally be asked, should the discovery of the Sanskrit have wrought so great a change in the classificatory study of languages? The answer is, that it furnished a key to the puzzle which had previously existed in the problem of languages.

It showed that the Sanskrit was intimately related to the Greek, Latin, and most of the European languages, not as their parent, but as a sister in the same family. And as the modern Italian, French, Spanish, and other Romance languages are sisters, derived from the Latin as their parent, so the Sanskrit, with its affiliated tongues, must have had a common parent. When this was ascertained, "all languages," says Müller, "seemed to fall of themselves into their right position;" i. e., they all took their places as members of groups having natural relations to each other. The classification, however, is not complete, there being some languages, as, for instance, the Chinese, respecting which philologists differ in opinion as to the place they should occupy.

Languages are comprehended, as is well known, by philologists under three general families — the Aryan, the Semitic, and the Turanian. My limits do not permit, nor does my object require, more than a bare enumeration of the different branches of these several families, with a mention of the geographical limits to which they properly belong.

I. The ARYAN * family, or, as it is frequently

---

* By some, *Arian*. Both forms are found in Müller's writings. The Sanskrit has *Aryâ*. It is the same as the *Arioi* of Herodotus and other Greek writers.

called, the INDO-EUROPEAN, the former "being the most ancient name by which the ancestors of this family distinguished themselves" (Müller), the latter indicating the geographical extent of the family in Asia and Europe. The former is the shortest, and contains a valuable historical reminiscence; the latter shows at a glance the localities where it is to be found. It is subdivided into two groups — the northern or European, and the southern or Asiatic.

At the head of the Asiatic group we, of course, place the Sanskrit with its dialects, the old Pali, and the Prakrit, ancient and modern, including the Bengali, the Hindi, the Punjaubi, and, according to some, the Urya, Marathi, and Guzerathi. Coming further west we find the languages of Afghanistan, Bokhara, Kurdistan, Media, Persia, Armenia, and some others, extending to the Black and Mediterranean Seas. The European group embraces the Greek, the Latin, the Sclavonic including the Lithuanian, the Germanic, and the Celtic, with the various dialects derived from them.

II. The SEMITIC family, so called because spoken mostly among the descendants of Shem. This has usually been subdivided into three branches — the Hebrew, the Aramaic, and the Arabic.

The Hebrew — now a dead language — was spoken in Palestine from or before the days of Moses to the time of Nehemiah and the Maccabees, when it was replaced by the Chaldee or Aramaic. The language of the Phœnicians and Carthaginians belonged to this branch.

The Aramaic consists of the Syrian (ancient and modern) and the Chaldean, the geographical limits of which are Syria, Mesopotamia, and part of Babylonia. Here are classed the dialects of the Assyrian and Babylonian ruins, written in the cuneiform or arrow-shaped characters.

The Arabic had for its original seat the Arabian peninsula. Here it is still spoken by a compact mass of aboriginal inhabitants, and the ancient inscriptions there (Himyaritic) testify to its early presence. In its more modern form, it has spread over Egypt and the northern coast of Africa, and is largely spoken in Turkey and Persia — indeed, wherever the Mohammedan religion has extended.

There is a fourth group of languages, which by many are assigned a place in the Semitic family, but by others are established as a distinct family by themselves, called The HAMITIC, from the Egyptian, — its most important member, — supposed to have been spoken by the descendants of Ham. This also is subdivided into three branches — the Egyptian — which was an older form of the modern Coptic, — the Ethiopian, the Libyan, or Berber, extending along the northern coast of Africa, and the Hottentot, embracing the dialects of tribes at the southern extremity of the continent. This family of languages present many analogies with the Semitic. Both the Egyptian and Babylonian, says Müller, "though clearly marked with a Semitic stamp, represent two scions of the Semitic stem, which branched off at a period of history so early, or rather so long before the beginning of all history, that they may be considered as independent colonies, rather than as constituent parts of the kingdom of Shem. The same remark applies to Semitic tribes in the north of Africa, the number and extent of which is almost daily increased by the researches of African travelers and missionaries." *

III. The third family of languages is the TURANIAN. The name is derived from *Tur*, who, in an old Persian legend, was one of the three brothers from whom, it is said, the races of mankind are descended. *Ircj*, another brother, was the founder of the race of Iran, i. e., the native Persians; *Tur*, of the Turans, their neighbors on the north-east, between which two races was an incessant warfare.† It comprises all the languages of Asia and Europe not included in the two preceding families, except,

---

* Languages spoken at the Seat of War, p. 23.
† Whitney, Language, etc., p. 325.

perhaps, the Chinese and its dialects. These are divided into two classes — the northern and southern. The first comprises the Tungusic, Mongolic, Turkic, Samoyedic, and Finnic, and occupies the regions to the north and west of China, as far as the Euxine and Mediterranean. To this division belong also the dialects of the Lapps and the Finns of Northern Europe, and the Magyars of Hungary. Its limits have been greatly extended in modern times by the conquests of the Turks, thus encroaching on the original territories of the Semites and the Aryans. The southern division comprises the Gangetic, i. e., the Thibetian and other dialects called Trans-Himmalayan and Sub-Himmalayan; the Taic, or the dialects of Siam; the Lohitic, i. e., dialects of Assam, Arakan, Burmah, and some others; the Malayic, comprising the languages of the Malayan peninsula and the Polynesian Islands; and the Tamulic, or the languages of Southern India, as the Canarese, Tamil, Telugu, Malayalam, and other minor dialects.*

* Müller, Sci. of Lang. vol. i. p. 398. For the last mentioned group, see likewise Caldwell's Comp. Grammar of the Dravidian Languages. But Professor Muller is the authority for the general classification and arrangement of this southern group, as well as for that of the northern. In regard to the last-mentioned group, the Tamulic, faithfulness to the subject requires me to add particularly, that the affiliation of those dialects with the Scythian or

Such is the classification of languages made by the masters in philology, as indicated in the tripartite division just named. In this the Chinese and the body of languages in Central Africa and in America — the speech of more than one third of mankind — are confessedly not included. Those also which are placed in the third family — the Turanian — are not grouped there, certainly not all of them, because of internal resemblances or affinities, but because they do not belong to either of the others. (Müller, p. 86.) These facts show how exceedingly imperfect the science of comparative philology still is, and ought to abate some of the confidence with which conclusions are drawn from it contrary to the teachings of the Scriptures. As it now stands, this classification, so far as respects the third family, is little more than a confession of ignorance as to the real character of the languages themselves. Some groups under it are, perhaps,

Turanian languages is doubted by some of our first linguists. Such affiliation can not, indeed, be positively denied, but the evidence is not regarded as conclusive. See some very judicious remarks on this point by Professor W. D. Whitney, Journ. Am. Or. Soc. vol. vii. p. 296, seq., appended to a valuable *résumé* of Caldwell's work above named, by Rev. E. Webb.

After all, we have here only another striking illustration of the indefiniteness of the classification of languages under the third division — the Turanian.

sufficiently defined to be set by themselves, others by themselves; yet the vast majority of the dialects are too little known or studied to have their true linguistic characteristics fully defined.*

There is still another classification of languages, founded upon their internal structure, which ought to be mentioned here. It divides them into three primary families, distinguished by the characteristics of their leading words. These are stated by Professor Müller as follows: —

"1. Roots may be used as words, each root preserving its full independence.

"2. Two roots may be joined together to form

---

* Since the above was written, the admirable work of Professor W. D. Whitney, "Language, and the Study of Language," has appeared, and I am pleased at finding my own opinions on many important points so much in accord with those he has expressed in this volume. He speaks rather disparagingly of the results of comparative philology, — as much so, perhaps, as I have myself. He of course accords a proper value to what has been settled by linguistic study respecting the Semitic and European families of languages, but is not satisfied with the classification of philologists in regard to the other languages. He prefers the term *Scythian* to *Turanian* for designating the third family (so called), and thinks the evidence on which dialects have been grouped together often unsatisfactory. He is eminently conservative. I approve of his use of Scythian for Turanian, and can not but wish he had done more to solve the problem of relationship between that vast number of dialects ranked in this family.

words, and in these compounds one root may lose its independence.

"3. Two roots may be joined together to form words, and in these compounds both roots may lose their independence." *

The first class gives rise to *monosyllabic* languages. These are "wholly unsusceptible of grammatical mutations; there is no formal distinction between verb and noun, substantive and adjective, preposition and conjunction; there are no inflections, no case- or person-terminations of any kind; the bare root forms the sole and whole substance of the language." † The following specimen of a Chinese sentence will illustrate this: "King speak: Sage! not far thousand mile and come; also will have use gain me realm, hey?" That is, "The king spoke, O Sage, since thou dost not count a thousand miles far to come, wilt thou not too have brought something for the weal of my realm?" ‡

The second class characterizes what are called *agglutinative* languages. Of the two or more roots of which its words are composed, one expressing the substantive idea is not liable to variation, and the others are somewhat loosely attached

---

* Lectures, first series, eighth lecture.
† Smith's Bib. Dict. art. *Confusion of Tongues.*
‡ Schleicher's Lang. of Europe, quoted by Whitney, p. 331.

or glued to it to express the various modifications, the latter losing their independent form in so doing, as *joy-ful-ly*, from the three roots *joy*, *full*, and *like*. So in Turkish, to the root *sev*, signifying love, are joined five formative roots, making the word *sev-ish-dir-il-eme-mek*, i. e., not capable of being made to love one another.*

The third class composes what are termed *inflectional* languages, where all the roots lose their independent form, and by fusion with each other constitute a new, indivisible word, as the root *true*, with its prefix and affixes, makes the word *untruthfulness*, etc.

Comparing these two modes of classification with each other, it is found that the Aryan and Semitic families are, for the most part, inflectional languages; the Turanian, including the dialects of Central Africa and America, agglutinative; and the Chinese, and its related dialects, monosyllabic. At the same time, words of each type are found more or less in them all. This fact, and the importance of it to the discussion in hand, will be again adverted to presently.

The question now recurs to us, How does the existence of these numerous families and groups of languages bear upon the antiquity of man on the

* Whitney, p. 319.

earth? Do not the radical differences between them — differences traceable back beyond the period of authentic history — prove that they could not have had a common origin in any one primitive tongue; or, if that were intrinsically possible, that it could not have been within the space of time which the Bible chronology allows subsequent to the date of Noah? To this inquiry we may reply, —

1. There stands at the very threshold of that period the recorded fact of a miraculous "*confusion of tongues*," by which the antecedent speech was broken up into a variety of dialects, each unintelligible to those who spoke the others. Before that time, "the whole earth was of one language and of one lip" (Gen. xi. 1, margin), i. e., probably one in substance and one in utterance. To defeat their design of building a city and tower, which should preserve them as one people in one locality forever, God "confounded their language, that they might not understand one another's speech." And this event is distinctly assigned as the reason why the one family was broken up and scattered into the various parts of the earth. Here, then, is an adequate and complete explanation of the origin of diversity in human speech. We know not, indeed, precisely what was the thing done, whether a change was wrought in the vocabulary or the gram-

mar of language, or in pronunciation only, nor into how many portions the one common speech was divided. From the analogy of other miracles, we should judge it probable that no more was done than was needful to effect the purpose in view. There is always, so to speak, a husbanding of divine power, by which the contravention or transcending of nature's laws is made as slight as possible. We may well suppose, that while real changes were introduced into the forms of language, its substance should have remained essentially the same. But be this as it may, here is the great fact of diversity accounted for. Neither the degree of that diversity, nor the length of time required for it on natural principles, affords any further difficulty.

And this fact, let me remark further, is to be taken *with* the Scripture chronology, both to explain and confirm it. If the latter fixes the confusion of language and the dispersion of the nations at a point no more remote than a few centuries before the era of history, it also affords the very key that was needed to show how those events were chronologically possible. If science, so called, rejects the miracle, she throws away the only key which can solve the mystery. Let her find a better one if she can.

2. In accordance with the supposition just made,

it is ascertained that under all the apparent differences existing among languages, there is very much also *in common* between them. Our space will not permit us to go into details on this point. They may be seen in the works on comparative grammar, and other treatises of philology. The article in Smith's Dictionary of the Bible, already referred to, mentions four particulars in which manifest tokens of unity between the families of languages may be discerned, viz., " in the *original material* out of which language was formed " (monosyllabic roots) ; " in the *stages of formation* through which it has passed ; in the general principle of *grammatical* expression ; and, lastly, in the *spirit and power* displayed in the development of these various formations." The article adds, " Such a result, though it does not prove the unity of language in respect to its radical elements, nevertheless tends to establish the *à priori* probability of this unity ; for if all connected with the forms of language may be referred to certain general laws, — if nothing in that department owes its origin to chance or arbitrary appointment, — it surely favors the presumption that the same principle would extend to the formation of the roots, which are the very core and kernel of language. Here, too, we might expect to find the operation of fixed laws of some kind or other producing results of a uniform character; here, too, actual variety may not be inconsistent with original unity."

On the question of an original identity in the *roots* of the different families, it seems to be agreed by philologers that the time has not come for pronouncing a positive opinion. Too little is yet known respecting the primary elements of languages to warrant definite conclusions. There certainly is no proof that the original roots were *not* identical. The most that can be affirmed seems to be, as expressed by Professor Whitney, "that language affords certain indications of doubtful value, which, taken along with certain other ethnological considerations, also of questionable pertinency, furnish ground for suspecting an ultimate relationship. The question, in short, is not yet ripe for settlement."*

3. In proportion as our knowledge of the various families of languages increases, the *differences between them diminish*, and new affinities come to light. It is ascertained that classes are not separated from each other so widely, and by such sharp lines of demarcation, as at first appeared. "The agglutinative languages are not wholly agglutinative; the Finnish and Turkish classes of the Ural-Altaian family are, in certain instances, inflectional, the relational adjunct being fully incorporated with

---

* Language, p. 308.

the predicable stem, and having undergone a large amount of attrition for that purpose. Nor, again, are the inflectional languages wholly inflectional; Hebrew, for instance, abounds with agglutinative forms, and also avails itself largely of separate particles for the expression of relational ideas. Our own language, though classed as inflectional, retains nothing more than the vestiges of inflection, and is, in many respects, as isolating and juxtapositional as any language of that class." * Thus not unfrequently resemblances and affinities are disclosed where they had not been suspected. I have already mentioned the results following the discovery of the Sanskrit and its literature, this proving to be the "missing link" requisite to complete the chain of connection between the various members of the Indo-European family. In the same way, what is of late taking the name of the Hamitic group, or, as Bunsen denominated it, *Khamism*, gives indications of becoming a connecting link between the Aryan and Semitic families.† Hence, too, the difficulties of classification which are found in many cases, cer-

---

* Smith's Dict. of the Bible, art. *Confusion of Tongues*.

† "The old Egyptian clearly stands between the Semitic and the Indo-European, for its forms and roots cannot be explained by either of them singly, but are evidently a combination of the two." — Bunsen, *Egypt's Place*, etc. p. 10. See also the remark of Osburn, cited on pp. 161, 162.

tain languages showing resemblances in opposite directions, leading them to be placed by one linguist in one class and by another in another. It is impossible to say, when all existing languages shall have been sufficiently studied, and their ultimate elements and principles of formation are known, how nearly they may be brought into affinity with each other. We hold the fact to be a significant one, that the *tendencies* are all one way, toward an original unity among the whole.

4. Languages, while in their unwritten and uncultivated state, are liable to *rapid changes*. There being nothing to retain them in their ancient forms, they are free to adapt themselves to the varying circumstances and necessities of the people who use them. There is, first, the law of " growth," already adverted to. In its earliest stage, language was monosyllabic, its words short, without grammatical variations, and with the simplest possible syntax — a fit vehicle for the simple thoughts of a primitive age. But gradually, as men's experience was enlarged, and new ideas were developed, this monosyllabic speech began to take on a more complex form, modifying and relational words attached or *glued* themselves to the roots, till another phase of language was reached, sufficiently removed from the former to rank it in a distinct class — the agglutinative. Later

still, by a continuation of the same process, the inflectional stage was reached, differing as much from the last as that did from the original. "Among all languages, ancient and modern," says M. Maury, " some have passed through the three phases; others have been arrested in their development. Thus agglutination includes the monosyllabic state, and inflection includes both the agglutinative and the monosyllabic states. Exactly as among species of animals, some remain as elementary organisms, whilst others progress, during the period of gestation, from that organism to a higher and more developed organization." *

Other changes also, equally important, have occurred in the ever-changing circumstances of mankind. Old languages have been broken up, and their fragments, assuming each a vitality of their own, have become separate living dialects, as the modern Romance languages of Europe have sprung from the Latin. Two or more languages, under outward force, have been compressed into one, as our own tongue sprung from the fusion of the Saxon and the Norman. And these changes have often taken place with great rapidity. In the instance last mentioned, two languages, greatly dissimilar in mate-

---

* Quoted in Anc. Hist. of the East, by Lenormant and Chevallier, p. 67.

rials and structure, were, in a little more than three centuries, wrought into a third, so unlike both that it would be wholly unintelligible to those who spoke either of the parent tongues.

Among savage nations this susceptibility to change is still greater. "We read," says Müller, "of missionaries in Central America who attempted to write down the language of savage tribes, and who compiled, with great care, a dictionary of all the words they could lay hold of. Returning to the same tribes after the lapse of only ten years, they found that this dictionary had become antiquated and useless. Old words had sunk to the ground, and new ones had risen to the surface, and, to all outward appearance, the language was completely changed." Again, he refers to tribes in the north of Asia, who "though really speaking the same language, have produced so many words and forms peculiar to each tribe, that even within the limits of twelve or twenty German miles, communication among them becomes extremely difficult." In a limited district in the mountain ranges of the Irrawaddy, "were collected no less than twelve dialects, some of them spoken by no more than thirty or forty families, yet so different from the rest as to be unintelligible to the nearest neighbor." *

* Science of Lang., vol. ii. pp. 62, 63.

With such evidences before us of the susceptibility of language to change, we have no need to resort to the theory of a plurality of origin to account for all the diversities now existing in human speech. Growth alone is sufficient to have originated the differing characteristics of the three leading families. If we suppose that the ancestors of the Chinese, for instance, and the other tribes of Eastern Asia, departed from the original abodes at a period when language was still monosyllabic, we are enabled to see that this archaic type of speech should have prevailed and been perpetuated among them. This principle is distinctly recognized by all the leading philologists, though perhaps not to the extent which facts would warrant. Bunsen refers to it in numerous instances in explaining the differences between groups of dialects. Müller, upon this ground, attempts to show the relative ages of the Turanian races. Muir remarks that "the ancestors of the Indians and Persians appear to have lived together as one nation to a later period than the other branches of the Aryan race." * We would not claim that this alone is sufficient to explain the whole problem before us, but it is enough to relieve us of its chief difficulties.

The results, then, to which we arrive on this sub-

* Sanskrit Texts, Part. II. chap. ii.

ject are twofold — negative and positive: 1. Comparative Philology has not proved, and can not prove, that all the languages of man did not have a common origin. 2.. She has proved that all the more important languages are spoken by nations whose ancestors were the direct descendants of Noah; and she exhibits many facts, both as to the materials and the form of all languages, which show traces of such original unity. Or, in the words of Professor Müller, —

"1. Nothing necessitates the admission of different independent beginnings for the *material* elements of the Turanian, Semitic, and Aryan branches of speech; nay, it is possible even now to point out radicals, which, under various changes and disguises, have been current in these branches ever since their first separation.

"2. Nothing necessitates the admission of different beginnings for the *formal* elements of the Turanian, Semitic, and Aryan branches of speech; and although it is not possible to derive the Aryan system of grammar from the Semitic, or the Semitic from the Aryan, we can perfectly understand how, either through individual influences, or by the wear and tear of speech in its own continuous working, the different systems of Asia and Europe may have been produced." *

* Science of Lang., vol. i. p. 340.

And says Professor Whitney, "Our general conclusion, which may be looked on as incontrovertibly established, is this: If the tribes of men are of different parentage, their languages could not be expected to be more unlike than they in fact are; while, on the other hand, if all mankind are of one blood, their tongues need not be more alike than we actually find them to be." *

* Language, p. 394.

CHAPTER X.

THE ARGUMENT FROM TRADITION.

Traditions of Primitive Ages to be expected. — Such Traditions found to exist. — Statement of Dr. Smyth. — Those only of Value in the Argument which are not derived from the Bible. — 1. Traditions of one God. — 2. Of the Creation. — 3. Of the Garden of Eden. — 4. Of the Temptation and Fall. — 5. Of the Weekly Division of Time. — 6. Of the Deluge of Noah.

'IF all men have descended from a single origin, and that so late as the flood of Noah, it might be expected that they would preserve some traditions of that fact, and of the chief events occurring in the infancy of the race. We should anticipate, indeed, that these would vary according to the genius and the outer history of the different nations, some retaining more vivid reminiscences than others, and all of them, perhaps, holding them in forms more or less disguised, with such additions or other modifications as might naturally arise in the lapse of centuries. And wherever such traditions are found, clearly defined and of unmistakable import, they afford strong collateral evidence as to the origin of the people who entertain them.

Such traditions, in fact, exist. "The primitive condition of mankind," says Dr. Smyth; "the purity and happiness of the golden age; the location of man in a garden; the tree of knowledge of good and evil; the influence of a serpent in the seduction and ruin of man; the consequent curse inflicted on man, on woman, and upon the earth; the promise of an incarnate Redeemer; traditions respecting Cain and Abel, Enoch and Noah; the longevity of the ancient patriarchs, and the existence of ten generations from Adam to Noah; the growing deteriorations of human nature; the reduction of man's age and power; the deluge and destruction of all mankind except a single family; the building of an ark, and its resting on a mountain, and the flying of the dove; the building of the Tower of Babel, and the miraculous confusion of languages; the institution of sacrifices; the rainbow, as the sign and symbol of destruction and of hope; the fable of the man in the moon — which is equally known in opposite quarters of the globe; the great mother, who is a *mythus* of the ark; the hermaphrodite unity of all the gods and goddesses, from a mistaken notion of the creation of Adam and Eve; the nature and purport of the mysteries in the Old and New World;

groves, and mountains, and caves, as places of worship; traditions also of Sodom and Gomorrah, of Abraham, Isaac, Jacob, Joseph, Moses, and the Red Sea; the division of time by weeks; and the explanation of the future conflagration of the earth; — these, and many other facts which lie at the foundation of sacred history, and the earliest events of humanity, are all found imbedded, like the fossils of the earth, in the traditionary legends, both written and oral, of every tribe and people under the whole heavens." *

I am inclined to think that this language is too strong, certainly as affirming the existence of these traditions among *every* tribe and people. There may be casual resemblances in some single particulars which have no proper historical character, just as there are striking coincidences in many facts of the natural world, which have no vital connection with each other. It must be borne in mind, also, that only those traditions which have not been *derived* from the Bible itself, have any value in this argument. The influence of the Jewish and Christian religions has been very great and very wide in the world, and many things contained in them may have made their way thence within the knowledge of surrounding nations. Such, for instance, was probably the gen-

* T. Smyth, On the Unity of the Human Races, pp. 237, 238.

eral expectation of the advent of some illustrious personage, about the time of Christ, who was to be a new Benefactor to the world.* It is only *independent* traditions, which have come down from remote antiquity within the bosom of the nations themselves, that can avail anything for proving their common origin. And of these, without going to the extent of the writer just quoted, there are not a few of great interest and importance, which I will mention.

1. The existence of *one supreme and eternal God*, the First Cause of all things. — "Those men," says Jablonski, "who were most distinguished for wisdom among the Egyptians, acknowledged God to be a certain unbegotten Eternal Spirit, prior to all things which exist; who created, preserves, contains, pervades, and vivifies everything; who is the spirit of the universe, but the guardian and protector of men." † Many of the Greek poets and philosophers held the same truth. In one of the Orphic Fragments preserved by Proclus, we find it expressly declared that "there is one Power, one Deity, the great Governor of all things." The verses which were sung in the Eleusinian mysteries contained

---

* Hesiod, Works and Days, 109; Ovid, Met. i. 89; Virgil, Ecl. iv., etc.

† Brande's Encyclopædia, art. *Monotheism*.

the following passage: "Pursue thy path rightly, and contemplate the King of the world. He is one and of himself alone, and to that One all things have owed their being. He encompasses them. No mortal hath beheld him; but he sees everything."*
Says Professor Wilson, "The Vedas are authority for the existence of one Divine Being, supreme over the universe, and existing before all worlds. In the beginning this all [the universe] was in darkness. He, the Supreme, was alone, without a second. He reflected, I am one; I will become many. Will was conceived in the divine mind, and creation ensued." In the Vishnu Purana it is said, "That which is imperceptible, undecaying, inconceivable, unborn, inexhaustible, indescribable; which has neither form, nor hands, nor feet; which is almighty, omnipresent, eternal; the cause of all things, and without cause; permeating all, itself unpenetrated, and from which all things proceed; — that is Brahma."†

2. The *Creation of the World and of Man.* — "The Greeks, in their legends, represented Prometheus as playing the part of a demiurgus, or secondary creator, who molded from clay the first individuals of our species, and gave them life by means of the fire which he stole from heaven. In the cosmogony of

---

* Brande's Encyclopœdia, art. *Monotheism.*
† Wilson's Translation, p. 642.

Peru the first man created by the divine power was called Alpa Camasca, 'animated earth.' Among the tribes of North America, the Mandans believed that the Great Spirit formed two figures of clay, which he dried and animated by the breath of his mouth; the one received the name of the 'first man,' the other that of 'companion.' The great god of Tahiti, Tœroa, made man of red earth, and the Dyacks of Borneo, stubbornly opposed to all Moslem influences, repeated from generation to generation that man had been formed from the earth." *

The following view of the Hindu cosmogony I take from the Laws of Manu, written probably in the seventh or eighth century before Christ. It is regarded by the Hindus as a revelation from Brahma.

"This universe existed only in darkness, imperceptible, undefinable, undiscoverable by reason, undiscovered, as if it were wholly immersed in sleep. Then the self-existing power, himself undiscovered, but making this world discernible with five elements and other principles, appeared with undiminished glory, dispelling the gloom. He whom the mind alone can perceive, whose essence eludes the external organs, who has no visible parts, who exists from eternity; even He, the soul of all beings, whom

* Anc. Hist. of the East, pp. 9, 10.

no being can comprehend, shone forth in person. He having willed to produce various beings from his own substance, first, with a thought, created the waters, and placed in them a productive seed. The seed became an egg, bright as gold, blazing like the luminary, with a thousand beams; and in that egg he was born himself in the form of *Brahma*,* the great forefather of all spirits. The waters are called Nara because they were the offspring of Nara, the Supreme Spirit, and as in them his first ayana (progress) in the character of Brahmā took place, he is thence *Narayana* (he whose place of moving was the waters). From that which is, the cause, not the object, of sense, existing everywhere *in substance*, not existing *to our perception*, without beginning or end, was produced the divine male, famed in all the worlds as Brahmā. In that egg the great power sat inactive a whole year of the Creator, at the close of which, by his thought alone, he caused the egg to divide itself, and from its two divisions he framed the heaven above and the earth beneath; in the midst he placed the subtile ether, the eight regions, and the permanent receptacle of

---

* The word *Brahma* — the final *a* short as in *America* — is a neuter noun, denoting the *abstract* Supreme Spirit. The masculine Brahmā — the final vowel having the long Italian sound of *ah* — denotes the *active* Creator.

the waters. . . . He gave being to time and the divisions of time; to the stars also, and the planets; to rivers, oceans, and mountains; to level plains and uneven valleys; to devotion, speech, complacency, desire, and wrath; and to creation. For the sake of distinguishing action, he made a total difference between right and wrong.

"That the human race might be multiplied, he caused the Brahman, the Kshatriya, the Vaishya, and the Shudra (the four castes) to proceed from his mouth, his arm, his thigh, and his foot. Having divided his own substance, the mighty power became half male and half female, and from that female he produced *Viraj*. Know me, O most excellent Brahmans, to be that person, whom the male power Viraj produced by himself — Me, the secondary framer of all this visible world."

The resemblances between this cosmogony and the Scripture account of the creation are striking. First, the Supreme Deity, shining forth upon the darkness of chaos; then the creation of the waters; the formation of the heaven above and the earth beneath, with the air and clouds between; the celestial bodies, and the divisions of time; the mountains, valleys, and plains; and, lastly, man himself. It is remarkable, also, that, as in the Bible, the act of creation is attributed not to the Supreme Spirit, the

Father, but to his Son. "No man hath seen God at any time; the only-begotten Son, which is in the bosom of the Father, he hath declared him." "All things were made by him, and without him was not anything made that was made."

3. *The Garden of Eden.* — The Vishnu Purana (p. 169) describes the city of Brahma, on Mount Meru, in the midst of the Jambu Dwipa, the inhabited world. I do not doubt that it is a tradition of Eden. The account is as follows: "On the summit of Meru is the vast city of Brahmā, extending fourteen thousand leagues, and renowned in heaven. The capital of Brahmā is enclosed by the River Ganges, which, issuing from the foot of Vishnu, and washing the lunar orb, falls here from the skies, and, after encircling the city, divides into four mighty rivers, and flows in opposite directions."

The Greeks had the fable of the garden of the Hesperides, which was shut in by high mountains on account of an oracle which predicted that, at a certain day, a person would come and carry off the golden apples that hung on a mysterious tree in the midst of the garden. Notwithstanding the precautions used, the hero Hercules came at last, destroyed the watchful serpent that kept the tree, and gathered the apples. This event was represented pictorially, the serpent being wreathed about the tree precisely as in the modern pictures of Eve's temptation. It is also a striking part of the legend, that Hercules is represented as the mortal son of Zeus, the Supreme God, and was attempted to be destroyed in his infancy by two serpents, which he slew.

4. *The Temptation and Fall of Man.* — The story of Pandora is the Grecian legend of Eve. She is represented as the first woman, exceedingly beautiful, sent by Zeus to be a punishment to man for the stolen fire of Prometheus. The gods each bestowed on her a gift, such as beauty, cunning, etc., which she was to use for the ruin of mankind. Prometheus had shut up in a box all the diseases and woes which the anger of the gods had denounced, but Pandora, lifting the cover of the box, let them loose upon the world, hope only remaining behind. The Chinese held that man was originally innocent and happy, and free from disease and death. In an evil hour he yielded to flattery, or, according to others, the inordinate thirst of knowledge, or, others still, the temptation of a woman, and sinned. He lost his purity, his self-control, and his intellectual pre-eminence, and the beasts, birds, and reptiles became his enemies.* Similar traditions exist among the worshippers of the Grand Lama, and the Buddhists of Ceylon, and are recounted, also, in the Vishnu

---

* Mémoires Chinoises, vol. i. 107.

Purana of the Hindus. The ancient Persians had, in a sacred book called Bundehesh, a story of the temptation, almost exactly like that of the Bible, in which all the essential features are found, even to that of the tempter having assumed the form of a serpent.*

5. *The Division of Time into Weeks.* — Such a division prevailed all over the East, from the earliest ages, among the Assyrians, Arabs, and Egyptians. To the last-named people, Dion Cassius ascribes its invention. Oldendorf found it among the tribes in the interior of Africa. The Peruvians and Mexicans had similar periods, derived from the phases of the moon. Many nations have named the days of the week after the gods, as did our own pagan ancestors. Among the Hindus the word *wara*, day, affixed to the names of the deities, constitutes the name, thus : —

Latin.	Saxon.	Hindu.
Sol, Dies Solis.	Sun, Sunday.	Aditya, Adityawara.
Luna, etc.	Moon, Monday.	Soma, Somawara.
Mars, "	Tuesco, Tuesday.	Mangala, Mangalawara.
Mercurius, "	Woden, Wednesday.	Budha, Budhawara.
Jupiter, "	Thor, Thursday.	Brahaspati, Brahaspatwara.
Venus, "	Freya, Friday.	Shuhra, Shuhrawara.
Saturnus, "	Sæter, Saturday.	Shani, Shaniwara.

* Anc. Hist. of the East, vol. i. p. 10.

Attempts have indeed been made to show that this world-wide observance is to be accounted for from natural causes, the observed phases of the moon, the occult properties of numbers, or, as Proudhon calls it, a certain "spontaneous genius, a sort of *magnetic vision*, which discovered primitive arts, developed language, invented writing, and created systems of religion and philosophy." * Far easier and more probable is the view which is admitted by nearly all writers, that it is due to a universal tradition, which has descended from the primary institution of the Sabbath, as recorded by Moses.

6. But the one tradition which, perhaps, more than any other, has been absolutely universal, both in ancient and modern times, is that of a *flood*, sent upon the world in punishment for the wickedness of man. Our space will not permit us to dwell at length on this very curious subject, and we can do little more than to allude to many of its details.

The Mexicans and Peruvians preserved this tradition in a form strikingly resembling that of the Bible. "The first age, called Atonatiuh, i. e., 'the sun of the waters,' was terminated by a universal deluge. The Noah of the Mexican cataclysm is Coxcox, called by some people Teo Cipactli, or

* Kitto's Bib. Cycl., new edition, art. *Sabbath*.

Tezpi. He saved himself, with his wife, Xochiquetzal, in a bark, or, according to other traditions, a raft of cypress-wood. . . . It is said that Tezpi embarked in a spacious vessel with his wife, his children, and many animals, and such seeds as were necessary for the subsistence of mankind. When the Great Spirit, Tezcatlicopa, ordered the waters to subside, Tezpi sent out of the ark a vulture. That bird, which lived on dead bodies, did not come back, on account of the great number of corpses scattered on the recently dried earth. Tezpi sent other birds, among which the humming-bird alone returned, holding in his mouth a branch with leaves. Then Tezpi, seeing that the soil was beginning to be covered with new verdure, came out of his ship on the mountain Colhuacan." * Traditions of a similar character are found among all the North American tribes.

Among the ancient Greeks, mention was made of two such catastrophes — the first called the deluge of Ogyges, which was placed by Varro about 1600 years before the first Olympiad, i. e., B. C. 2376, which differs from the Hebrew date of Noah only twenty-eight years. This, however, was only a local inundation, of no great extent, it being the overflow of the Lake Copais, which submerged the

* Anc. Hist. of the East, vol. i. p. 17.

valley of Bœotia. The other, which far more nearly resembled the Scripture narrative of the deluge, was called the flood of Deucalion. Even Bunsen is constrained to say, "Our previous researches will not permit us to doubt that the oldest Hellenic tradition about the flood of Deucalion was a legendary reminiscence of that great historical deluge." The account of it, as given by Lucian, is as follows: —

"I have heard, among the Greeks, the story of Deucalion, which they relate respecting him. They fable it as follows: The present generation of men is not the same as the former. That generation all perished; the men of the present are immediately descended from Deucalion. Mankind, having become exceedingly haughty, were lawless, for they did not regard their oaths, perform the rights of hospitality, or spare the suppliants. On account of these things, a great calamity came upon them; the earth suddenly poured forth floods of water, great rains fell, the rivers were swollen, and the sea overflowed, until all became submerged under water, and all flesh perished. Deucalion alone of men was preserved for a second race; this was on account both of his justice and piety. His deliverance was in this wise: Having put his sons and their wives into a great ark, which he had prepared, he went in himself, and the animals, swine, horses, lions, and whatever else lived on the earth, all came to him in pairs. He received them all, and was not injured by them, but there was great harmony throughout. In this one ark they all floated as long as the waters prevailed. These things are related by the Greeks respecting Deucalion." *

The sequel to this story represents the ark to have floated on the waters nine days, when it landed on Mount Parnassus, or, according to others, on Mount Athos. When the flood had subsided, Deucalion offered a sacrifice to Jupiter, who sent to him Mercury, with a promise that he would grant any prayer he might offer. Deucalion asked that Jupiter would restore mankind. He and his wife Pyrrha were directed to cover their heads and throw the bones of their mother behind them. After some doubts and scruples as to the meaning of this command, they agreed that the bones of their mother must be the stones of the earth. They accordingly threw these behind them, and those thrown by Deucalion became men, and those by Pyrrha women. From these the present family of mankind are descended.

Still more remarkable than this is the Phrygian tradition relating to the city of Apamea, where, it is said, the ark rested after the flood. The city itself

* Lucian's Works, Paris, 1840, p. 735.

was anciently called "Kibotos," or the Ark, and a medal was struck on which a representation of that vessel was shown, with two persons going forth from it, and two birds, one flying, the other resting upon it, with the name $N\Omega E$ inscribed on the side.

Among the Chaldeans, frequent mention is made of the flood of Xisuthrus, of which Berosus gives the following account: "After the death of Ardatus, his son Xisuthrus reigned 18 *sari*. In his time occurred a great deluge, which is thus described: The deity Kronus appeared to him in his sleep, and made known to him that upon the 15th day of the month Dæsius there would be a flood by which mankind would be destroyed. He therefore commanded him to write a history of the beginning, progress, and conclusion of all things, and bury it in the city of the sun at Sippara; also to build a vessel, and take with him into it his friends and relatives, with food and drink, and the different animals, both birds and quadrupeds, preparing all for the voyage. Having asked the deity whither he was to sail, he was answered, 'To the gods.' Offering up a prayer for the good of mankind, he obeyed the divine injunction, and built a vessel five stadia in length and two in breadth. Into this he put everything he had prepared, with his wife, children, and friends.

"After the flood had been long upon the earth, and had somewhat abated, Xisuthrus sent out certain birds, which, not finding any food, or place whereon to rest their feet, returned to the vessel. After some days, he sent forth birds a second time. These returned with their feet smeared with mud. He sent them forth a third time, and they returned no more. From this Xisuthrus knew that the earth had appeared above the waters, and, making an opening in the sides of the vessel, he perceived that it was stranded upon a mountain. He then left the vessel, with his wife, and daughter, and the pilot, and, having worshiped the earth, he built an altar, and offered sacrifice to the gods. Then, with those who had come out of the vessel with him, he disappeared.

"Those that remained in the vessel, finding that Xisuthrus and his company did not return, went out to seek him, calling him loudly by name. They saw him no more, but they heard his voice in the air commanding them to pay proper regard to religion, for he, on account of his piety, had gone to dwell with the gods, and his wife, his daughter, and the pilot, had been made partakers of the same honor. He further directed them to repair to Babylon, and, as had been commanded, search for the books he had buried at Sippara, and give them to mankind. They were then in the country of Armenia. Having heard these words, they, too, sacrificed to the gods, and proceeded to Babylon.

"Of this vessel, thus stranded in Armenia, it is said that a part still remains in the Corcyræan mountains of Armenia, and that the people, scraping off the bitumen with which it was coated, carry it away to keep it for charms and amulets. The comrades of Xisuthrus, having arrived at Babylon, dug up the writings buried at Sippara; they also built cities and temples, and Babylon was again inhabited." *

The resemblance between this account and that given in the Hebrew Scriptures is very striking. It has been suggested † that Berosus was acquainted with the latter, and drew his statement from them. There is no evidence, however, of this fact. On the contrary, while his narrative in general so much resembles that of Moses, there is sufficient discrepancy in details to show that he could not have borrowed it from him. It is much more probable that he derived the incidents of his story from traditions, either oral or written, preserved at Babylon, which embodied the memory of an event common to the history of all nations.

The Chinese preserve a striking tradition of the

* Cory's Ancient Fragments.
† Smith's Dict. Gr. and Rom. Biog., art. *Berosus*.

flood, which they say took place in the reign of Fuh-hi, 4000 years B. C. He, his wife, three sons, and three daughters, alone escaped, and from these the whole circle of the universe was repeopled. Dr. Gutzlaff relates that he saw in one of the Buddhist temples, "in beautiful stucco, the scene where Kwan-Yin, the goddess of mercy, looks down from heaven upon the lonely Noah in his ark, amidst the raging waves of the deluge, with the dolphins swimming round, as his last means of safety, and the dove, with an olive branch in its beak, flying toward the vessel. Nothing could have exceeded the beauty of the execution." *

It has been frequently said (by Lepsius and others) that there was no trace of the tradition of a deluge among the ancient Egyptians, the only flood of which they knew anything being the harbinger of fertility and plenty. This statement, however, is fully refuted by Osburn. He says, as to there being "no trace of Noah or the deluge in the hieroglyphic legends, we have no hesitation whatever in stating our conviction that Lepsius is mistaken. Our proof is a very direct and plain appeal to the senses. . . . It is to be found in the name of one of the most ancient gods

* Smith's Bib. Dict., art. *Noah.*

of Egypt, who was entitled 'the father of the gods,' 'the giver of mythic life to all beneath him.' Birch has truly identified this god with water. He was in reality the mythic impersonation of the annual overflow of the Nile. His name is written ⟨hieroglyph⟩ . . . Champollion and Birch identified the name of this god with the word ⟨hieroglyph⟩, *nou* or *nh*, which signifies 'the primordial water,' 'the abyss.' How it is possible not to recognize in this idol the apotheosis of the patriarch Noah (Hebrew, N-h or Nuh), we must confess ourselves unable to understand, especially when we call to mind that so indissolubly was the name of Noah linked with the remembrance of the general deluge, that it was afterward called by the Hebrews 'the waters of Noah.' (Isa. iv. 9.)" *

Nowhere, however, is the tradition of the flood more remarkable for its conformity to the Mosaic narrative than in the Hindu Vedas, which relate the *Avataras,* or incarnations of Vishnu. It is generally agreed that the first three of these owe their origin to that tradition. The first is called the *Matsya*, or Fish-Avatara. The legend is found in the Mahabharata, one of the great epic poems of the Sanskrit. It is likewise repeated in several of the Puranas, with slight variations. The substance of

---

* Monum. Hist. of Egypt, vol. i. pp. 239, 240.

it is, that Brahma, — in the Puranas, Vishnu, — assuming the form of a fish, informs Manu, a holy sage, that the earth is to be overwhelmed by a flood of waters, and directs him to build a ship, in which himself and seven other holy sages, with the living seeds of all things, will be preserved. When well secured in the great ship, the deity would appear in the form of a fish. The holy sage was to fasten the vessel to the fish's horn, and it would then ride safe over the turbulent waters. All this took place as predicted, and the ship, with its precious freight, rested at last on the loftiest peak of the Himalaya Mountains.

But the points of resemblance between the Hindu legend and the Mosaic account will best be seen from an extract. It is taken from the poetic version of Milman, late professor of poetry in Oxford University. Though clothed in poetic language, it appears to be a correct version of the original, preserving at the same time, in good degree, its measure and form of verse.

Passing over the introduction, which contains some unimportant particulars respecting the manner in which the fish-form deity was introduced to Manu,*

* The name Manuja, Manu-born, as the appellative of the human race (in Sanskrit books) is from Manu; from thence the Gothic Manu, which we have preserved. Manu is the representative of man. — *Milman's Version*, p. 11.

the holy sage, the account is as follows — the fish
continuing his divine directions : —

  "When the awful time approaches,
    hear from me what thou must do.
  In a little time, O blessed,
    all this firm and seated earth,
  All that moves upon its surface,
    shall a deluge sweep away.
  Near it comes, of all creation
    the ablution day is near;
  Therefore what I now forewarn thee
    may thy highest weal secure.
  All the fixed and all the moving,
    all that stirs, or stirreth not,
  Lo, of all the time approaches,
    the tremendous time of doom.
  Build thyself a ship, O Manu!
    strong with cables well prepared,
  And thyself, with the seven sages,
    mighty Manu, enter in.
  All the living seeds of all things,
    by the Brahmans named of yore,
  Place thou first within thy vessel,
    well secured, divided well.
  From thy ship keep watch, O hermit,
    watch for me as I draw near;
  Hornèd shall I swim before thee;
    by my horn thou't know me well.
  This the work thou must accomplish.
    I depart; so fare thee well.
  Over those tumultuous waters
    none without mine aid can sail.

Doubt not thou, O lofty minded,
    of my warning speech the truth.'
To the fish thus answered Manu;
    'All that thou requirest I will do.'"

Manu, having done as directed, and launched his vessel on the sea with its precious freight, the fish appears, and the vessel is bound to his head, and—

"Dancing with the tumbling billows,
    dashing through the roaring spray,
Tossed about with winds tumultuous,
    in the vast and heaving sea,
Like a trembling, drunken woman,
    reeled that ship, O king of men.
Earth was seen no more, no region,
    nor the intermediate space;
All around a waste of waters,
    water all, and air, and sky.
In the whole world of creation,
    princely son of Bharata,
None was seen, but those seven sages,
    Manu only and the fish.
Years on years, and still unwearied
    drew that fish the bark along,
Till at length it came, where lifted
    Himavan its loftiest peak.
There at length it came, and smiling,
    thus the fish addressed the sage:
'To the peak of Himalaya
    bind thou now thy stately ship.'
At the fish's mandate quickly,
    to the peak of Himavan

Bound the sage his bark, and ever
    to this day, that loftiest peak
Bears the name of Manhubandhan,
    from the binding of the bark.
To the sage, the god of mercy,
    thus with fixéd look bespake:
'I am Lord of all creation,
    Brahmá, higher than all height;
I in fish-like form have saved thee,
    Manu, in the perilous hour;
But from thee new tribes of creatures,
    gods, asuras, men, must spring.
All the worlds must be created,
    all that moves, or moveth not,
By an all-surpassing penance,
    this great work must be achieved.
Through my mercy, thy creation
    to confusion ne'er shall run.'
Spake the fish, and on the instant,
    to the invisible he passed."

Manu immediately begins his penance and the work of creation. The legend closes, —

"Such the old, the famous legend,
    named the Story of the Fish,
Which to thee I have related;
    this for all our sins atones.
He that hears it, — Manu's legend, —
    in the full possession he
Of all things complete and perfect,
    to the heavenly world ascends."

While the ark floats fastened to the fish, Manu

enters into conversation with his divine guide and preserver; and his questions and the replies of the deity form, in the Purana, the main substance of the compilation. The principal subjects are, as usual in these books, an account of the creation, the royal dynasties, the duties of the different orders, and various mythological legends.

The foregoing are but specimens of the traditions which are found among all nations respecting the great events of the primitive ages. The curious reader will find very much in the authorities cited, and others, that will well repay his researches into this subject. We ask now, in view of these facts, of the number of these traditions, their striking resemblances both to the Bible narrative and to each other, with just those differences that show independent lines of descent from the beginning, how they can be explained but upon the supposition that they are reminiscences coming down from a period in the history of mankind when as yet they were an unbroken family. That they could have been derived by one nation from another, will be conceded, by all familiar with the history of these nations, to be impossible. That they should have sprung up spontaneously among peoples so wide apart in lineage, in abode, and in speech, no one will maintain. We regard them, as they have ever been regarded by scholars and historians, as among the most conclusive evidences both of the unity of the race and of the commencement of the separate existence of those peoples since the time of Noah.

CHAPTER XI.

THE ARGUMENT FROM MYTHOLOGY.

Mythology, its Nature. — All Myths founded in Fact. — Instances of the Origin of modern Myths. — Character of Greek Writers. — Specimens of their Mistakes respecting foreign Names and Personages. — I. All Mythologies had a common Origin. — The Roman and Greek. — The Egyptian. — The Phœnician. — The Chaldean. — The Hindu. — II. That Origin in the Bible Narrative of the Creation and the Flood. — Myths of the Creation. — Of the Antediluvians. — of Noah. — Of the Ark. — Of the Dove. — of the Rainbow. — Of the eight Persons saved. — Of Noah's three Sons. — Results.

MYTHOLOGY is a species of tradition which, among pagan nations, embraces the facts and principles of religion. It is true that there are secular myths, — legendary stories of individuals and tribes, — having no sacred import. Still, so active was the supposed participation of the gods in human affairs, that few of these fables are entirely destitute of allusions to them. Indeed, the whole theology of the ancient pagan world was essentially mythical; the names, characters, and actions of the gods, their relations to men, and the modes in which they were to be worshiped, were recounted by the poets and fabulists, and formed collectively that mass of traditions and writings which we call mythology.

It is apparent, then, that the field which mythology opens to us may afford important aid in the consideration of the question now in hand. Religious belief has the strongest hold upon the heart, and is transmitted with the greatest care from one generation to another. If all men have sprung from a common parentage, we ought to find, as we ascend the stream of history, traces of a similarity in faith and religious rites among them. Even though the primitive belief and worship of one God were early lost through that depravity of heart which the apostle Paul so graphically describes in the first chapter of Romans, still the idolatry which came in its place, having been derived from common sources in the traditions of the past, ought to show those evidences of the fact which will powerfully demonstrate the original unity of those who hold it.

It is important to observe that all myths, however absurd and incredible their form, were *founded upon fact*. Thus says C. O. Müller: "It is quite clear that two distinct ingredients enter into mythology, viz., the statement of things done and things imagined. . . . We always find a chain of

facts leading from history into mythology."* That is, some actual person existed, or was believed to have existed, or some event, real or supposed, took place, which formed, as it were, the nucleus of the tradition, round which, in the lapse of time, was gathered, under the influence of an active imagination, a mass of fictitious incident, until it finally reached its present form. I am aware that some have held a different theory as to the process of its growth, believing that some abstract idea, philosophical or ethical, was the germ, which created for itself a legend of personification and narrative for its expression. Thus says George: †
" Mythus is the creation of a fact out of an idea." Professor Powell says, " A myth is a doctrine expressed in a narrative form; an abstract moral or spiritual truth, dramatized in action and personification, where the object is to enforce faith, not in the parable, but in the moral." ‡ I think these definitions are quite wrong. I do not believe a myth, properly so called, ever originated in an idea, but exactly the reverse. There is first the fact, real or supposed; then a distortion of it through misapprehension, or an amplification of it for ornament or

---

* Introd. to a Scientific System of Mythology, p. 9.
† Mythus and Sage, quoted by Rawlinson Hist. So., p. 231.
‡ Ibid.

explanation; a personification, apotheosis, and the like. I know that myths frequently reach that form in which an idea or a doctrine becomes their chief import; but still I maintain that they began with simple facts or actual beings. The opposite theory, that abstract ideas or principles, in primitive times, clothed themselves in mythical forms, creating gods, and heroes, and fictitious events, as a mode of expression, endows the infancy of the race with too much of a philosophic sense. It reverses the natural order of development, imaginative childhood first, reflective and reasoning manhood afterward.

I have said that misapprehension of the original facts was a fruitful source of mythology. Professor M. Müller gives several curious instances illustrative of this in modern times.

"Many of the old signs of taverns contain what we may call hieroglyphic mythology. There was a house on Stoken-church Hill, near Oxford, exhibiting on its sign-board 'Feathers and a Plum.' The house itself was vulgarly called the 'Plum and Feathers;' it was originally the 'Plume of Feathers,' from the crest of the Prince of Wales.

"'A Cat with a Wheel' is the corrupt emblem of 'St. Catharine's Wheel;' the 'Bull and Gate' was originally intended as a trophy of the taking of Boulogne by Henry VIII.; and the 'Goat and Compasses' have taken the place of the fine old Puritan sign-board, 'God encompasses us.'

"There is much of this popular mythology floating about among the people, arising from a very natural and very general tendency, viz., from a conviction that every name must have a meaning. At Lincoln, immediately below the High Bridge, there is an inn bearing now the sign of the 'Black Goats.' It formerly had the sign of the 'Three Goats,' a name derived from the three *gowts* or drains by which the water from the Swan Pool, a large lake which formerly existed to the west of the city, was conducted into the bed of the Witham below. A public house having arisen on the bank of the principal of these *gowts*, in honor, probably, of the work when it was made, the name became corrupted into 'Three Goats' — a corruption easily accomplished in the Lincolnshire dialect.

"One of our colleges at Oxford is now called and spelled *Brasenose*. Over the gate of the college there is a brazen nose, and the arms of the college display the same shield, and have done so for several centuries. I have not heard of any legend to account for the startling presence of that emblem over the gate of the college; but this is simply owing to the want of poetic imagination on the part of the Oxford ciceroni. In Greece, Pausanias would have told us ever so many traditions commemorated by such a monument. At Oxford we are simply told that the college was originally a brew-house, and that its original name, *Brasen-huis* (brasserie), was gradually changed to Brasenose."

Mistakes of this nature, sometimes originating in ignorance and sometimes in design, were exceedingly common among the Greeks, from whose writers we derive our chief knowledge, not only of their own mythology, but of those of other peoples. Of this propensity Bryant speaks as follows : —

"As their traditions were obsolete, and filled with extraneous matter, it rendered it impossible for them to arrange properly the principal events of their country. They did not separate and distinguish, but often took to themselves the merit of transactions which were of a prior date and of another clime. These they adopted, and made their own. Hence, when they came to digest their history, it was all confused, and they were embarrassed with numberless contradictions and absurdities which it was impossible to remedy. . . . They had a childish antipathy to every foreign language, and were equally prejudiced in favor of their own. This was attended with the most fatal consequences. They were misled by the too great delicacy of their ear, and could not bear any term which appeared to them barbarous and uncouth. On this account they either rejected foreign appellations, or so modeled and changed them, that they became, in sound and meaning, essentially different. And as they were attached to their own country and its customs, they presumed that everything was to be looked for among themselves. They did not consider that the titles of their gods, the names of cities, and their terms of worship were imported, that their ancient hymns were grown obsolete, and that time had wrought a great change. They explained everything by the language in use, without the least retrospect or allowance, and all names and titles from other countries were liable to the same rule. If the name were dissonant and disagreeable to their ear, it was rejected as barbarous; but if it were at all similar in sound to any word in their language, they changed it to that word, though the name were of Syriac original, or introduced from Egypt or Babylonia. The purport of the term was by these means changed, and the history which depended upon it either perverted or effaced." *

Many examples are given by this author in illustration of these statements, of which only a specimen or two can here be mentioned. The myth of Mount Olympus being the residence of the gods originated

* Ancient Mythology, vol. i. pp. 204, 210.

thus: *Ham*, the progenitor of the Egyptians, was worshiped as a god (*El*), being the same that the Greeks called Amun, or Ammon. *Phi* signifies a mouth,* and was used especially to denote the voice or oracle of a god. Hence El-Ham-Phi, or Elampi, would mean the oracle of the god Amun. The Greeks, knowing or caring nothing for the etymology, wrote it Ol-um-pos (Olympus), and then invented the legend corresponding, locating it, as oracles were generally placed, on a mountain, and making it the home of Zeus (the Greek equivalent of Amun), and of course of his divine court.

The same word, slightly changed, *Am-phi-el*, gave rise to another notion equally absurd. The sound of it somewhat resembled that of their own word *omphalos*, a navel. Hence they fabled that Delphi, the seat of the oracle of Apollo, was the *navel*, i. e., the center of the world. Sophocles calls it the "umbilical oracle of the earth," † and Livy, "umbilicum orbis terrarum." ‡ Towns and cities, where similar oracles existed, were often called Omphalian, and their people Omphalians; and Quintus Curtius, describing the temple of Jupi-

---

* As in the Hebrew words Peniel, Pibeseth, Pihahiroth, Phicol, etc.

† Μεσόμφαλα Γῆς μαντεῖα. Œdip. Tyr., v. 487.

‡ L. 38, c. 47.

ter Amun, gravely informs us that there was an Omphalus there, and that the deity was represented in the form of a *Navel*, set around with precious stones.*

In like manner the Egyptian *Cahen-Caph-El*, meaning the "priests of the temple of the god" (the sun), was, from a rude similarity of sound, transformed into *Cyno-ceph-al-oi*, i. e., "beings with dogs' heads;" and the absurd story invented that the Egyptians kept in their temples baboons with dogs' heads, who were wonderfully skilled in the motions of the heavenly bodies, who could read and write, and "whenever one of them was introduced into the sacred apartments for probation, the priest presented him with a tablet, and with a pen and ink, and, by his writing, could immediately find out if he were of the true intelligent breed," † the latter circumstance referring to the examination to which novices were subjected before they were admitted to the priesthood. ‡

These illustrations we deem very valuable, as throwing a flood of light on the whole subject of the heathen mythology, enabling us to account for many

---

* *Umbilico* maxime similis est habitus, smaragdo et gemmis coagmentus, l. 4, c. 7.
† Horapollo, l. 1, c. 14, p. 28.
‡ Bryant, Anc. Myth., vol. ii. pp. 20-23.

of its wildest absurdities. Not that we are able to trace the rise and progress of every myth, but we can easily imagine, after these examples, modern as well as ancient, how they may have risen and run a wild course to the shape in which we now find them. If the name of an old brew-house can be so changed as to become a *brazen nose*, if three drains for conducting off the waters of a lake can become, even on the very spot, *Three Goats*, if the pious expression of confidence in the divine care can be transformed into the *Goat and Compasses*, and all this in recent historic times, and near the very seats of modern science, what might we not expect among the ignorant and superstitious peoples of other lands and other times?

The views thus exhibited of the nature of myths, and the origin and growth of mythology in general, will prepare the way for the proposition which will bring the subject into connection with our present discussion, viz., *That all the systems of ancient mythology had a common origin, and that origin was in the persons and events described in the Mosaic account of the primeval ages of man, in the first chapters of Genesis.*

I. The first part of this proposition, that all the systems of ancient mythology had a common origin, need not detain us long.

That the Roman mythology was essentially the same as the Greek is familiar to every classical scholar. The names of the gods were, indeed, for the most part, different; but their characters and histories were sufficiently alike to cause them to be recognized by the writers of both countries as substantially the same. I speak now of the chief deities only, for there were numerous local and subordinate divinities, both in Greece and Italy, who were not known elsewhere. Nor are we to understand that the Roman mythology, except partially, in later times, when intercourse between the two countries became frequent, was borrowed from the Greek. Rather, the two mythologies, like the two languages, were sisters, being each derived from a common source, in a period antecedent to the settlement of either country.

In like manner the Greek mythology, in its main elements, was the same as that of Egypt. The Grecian writers, from Herodotus down, represent that the names and characters of the principal gods and goddesses were derived from the East, mostly from Egypt. Herodotus (ii. 52) says this expressly, and Diodorus Siculus dwells upon it at great length. All that was peculiarly Grecian was the localizing and modifying of the names in the manner already described, with the invention of new fictions to correspond to those alterations. I think it a mistake, however, to affirm that the Greek mythology was *derived* from Egypt, and would prefer to say that both the Egyptian and the Grecian were originally from a common source, and owe to this their mutual resemblance to each other.

This resemblance, again, is found between the Egyptian, Phœnician, and Chaldean or Babylonian systems. Bunsen expressly says, " All Egypt's roots are in Asia," and he gives very conclusive examples of such derivation. The Jupiter, Mars, Venus, and Mercury of the West, and the Amun, Muntru, Athor, and Thoth of Egypt, are at Nineveh and Babylon, Bel-Merodach, Nergal, Ishtar, and Nebo.

And so in numerous other instances. There is some reason to think that the gods of the Assyrian and Babylonian mythologies, as deciphered from the cuneiform inscriptions, are nearer the common source from which all are derived, than any other.

In the Hindu mythology, we are met again by striking points of resemblance to those already mentioned. It is, says M. Müller, a "fact which can not be doubted, and which, if fully appreciated, will be felt to be pregnant with the most startling and the most instructive lessons of antiquity — the fact, I mean, that *Zeus*, the most sacred name in Greek mythology, is the same word as *Dyaus*, or *Dyu* in Sanskrit, *Jovis* or *Ju* in Jupiter in Latin, *Tiw* in Anglo-Saxon (preserved in Tiwsdæg, Tuesday, the day of the Eddic god Tyr), *Zio* in old High German," * and, he might have added, *Ti* in Chinese, and *Teo* in Mexican. And a writer in the Christian Examiner,† reviewing this work of Müller, remarks further, " As the Sanskrit has, in most cases, preserved its roots in a more primitive form than the other Aryan languages, so in the Rig-Veda we find the same mythic phraseology as in Homer and Hesiod, but in a far more rudimentary and unintelligible condition. Zeus, Eros, Helena, Ouranos, and Cerberus reappear as Dyaus, Arusha, Sarameias, Sarama, Varuna, and Sawara; but instead of completely developed personalities, they are presented to us only as vague powers, with their nature and attributes dimly defined, and their relations to each other fluctuating, and often contradictory. There is no theogony, no mythologic system. The same pair of divinities appear now as father and daughter, now as brother and sister, now as husband and wife; now they entirely lose their personality, and become undifferentiated Forces. In the Vedas, the early significancy of myths has not faded, but continually recurs to the mind of the

* Science of Lang., second series, p. 444.
† May, 1865, p. 380.

poet. In the Homeric poems, that significance is almost entirely lost sight of, and its influence upon the poet is an unconscious influence."

I remark here, as before, that these resemblances do not prove that the Greeks *derived* their mythology from India. In the mass, and in details, it has very little in common with that of the latter country, although many of the names in them are etymologically the same. The most that I would claim is, that the elementary roots of the two systems were derived from a common source. Or, rather, those roots existed as a common stock among the remote ancestors of the two peoples before they separated in the primeval times, and when the separations took place, these elementary roots developed, in the different countries to which they were carried into the different systems subsequently found there.

II. The second part of our proposition is, that all the various systems of mythology existing among the ancient nations had their origin in the persons and events mentioned by Moses in the earliest chapters of Genesis.

The full exhibition of this fact would require a volume, or rather many volumes. Of course only some hints of the argument can be given here. The reader is referred, for a detailed view, to Bryant's

Ancient Mythology, Faber's *Origin of Pagan Idolatry*, Kitto's *Daily Bible Illustrations*, vol. i., etc.

It is not meant, of course, that every particular of the vast mass of fable, poetry, and song, which constitute those mythologies, was derived from the source mentioned, but only their *roots*, or the primary and leading facts from which all the rest have been developed. Some of these primary facts are the following: —

The creation of the world. According to Moses, the earth was originally "without form and void" (Heb., emptiness and desolation), "and darkness was upon the face of the deep." The first thing formed was light, or the Day; then the firmament called Heaven; the dry land, Earth; the collections of waters, Seas; next vegetable life, yielding seed and fruit; after that, the sun, moon, and stars. Now, all this, told in the Greek and Roman mythologies, is as follows: —

First was Chaos, "the confused mass containing the elements of all things," * who was the mother of *Erebos* and *Nyx*, i. e., Darkness and Night. These intermarrying, begat *Æther* and *Hemera*, the Air,

---

* Smith's Dict. of Biog. and Myth., which will be our authority in the subsequent statements, unless otherwise noticed. Where two names are given together, the first is Greek, and the second its Latin equivalent.

or Welkin, and the Day. The eldest of the gods was *Ouranos*, Cœlus, who married *Ge*, Terra, i. e., the Heaven and Earth, and was the father of the Titans, viz., Oceanus, Cronus, Hyperion, Iapetus, Cœus, and Crius. *Oceanus*, the ocean, married his sister Tethys, and begat the *Oceanides*, nymphs of the ocean; the *Nereides*, nymphs of the Mediterranean; the *Potameides*, nymphs of the rivers; the *Naiades*, nymphs of fountains, etc. *Kronos*, Saturn, marrying his sister Rhea, was the father of *Hestia*, Vesta, i. e., fire; *Demeter*, Ceres, i. e., mother-earth, the goddess of corn and fertility; *Zeus*, Jupiter, and his sister-wife *Hera*, Juno, the gods of the sky or upper air; *Poseidon*, Neptune, the sea (Mediterranean); and *Hades*, Pluto, the under-world, hell. *Hyperion*, marrying another sister, Theia, was the father of *Helios*, Sol, the sun; *Selene*, Luna, the moon, and *Eos*, Aurora, the dawn.

Equally fruitful in fable has been the record of man's creation and fall. In Genesis, God is represented as taking counsel with himself, and then making man out of the dust of the earth, and animating him with an immortal soul, endowed with the divine image. Subsequently woman was made, and brought to the man, who, being tempted, brings sin and death into the world, "and all our woe," but to whom is given in mercy the hope of a Deliverer. This is told, mythologically, thus: —

Iapetus, one of the Titans, was the father of *Prometheus*, i. e., forethought or counsel. He made the first man of clay, and then, with the aid of Athene, stole from heaven a celestial spark, with which to animate him. In punishment for this theft, Zeus ordered Hephæstus to make a woman, *Pandora*, — so called because endowed with " every gift," beauty, wisdom, etc., — and gave her in marriage to *Epimetheus*, i. e., afterthought or repentance. She, led by curiosity, lifted the lid of the box in which Prometheus had confined diseases, misfortunes, and other woes, and let them loose to afflict mankind. In the bottom of the vessel, however, hope remained, which is appointed to solace man under his sufferings.

Before the flood there was, according to the Bible, a succession of ten patriarchs, who lived each many hundred years. From these, we cannot doubt, originated the idea, which prevailed among nearly all nations, of a series of antediluvian kings, sometimes regarded as divine, sometimes as human, whose reigns covered immense periods of time. These were the gods, demigods, and manes, of Egyptian chronology, that reigned before Menes, who, I doubt not, was Noah. In respect to the term *Manes* (Gr. νέκυες), Bryant remarks (iv. 441), that the Egyptian word was *Nechus*, or *Necho*, signifying a king, as seen in the name Pharaoh-Necho (2 Kings xxiii. 29), also in Nech-epsos, Nech-aos, etc., and that the Greeks, not understanding it, rendered it by νέκυς, a dead person; hence *manes*, or spirits of the dead. Instead, therefore, of "gods, demigods, and manes," he would read, "gods, and demigods, and kings who were mortals." These, it is said, reigned in all 24,900 years.* The Chaldeans, as we have seen (p. 94), enumerated ten kings before Xisuthrus and the flood, who reigned 432,000 years. So among the Hindus there were ten lords of created beings, and among the Chinese the first man, Pan-kou, who chiseled the heavens and earth out of granite, lived 18,000 years, and was followed by a succession of sovereigns called celestial, terrestrial, and human, until Fuh-hi (Noah), covering a period variously given as from 45,000 to 500,000 years.†

In consequence of the wickedness of the race, God, it is said, repented him that he had made man, and determined to destroy them with a deluge. What else could have originated the legend that Uranus hated his children, and sent them all, immediately after their birth, to Tartarus?

* Appendix, E., p. 362.
† pp. 121, 122. — William, Mid. King., vol. ii. pp. 196, 199.

But the most fruitful source of mythology was the flood itself, with the persons and objects connected with it — the event which, as we have seen, is preserved in the traditions of all the ancient nations.

First, the patriarch himself is described to us in the stories of Deucalion, Xisuthrus, Coxcox, etc., the particulars of which have before been given. Next, his name appears in numerous languages, and in a great variety of forms, often disguised, but still showing evidences of their original identity. That name in Hebrew is N-ch, or N-u-ch, the final hard guttural of which is in Greek represented by κ, or more commonly softened into ς, as Nus, Nusus, Naus, Noas, Noe, etc. "Its fundamental root is *Na*, to which, in all the languages of the latter (Aryan) race, is attached the meaning of water — ναειν, to flow, ναμα, water, νηχειν, to swim; Nympha, Neptunus, water deities; Nix, Nick, the Undine of the northern races," * to which I may add ναῦς, navis, a ship, navy, nautical, etc. Thus Suidas tells us of a king Nan-nakus, or An-nakus, who foretold the flood of Deucalion, and warned men to repent. I-nachus was represented as the son of Oceanus, who, after the flood, led his people from the mountains into the plains, and confined the waters within their proper channels. The name

---

* Hist. of the East, Lenormant, vol. i. p. 15.

again appears in *Dionysus*, the Greek appellation of Bacchus, meaning Dio, or Dius-Nus, the divine Nus. He was the god of wine and drunkenness — a plain allusion to Noah's intoxication from wine. It is said that he was the son of Zeus and Semele, and that to escape the anger of Juno, Zeus put the mother and child into a chest (ark), and threw it into the sea. The vessel arrived safely to land, and the god was carried to Mount *Nysa*, where he was brought up. The Scriptures say that, after the flood, Noah began to be a husbandman (Heb., man of the ground); and this very epithet ($\theta\epsilon\grave{o}\varsigma$ $\chi\theta\acute{o}\nu\iota o\varsigma$) is one of the titles of Dionysus. He invented the cultivation of the vine, and, leaving Mount Nysa, traveled over the world teaching men the use of wine, the worship of the gods, the observance of the laws, etc.* Among the Egyptians he was recognized under the name of 〔hieroglyphs〕 or 〔hieroglyphs〕 Nou or Nuh, signifying the "primordial water," also in Kneph, Chnoubis, Chnouphis, and in the city No-Amun, etc. In the Vedas, the name of the person saved from the flood is Ma-nu, and one of the earliest Chinese kings is Nau the Great, to whom is attributed the invention of the cycle of 60 years. The so-called first man, Pan-kou, or, as it may equally well be pronounced Man-hou, is probably, also, the same name. †

* Appendix L. † Appendix M.

The tradition of the ark itself is preserved in many ways. Its name in Hebrew was תֵּבָה, *tcba,* or *thcba*, which was the name given to numerous cities, all of which show some traces of connection with Noah. Thebes, in Egypt, was said to have been founded by Menes (Noah), and was called *No* (Ezek. xxx. 14, 15, 16; Nah. iii. 8). From this city Osiris set forth on a tour of the world to teach men agriculture. During his absence Typhon (signifying storm, or deluge) conspired against him, and let loose a flood upon the world, and, on his return, Typhon killed him, and placed the body in a beautiful ark, which he threw upon the waters. This was cast upon the shore of Phœnicia, where Osiris returned to life, and became the patron of agriculture, etc. Thebes, in Greece, was the birth-place of Dio-nysus, or Bacchus, the god of wine, another name for Noah, as already seen. There was also a Thiba in Pontus, in regard to which there was a tradition that its inhabitants could not be drowned. Another Hebrew word for ark was אַרְגָּז, *argoz*, translated *coffer* in 1 Sam. vi. 8, 11, which doubtless gave its name to the various cities called Argos. Argos, in Achaia, was founded by *I-nachus* (Noah), and its citadel built by *Da-naus* (another name of Noah), who is said to have come in a large ship from Egypt, with his fifty daughters, and who deposited in the citadel a model of the vessel called the *Amphiprumnon*, i. e., having two prows, hence lunar-shaped. Here lived *Argus*, the builder of the ship Argo, who went on the famous Argonautic expedition, and *Da-nae*, the mother of Perseus, who conceived by Zeus, who came to her in a golden shower, and was afterwards shut up with her infant in an ark, and thrown into the sea, where she floated to an island, and was saved by a fisherman named Dictys. In Greek the ark was called *Kibotos*, which was another name of Apamea in Phrygia, where was struck the famous medal, having on it the representation of the ark and dove with Noah and his wife.

The dove which Noah sent from the ark has given rise to a multitude of traditions. The word in Hebrew is יוֹנָה, Yonah, in Greek οἰνάς, whence probably *Venus*, in Latin, the goddess of love. She is said to have risen from the foam of the sea, hence called Venus Anadyomene. She presided over the waters, and had power to appease the troubled ocean, and cause a universal calm. The dove was especially sacred to her, and she was represented in a chariot drawn by these birds. All this is plainly suggestive of the dove sent forth from the ark, who flew to and fro on the waters, finding no rest for the sole of her foot, and whose return was the signal that the flood had abated, and fair weather returned to the earth. As the prophet who preached to the Ninevites was named Jonah, so the patriarch who preached to the antediluvians was called by Berosus *Oan,* or *Oannes,* which are the same name. He is represented, with evident allusion to the flood, as being below the waist a fish (dag); hence *Dag-on,* the fish deity of the Babylonians and Phœnicians. He is said to have been a benevolent being, who came out of the sea, taught mankind to build temples and cities, and cultivate the earth, etc.

From the same source, also, probably originated *Juno,* the queen of the gods. She was called I-nachia by the poets, and was accompanied by *Iris,* the rainbow, etc.

The eight persons saved in the ark are supposed to be represented by the *Cabiri,* who were four gods and four goddesses, children of *Zadik,* i. e., the righteous one, the first of whom, as deciphered by Wilkinson from the monuments, bore the well-known Egyptian names of the patriarch Nou, Noub, Cnoubis, Cnouphis, Kneph, etc. In other combinations we have the names of three gods and goddesses, and of twelve, the number being doubled, as is not uncommon in mythology; as Herodotus says, " The twelve gods were, they affirm, produced from the eight." It is remarkable, also, how triads abound in almost all mythologies, as among the Greeks, Zeus, Poseidon, and Hades; among the Romans, Jupiter, Neptune, and Pluto; in Egypt, Osiris, Isis, Horus, etc. Wilkinson says, "If, in every town or district of Egypt, the principal temple had been preserved, we might discover the nature of the triad worshiped there, as well as the name of the chief deity who presided in it."* Tacitus relates that the ancient Germans celebrated in songs the praises of their god *Tuisco* and his son *Man-nus*, the founders of three Germanic nations. To Man-nus (compare Egyptian, Menes, Hindu, Manu, etc.) they assign three sons, by whose names the people occupying different parts of the country were called. Among the Persians, Feridun had three sons, Selim, Tur, and Irij, to whom he gave respectively Rum, Turan, and Iran.

But we can pursue these illustrations no further. The subject is certainly a curious one, and will amply repay the investigations of every scholar of antiquity. Making, now, all due allowances for mistake in some particulars, from erroneous etymologies, or insufficient points of resemblance, we are sure that the general conclusion can not well be disputed. In some respects it seems

---

* Anc. Egypt, second series, vol. i. p. 230.

even more reliable than that derived from History, Ethnology, or Language. Mythology has to deal with *the origin of things*, especially of *religious* things, and seems to carry us further back than either of its sister sciences. And though at first view the vast mass of fiction and fable which it presents to us seems scarcely less confused than the original chaos of the earth, yet a little patient study will enable us to find the clew which will lead us intelligently and safely through it, and show a very simple origin for the whole, in the inspired account of creation, the antediluvian world, and the flood; thus corroborating the truth of that narrative, and proving the descent of all nations from one common source.

CHAPTER XII.

THE ARGUMENT FROM GEOLOGY.

Lyell's "Geological Evidences." — Alleged Facts proving a Remote Antiquity for the Race. — 1. Fragments of Brick and Pottery from Egypt. — The Data not verified. — Changes in the Nile Valley. — Burnt Brick unknown to the Ancient Egyptians. — 2. Human Fossil in Mississippi Valley. — 3. Skeleton found near New Orleans. — 4. Remains in the Florida Coral Reefs. — 5. Flint Implements in the Valley of the Somme. — Diagram of the Valley. — Its assumed Geological History. — The Association of Human and Animal Remains no Proof that they were contemporaneous. — If contemporaneous, no proof of extreme Antiquity. — Opinion of Westminster Review. — Opinion of Professor Rogers. — Alleged Geological Changes in the Somme Valley. — Assumed to be wrought by existing Agencies. — Uniformitarians. — Testimony of President Hitchcock. — Of Professor Duns. — Of Sir R. Murchison. — Of Professor Wilson. — Of Elie de Beaumont. — Of Professor Rogers. — 6. Human Remains in Peat-bogs, Shell-mounds, and Lakes. — The Stone, the Bronze, and the Iron Age. — All pertaining to the Celtic Race. — Opinion of Dr. Keller. — Of Troyon. — Conclusion.

I PROPOSE now to pass under review the leading facts presented us in Geology, which are relied on by many to prove a very high antiquity. They are taken chiefly from the elaborate work of Sir Charles Lyell, entitled, "The Geological Evidences of the Antiquity of Man" (Am. edition, 1863). In that volume the distinguished author has collected all the important facts furnished by his favorite science, whether brought to light by himself or by the labors of others. The work may be regarded as exhaustive on that side of the question. .

1. The first case that I will notice of alleged geological discoveries, which are supposed to prove the very remote antiquity of our race, is that of the fragments of brick and pottery dug up from the valley of the Nile. This case is the more important, as it is cited by almost every author who avowedly opposes the Bible chronology.

In the year 1851, the Royal Society of London instituted a series of borings in the sediment of the Nile valley, under the care of Mr. Leonard Horner, the expense of which was partly sustained by the viceroy. Sixty workmen, with several engineers, were employed for this purpose — men accustomed to the climate, and capable of pursuing the work during the hot months, after the annual inundation was passed. "The results," says Sir Charles Lyell, "of chief importance were obtained from two sets of shafts and borings, sunk at intervals in lines crossing the great valley from east to west. One of these consisted of no less than fifty-one pits and artesian perforations made where the valley is sixteen miles wide from side to side, between the Arabian and Libyan deserts, in the latitude of Heliopolis, about eight miles above the apex of the delta. The other line of borings and pits, twenty-seven in number, was in the parallel of Memphis, where the valley is only five miles broad. . . .

"In some instances the excavations were on a large scale for the first sixteen or twenty-four feet, in which cases jars, vases, pots, and a small human figure in burnt clay, a copper knife, and other entire articles were dug up; but when water, soaking through from the Nile, was reached, the boring instrument used was too small to allow of more than fragments of works of art being brought up. *Pieces of burnt brick and pottery* were extracted almost everywhere, and from all depths, even where they sank sixty feet below the surface toward the central parts of the valley. In none of these cases did they get to the bottom of the alluvial soil." *

The mode in which these pieces of brick and pot-

---

* Geological Evidences, etc., pp. 34, 36.

tery are made to testify to the antiquity of man, is by estimating the length of time requisite for their burial at the alleged depth under the sediment deposited by the overflow of the Nile. "M. Girard, of the French expedition to Egypt, supposed the average rate of the increase of Nile mud in the plain between Assouan and Cairo to be five English inches in a century. This conclusion, according to Mr. Horner, is very vague, and founded on insufficient data; the amount of matter thrown down by the waters in different parts of the plain varying so much that to strike an average with any approach to accuracy must be most difficult. Were we to assume six inches in a century, the burnt brick met with at a depth of sixty feet would be 12,000 years old.

"Another fragment of red brick was found by Linant Bey in a boring seventy-two feet deep, being two or three feet below the level of the Mediterranean, in the parallel of the apex of the delta, 200 metres distant from the river, on the Libyan side of the Rosetta branch. M. Rosière, in the great French work on Egypt,* has estimated the mean rate of deposit of sediment in the delta at two inches and three lines in a century. Were we to take two and a half inches, a work of art seventy-

* Description de l'Egypt (Histoire Naturelle, tom. ii. p. 494).

two feet deep must have been buried more than 30,000 years ago. But if the boring of Linant Bey was made where an arm of the river had been silted up at a time when the apex of the delta was somewhat further south, or more distant from the sea than now, the brick in question might be comparatively very modern." (pp. 37, 38.)

It is truly surprising that any author of repute should build such a conclusion on data so imperfect, and involving so many elements of doubt. What assurance have we that these fragments of brick and pottery were actually found in the places alleged? In Egypt, and throughout the East generally, the native population are skilled in the art of furnishing artificial antiques, and will always produce whatever specimens are supposed to be wanted. Or, conceding their genuineness, what evidence is there of a *uniform* rate of increase in the Nile deposits for so many thousands of years. Lyell himself admits that the Egyptians were "in the habit of inclosing with embankments the areas on which they erected temples, statues, and obelisks, so as to exclude the waters of the Nile," and " Herodotus tells us that in his time those spots from which the Nile waters had been shut out for centuries, appeared sunk, and could be looked down into from the surrounding grounds, which had been raised by the gradual accumulation over them of sediment annually thrown down. If the waters at length should break into such depressions, they must at first carry with them into the inclosure much mud, washed from the steep surrounding banks, so that a greater quantity would be deposited in a few years than perhaps in as many centuries on the great plain outside the depressed area where no such disturbing causes intervened." (pp. 38, 39.)

It has been suggested, also, that these fragments may have fallen into wells, or into some of the innumerable fissures into which the soil is rent in the dry season, which are often very deep. The bed of the Nile itself has often changed its site. "According to an ancient tradition (Herod. ii. 99), Menes, . . . when he founded Memphis, is related to have diverted the course of the Nile, by a dam, about one hundred stadia (12 miles) south of the city, and thus to have dried up the old bed." * " We know from the testimony of Makrizi, that less than a thousand years ago the Nile flowed close by the western limits of Cairo, from which it is now separated by a plain extending to the width of more than a mile. In this plain, therefore, one might now dig to the depth of twenty feet or more, and find plenty of fragments of pottery and other remains, less than a thousand

* Quarterly Rev., 1859, p. 420.

years old. Natural changes in the course of the Nile, similar to that which we have here mentioned, and some of them, doubtless, much greater have taken place in almost every part of its passage through Egypt." *

It is further alleged, that *burnt* brick was unknown in Egypt till the time of the Romans. " If a coin of Trajan or Diocletian had been found in these spots, even Mr. Horner would have been obliged to admit that he had made a fatal mistake in his conclusions; but a piece of *burnt* brick, found beneath the soil, tells the same tale that a Roman coin would tell under the same circumstances. . . . There is not a single known structure of burnt brick, from one end of Egypt to the other, earlier than the period of the Roman dominion. These ' fragments of burnt brick,' therefore, have been deposited after the Christian era, and, instead of establishing the existence of man in Egypt more than 13,000 years, supply a convincing proof of the worthlessness of Mr. Horner's theory." †

Sir Charles Lyell notices most of these objections to his theory, and attempts to parry the force of them, but with indifferent success. As to the last, he claims, on the authority of Mr. Birch, of the British Museum, that it is erroneous in fact, there

---

* Quarterly Rev., 1859, p. 420. † Ibid.

being two burnt bricks in the Museum, with inscriptions that refer them to the 18th and 19th dynasties (B. C. 1250–1300). But on the main point of the argument, he confesses what is a virtual abandonment of it. "This conclusion," according to Mr. Horner, "of an average rate of increase of Nile mud equaling five inches in a century, is *very vague, and founded on insufficient data*, the amount of matter thrown down by the waters in different parts of the plain varying so much that *to strike an average with any approach to accuracy must be most difficult.*" Again, "The experiments instituted by Mr. Horner, in the hope of obtaining an accurate chronometric scale for testing the thickness of Nile sediment, *are not considered, by experienced Egyptologists, to have been satisfactory.*" (pp. 37, 38.)

2. The next instance which I will notice is that of the human fossil discovered in a ravine near Natchez, Miss. The ravine was caused by the earthquakes which occurred in the Mississippi valley in 1811–12, and is named, from the bones found in it, the Mammoth Ravine. Mr. Lyell describes the fossil referred to as follows: —

" I satisfied myself that the ravine had been considerably enlarged and lengthened, a short time before my visit, and it was then freshly undermined, and undergoing constant waste. From a clayey deposit, immediately below the yellow loam, bones of the *Mastodon Ohioticus*, a species of megalonyx, bones of the genera *Equus*, *Bos*, and others, some of extinct and some presumed to be of living species, had been detached, and had fallen to the base of the cliffs. Mingled with the rest, the pelvic bone of a man (*os innominatum*) was obtained by Dr. Dickeson, of Natchez, in whose collection I saw it. It appeared to be quite in the same state of preservation, and was of the same black color, as the other fossils, and was believed to have come, like them, from a depth of about thirty feet from the surface. In my 'Second Visit to America,' in 1846,* I suggested, as a possible explanation of this association of a human bone with the remains of a mastodon and megalonyx, that the former may possibly have been derived from the vegetable soil at the top of the cliff, whereas the remains of extinct mammalia were dislodged from a lower position, and both may have fallen into the same heap, or talus, at the bottom of the ravine. The pelvic bone might, I conceived, have acquired its black color by having lain, for years or centuries, in a dark, superficial, peaty soil, common in that region. I was informed that there were many human bones in old Indian graves in the same district, stained of as black a dye. On suggesting this hypothesis to Colonel Wiley, of Natchez, I found that the same idea had already occurred to his mind. No doubt, had the pelvic bone belonged to any recent mammifer other than man, such a theory would never have been resorted to; but so long as we have only

* Vol. ii. p. 197.

one isolated case, and are without the testimony of a geologist who was present to behold the bone when still engaged in the matrix, and to extract it with his own hands, it is allowable to suspend our judgment as to the high antiquity of the fossil." *

Allowable! And is this *science*, which from the finding of a bone that confessedly may have come from the soil itself, — possibly from an old Indian grave, — makes a merit of its candor in only not claiming it as demonstration that man lived in the Mississippi valley "more than a thousand centuries ago"? Why did not Sir Charles say as much, at least, as that we are *required* to suspend judgment; or, rather, that the case proves nothing at all, except the willingness of the author to find evidence in support of what was, in his mind, already a foregone conclusion?

3. The next case adduced for the same purpose is that of the skeleton found near New Orleans.

"In one part of the modern delta, near New Orleans, a large excavation has been made for gas works, where a succession of beds, almost wholly made up of vegetable matter, has been passed through, such as we now see forming in the cypress swamps of the neighborhood, where the deciduous cypress (*Taxodium distichum*), with its strong and spreading roots, plays a conspicuous

* Geological Evidences, pp. 202, 203.

part. In this excavation, at the depth of sixteen feet from the surface, beneath four buried forests, superimposed one upon the other, the workmen are stated by Dr. B. Dowler, to have found some charcoal and a human skeleton, the cranium of which is said to belong to the aboriginal type of the red Indian race. As the discovery in question had not been made when I saw the excavation in progress at the gas works in 1846, I can not form an opinion as to the value of the chronological calculations which have led Dr. Dowler to ascribe to this skeleton an antiquity of 50,000 years." *

This case has always been regarded as an important one by the advocates of a high human antiquity. Who has not heard of this skeleton, under the "four buried forests"! And yet how very uncertain the data! Mr. Lyell gives them at second or third hand, and admits that he can not judge of the evidence adduced as to the great age of this fossil. In his "Second Visit to the United States" (vol. ii. p. 191), he describes the growth of the cypress swamp, and quotes from a writer in Silliman's Journal (Sec. series, vol. v. p. 17), as follows: "Sections of such filled-up cypress basins, exposed by the changes in the position of the river, exhibit undisturbed, perfect, and erect stumps, in a series of every elevation with respect to each other, extending from

* Geological Evidence, pp. 43, 44.

high-water mark down to at least twenty-five feet below, measuring out a time when not less than *ten fully matured cypress growths* must have succeeded each other, the average of whose age could not have been less than four hundred years, thus making an aggregate of 4000 years since the first cypress tree vegetated in the basin. There are also instances where prostrate trunks, of huge dimensions, are found imbedded in the clay, immediately over which are erect stumps of trees numbering no less than 800 concentric layers." But the skeleton referred to was found under four of these "buried forests," or "cypress growths;" so that, according to the mode of calculation here proposed, its antiquity is only 1600 years. And we venture to suggest, what to our view is at least equally probable, that if it was sunk in the soft mud of the swamp, or in some ancient grave, it may have reached the place where it was found even within the time since Europeans settled in the country.

Sir Charles Lyell is inclined to think the delta of the Mississippi very ancient. "Although we can not estimate correctly how many years it may have required for the river to bring down from the upper country so large a quantity of earthy matter, — the data for such computation being as yet incomplete, — we may still approximate to a minimum of the time which such an operation must have taken, by ascertaining, experimentally, the annual discharge of water by the Mississippi, and the mean annual amount of solid matter contained in its waters. The lowest estimate of the time required would lead us to assign a high antiquity, amounting to many tens of thousands of years (probably more than 100,000), to the existing Delta." (p. 43.) But a recent "Report upon the Physics and Hydraulics of the Mississippi River," by Captain A. A. Humphreys, and Lieutenant H. L. Abbot, of the United States Topographical Engineers, states that it is apparent " from many considerations, that the mouth of the river was once more than two hundred miles above where it now is, and that it is building out into the gulf new land at the rate of 262 feet every year." * Assuming this as the basis of calculation, we find but little more than 4000 years requisite for the formation of the Delta from at least one hundred miles above New Orleans. Still another estimate is that of Major Stoddard, in a treatise on the State of Louisiana,† who says, "It is calculated that from 1720, a period of eighty years, the land has advanced fifteen miles into the sea; and there are those who assert that it

---

* N. Am. Rev. for April, 1862.

† Quoted in " Campaign to the Rocky Mountains," p. 240, by James Hildreth.

has advanced three miles within the memory of middle-aged men." These data give an increase of 990 feet in a year, requiring no more than 1160 years for the formation of the entire Delta.

These methods of computation are all too uncertain to have any value in discussions like this. Many geologists frankly confess that they are wholly unreliable. "Many ingenious calculations," says Page,[*] "have, no doubt, been made to approximate the dates of certain geological events; but these, it must be confessed, are more amusing than instructive. For example, so many inches of silt are yearly laid down in the Delta of the Mississippi — how many centuries will it have taken to accumulate a thickness of 30, 60, or 100 feet? Again, the ledges of Niagara are wasting at the rate of so many feet per century — how many years must the river have taken to cut its way back from Queenstown to the present falls? . . . For these and similar computations, the student will at once perceive we want the necessary uniformity of factor; and, until we can bring elements of calculation as exact as those of astronomy to bear on geological chronology, it will be better to regard our 'eras,' and 'epochs,' and 'systems,' as so many terms, indefinite in their

[*] Advanced Text-book of Geology, by David Page, F. G. S. Edinburgh, 1861, p. 385.

duration, but sufficient for the magnitude of the operations embraced within their limits."

4. Sir Charles Lyell mentions, but does not dwell upon, an alleged discovery of human remains in certain coral reefs on the coast of Florida. These reefs are in a process of growth by which it is estimated that the land advances upon the sea at the rate of one foot in a century. "In a calcareous conglomerate forming part of the above-mentioned series of reefs, and supposed by Agassiz, in accordance with his mode of estimating the rate of growth of those reefs, to be about 10,000 years old, some fossil human remains were found by Count Pourtalis. They consist of jaws and teeth, with some bones of the foot." (Geol. Ev. p. 44.) This case is too indefinite to have any value. Nothing is stated as to the position of these remains, or the reasons for attributing to them an antiquity equal to that of the reef itself. For aught that appears, they may be of a similar class with the famous Guadaloupe skeleton found in a ledge of shell limestone now in process of formation on the shore of that island, which is now ascertained to be the remains of a Carib Indian killed in battle about two hundred years ago.*

5. But the case most relied on to prove the re-

* Dana's Manual of Geology, p. 580.

mote antiquity of man on earth appears to be that of the discovery of flint implements, constructed by man, in certain beds of river drift, accompanied by the remains of ancient animals in the valley of the Somme, in Picardy, France.

The above diagram will aid us in comprehending the phenomena of this valley. "It is situated geologically in a region of white chalk, with flints, the strata of which are nearly horizontal. The chalk hills which bound the valley are almost everywhere between 200 and 300 feet in height. On ascending to that elevation, we find ourselves on an extensive table-land, in which there are slight elevations and depressions. The white chalk itself is scarcely ever exposed at the surface on this plateau, although seen on the slopes of the hills as at a and b. The general surface of the upland region is covered continuously for miles in every direction by loam or brick earth (5), about five feet thick, devoid of fossils. To the wide extent of this loam the soil of Picardy chiefly owes its great fertility. Here and there we also observe on the chalk outlying patches of tertiary sand and clay (6), with eocene fossils, the remnants of a formation once more extensive, and which probably once spread in one continuous mass over the chalk, before the present system of valleys had begun to be shaped out." (Geol. Ev. p. 106.) In the bottom of the valley, which has an average width of one mile, there is a bed of gravel (1) from three to fourteen feet thick, and upon this, separated by a thin layer of impervious clay, a growth of peat (2) from ten to thirty feet in depth, through which the river now flows (*c*). Upon the sides of the valley (3 and 4) are beds of gravel, resembling ancient river banks, the lower one but little above the peat, the upper from eighty to a hundred feet higher. In these gravel beds are found the bones of numerous animals of races now extinct, such as the elephant, the rhinoceros, the horse, ox, deer, tiger, hyena, and others, and, mingled with these, various tools of flint, supposed to have been used for hatchets, spear-heads, knives, etc.

The geological *history* of this valley is assumed to have been as follows: Originally the chalk formation was continuous, filling the entire space. In some way a stream of water began to flow across this formation, by which the chalk was gradually worn away to the level of the upper gravel beds (4), and of a width equal to the present breadth of the valley at that level. Here the process was for a time arrested, and the gravel bed, formed of the insoluble materials not carried away, settled itself in the then bottom of the valley, reaching, of course, from side to side. During this period lived and died the animals above named, and their remains were mingled and imbedded in the alluvium of the stream. At the same time, some of the primitive race of men lived there, who, not knowing the use of iron, fashioned for themselves rude instruments out of the flints once contained in the chalk formation, which they used for defense, and hunting, and for digging canoes, building huts, and the like; which implements, also, as they became worn or lost, were buried in the earth, along with the remains of the animals that perished there. After a long period, owing, probably, to an elevation of the land, the process of washing away was resumed, and the valley was further excavated to the level of the lower gravel beds (3), leaving behind the traces of the earlier alluvium, as we now find them. Then a like period of repose, followed by similar results, gave rise to the lower beds. Still another elevation caused a further scooping out of the valley to its present depth, leaving it filled with the bottom bed of gravel, which still remains. Upon this have since accumulated the vegetable remains which have covered it with a bed of peat in some places more than thirty feet in thickness.

In the facts and theory thus succinctly stated are found the data on which is based the remote antiquity of our race. The argument is twofold; first, from the intermixture of the flint implements with the animal remains, showing that the men who fashioned and used the former were contemporaneous with the latter, and secondly, from the immense periods of time necessary to the geological changes described. We may consider these two classes of proof separately.

First: does the association of human remains with those of animals now extinct, prove that they existed contemporaneously in a former geological period? On this point I can not claim to advance an independent opinion of my own of any value, neither have I room for the details of this argument. I shall content myself with citing the testimony of *savants* who, if any, are competent to speak concerning it, and whose names are at least equal in weight with those of any who have spoken on the other side.

Professor H. D. Rogers sums up the evidence in reference to this question as follows:—

" The argument which we erect upon all these manifest indications of turbulent action in the waters which left this very promiscuous deposit is, that by pointing to an agency — an incursion, we mean, of the by no means distant ocean — perfectly capable of invading the dry land within historic times, and mixing up its more recent surface objects with previously buried relics of an earlier or pre-historic epoch, *we are debarred from assuming that the two classes of monuments were coeval*, and that from the imputed age of the one we are to infer the antiquity of the other. This is what those do who view all the surface drifts as but one formation, pointing to but one date, calling it the Diluvium. We pray the reader to observe that it is far from our meaning here that we can *disprove* the contemporaneousness of the flint-shaping men and the great antediluvian quadrupeds. We only assert, but assert confidently, that *the phenomena utterly fail to prove it*. The burden of the case is with those who, treating the Diluvium as one and indivisible in the mode of formation, and in date, accept the mere fact of present association in it as evidence of co-existence in time. If, therefore, it can be shown, on an interpretation of geology in accordance with sound physical principles, that a redressing of the deposit *may* have taken place, the verdict must be, that this co-existence in time is not established, and the antediluvian antiquity of man must be cast out of the high court of science with a verdict of *Not Proven.*" *

But it is not necessary to insist upon this negative conclusion. Let it be conceded that man was contemporaneous with those ancient quadrupeds, the

* Blackwood's Mag., Oct., 1860, p. 430, Am. ed.

question of their actual date remains still undetermined. Says a writer in the Westminster Review for April, 1863, who is evidently an able geologist and an ardent advocate of the doctrine of man's remote antiquity, —

" Regarding the contemporaneousness of man with the great extinct Pachyderms as fully proved by the facts and reasonings already adduced, we have now to inquire how this contemporaneousness is to be accounted for; whether by affirming the prolonged existence of these mammals into the human period, as ordinarily understood, or by antedating the commencement of the human period so as to place it in some part of what has been designated the Post-pliocene, as distinguished from the Recent epoch. The acceptance of the former solution might be justified by the unquestionable fact that the existence of the *Bos Primogenius* was prolonged even into the historic period, and seems favored by the preservation of the carcasses of the mammoth and rhinoceros. But it is obviously not required by either of these facts; since many species of animals, whose first introduction dates much further back in geological time, are at present contemporaneous with man; and carcasses once frozen up might be preserved for thousands of years as well as for hundreds, for millions as well as for thousands."

That is, the mere fact that man was contemporary with those extinct animal tribes proves nothing as to his antiquity. They may have come down to his day, or he may have begun to be in theirs; and the bare juxtaposition of their remains in a geological formation can not tell us which.

Professor Rogers is very explicit to the same effect: —

"Let us admit that the wrought flints are truly contemporaneous with the animals whose bones lie side by side with them, and that the deposit imbedding both is the general Diluvium or mammalian drift, do these facts determine the flints to have been fashioned in an age preceding the usually assigned date of the birth of man? Logically, it must be conceded they do not; for, independent of the absence or presence of these or other vestiges of man in the Diluvium, its antiquity, or relation to historic time, is obviously not ascertainable. Apart from human relics in, or over, or under the drift, how can we link it on to historic time at all? Before the flint implements were found in this superficial formation, or so long as the traces of man were known only in deposits later than the Diluvium, it was deemed to belong to an age antecedent to the creation of man, and had, therefore, a relatively high antiquity assigned to it; but now, granting that the relics of man have been authenticated as buried in it, is it sound reasoning, we would ask, to infer for these relics the very antiquity which was only attributable to the Diluvium because it was believed *destitute* of all such human vestiges? The Diluvium of the geologists has, since the illustrious Cuvier, been always looked upon as something very ancient, simply because he and his successors, finding it replete with the remains of huge land mammals no longer living, never succeeded in detecting in it a solitary bone or tooth of any human being, nor indeed of anything indicative of man's existence; but now that things indicative of man have been found, it is surely illogical, and a begging of the very question itself, to impute an age incompatible with his then existing.

" As matters now stand, is it not as natural to infer the relative recency of the extinct *Elephas Primogenius*, and the other mammals of the Diluvium, from the co-existence of the works of man with them, on the ground that the human is the living and the modern race, as it is to deduce the antiquity of man from the once erroneously assumed greater age of those animals? I would repeat, then, that a specially remote age is not attributable to the flint-carrying men of the Diluvium, simply because it is the Diluvium or the mammoth-imbedding gravel which contains them. If the association with these extinct animals does intimate a long pre-historic antiquity, the evidences of this are to be sought in some of the other attendant phenomena." *

We come, then, to the second argument derived from these alleged " attendant phenomena," viz., the geological changes recorded in the features of the Somme valley, and the immense periods of time which they must have required.

---

* Blackwood's Mag., Oct., 1860, pp. 428–431.

The most recent fact is the deposit of the peat-bed in the bottom of the valley. (See the diagram, p. 301.) "Careful observations," says Sir Charles Lyell, "have not been made with a view of calculating the minimum of time which the accumulation of so dense a mass of vegetable matter must have taken. A foot in thickness of highly compressed peat, such as is sometimes reached in the bottom of the bogs, is obviously the equivalent in time of a much greater thickness of peat of spongy and loose texture, found near the surface. The workmen who cut peat, or dredge it up from the bottom of swamps and ponds, declare that, in the course of their lives, none of the hollows which they have found, or caused by extracting peat, have ever been refilled, even to a small extent. They deny, therefore, that the peat grows. This, as M. Boucher de Perthes observes, is a mistake; but it implies that the increase in one generation is not very appreciable by the unscientific.

"The antiquary finds near the surface Gallo-Roman remains, and, still deeper, Celtic weapons of the stone period. But the depth at which Roman works of art occur varies in different places, and is no sure test of age, because in some parts of the swamps, especially near the river, the peat is often so fluid that heavy substances may sink through it, carried down by their own gravity. In one case, however, M. Boucher de Perthes observed several large flat dishes of Roman pottery lying in a horizontal position in the peat, the shape of which must have prevented them from sinking or penetrating through the underlying peat. Allowing about fourteen centuries for the growth of the superincumbent vegetable matter, he calculated that the thickness gained in a hundred years would be no more than three French centimetres (1.17 inches). This rate of increase would demand many tens of thousands of years (30,000) for the formation of the entire thickness of thirty feet."— *Geolog. Evid.*, pp. 110, 111.

But the formation of the peat could not have commenced till after the process of excavating the valley was completed. The gravel bed, next above it, was carried away, leaving only the small portions, 3, 3. (See diagram.) Previous to this was the formation of that bed; still further back, the denudation of the upper gravel bed, 4, and the wearing away of the rock eighty feet or more between it and 3; and lastly, the formation of the upper bed with its inclosed bones and flint implements — a series of events involving an ascending scale of time into the past, the lower step of which was not less than 30,000 years, and each higher one possibly still longer. "No one," says the writer before quoted (p. 306), "who gives to these considerations their due weight, can hesitate in admitting that they carry back the origin of man into that dim remoteness in which all account of time is lost." *

It is to be observed, that this computation assumes that the only agencies which have been concerned in producing the phenomena of this valley, are *those that now exist*, both in kind and degree of activity. Sir Charles Lyell, and those who agree with him in his views on this subject, are, in geological parlance, *Uniformitarians* ; † and his reasonings throughout, whether having relation to the filling of river deltas, the growth of peat, the denudation of valleys, and the like, are all based upon this assumption as a first principle of geological science.

---

* Westm. Rev., April, 1863, p. 281.

† Professor Rogers describes the two schools of geologists thus: "The *Uniformitarian* School, or, as sometimes designated, *Quietists*, who, interpreting the past changes in the earth's surface by the natural forces, especially the gentler ones, now in operation, overlook the more energetic and promptly acting ones; the other, the School of the *Catastrophists*, perhaps more fitly termed the *Paroxysmists*, who, blind in the opposite eye, see only the most vehement energies of nature, the earthquake and the inundation, and take no account of the softer but unceasingly efficient agencies which gradually depress and lift the land, or silently erode and reconstruct it." — *Blackw. Mag.*, Oct., 1860, p. 432.

Such assumption, however, is not to be conceded without question. Even if the growth of peat by vegetable deposit, under the present conditions of the surrounding country, is as slow as alleged, what does this prove as to its rate at a former period, when the land was covered with forests and dense undergrowths, and when, being so covered, its climatal conditions probably differed widely from those of the present time? So with the formation of the valley; what evidence is there that it was ever caused by the action of running water at all, and not by those great subterranean powers to which both mountain ranges and valleys so generally owe their origin, becoming the bed of the Somme, not because excavated by it, but because previously existing, and therefore determining the direction of the flow of the surface waters of that district? But without multiplying these inquiries, which so readily suggest themselves even to persons unskilled in geological speculations, let us listen to some who are worthy to speak authoritatively on the subject.

Says the late President Hitchcock,* "The increase of peat varies so much, under different circumstances, that *it is of no use to attempt to ascertain its rate of growth.* On the continent of Europe it is stated to have gained seven feet in thirty

* Elem. Geology, p. 222.

years. — *Macculloch's Sys. of Geology*, vol. ii. p. 344."

Professor J. Duns, of New College, Edinburgh, relates, on the authority of Captain F. L. N. Thomas, that in the Hebrides peat has accumulated over some of the ancient pagan monuments to the depth of six feet in 1000 years.*

As to the origin of the Somme valley, Professor Duns says, "Taking the depths of the valley as given above, are we warranted to conclude that the Somme once ran at the level of the higher gravels, and that it has cut a path for itself to its present depths? I believe that *other and more powerful agencies* than the erosive power of running water have been at work in that part of France. Yet this question might be answered in the affirmative, and its value, as favorable to Sir Charles Lyell's views of the antiquity of man, destroyed by an appeal to facts for whose truth he himself is the voucher." Professor D. then refers to the facts adduced in Lyell's "Principles of Geology," in regard to the erosive power of running water, among which is the following : —

"At the western base of Ætna, a current of lava, descending from near the summit of the great volcano, has flowed to the distance of five or six miles, and then reached

* Science and Christian Thought, p. 249.

the alluvial plain of the Simeto, the largest of the Sicilian rivers, which skirts the base of Ætna, and falls into the sea a few miles south of Catania. The lava entered the river about three miles above the town of Adano, and not only occupied its channel for some distance, but, crossing to the opposite side of the valley, accumulated there in a rocky mass. Gemmellaro gives the year 1603 as the date of the eruption. . . . In the course, therefore, of about two centuries, the Simeto has eroded a passage from fifty to several hundred feet wide, and in some parts from forty to fifty feet deep. The portion of lava cut through is in no part porous or scoriaceous, but consists of a homogeneous mass of hard blue rock, somewhat inferior in weight to ordinary basalt, and containing crystals of olivine and glassy felspar. The general declivity of this part of the bed of the Simeto is not considerable. . . . The external forms of the hard blue lava are as massive as any of the most ancient trap rocks of Scotland."

"From this point of view, then," remarks Professor Duns, "the question comes to be a very simple one. If the Simeto has in two hundred years cut a ravine, through hard volcanic rock, a hundred feet wide and fifty feet deep, how long would the Somme require to excavate its present valley in the soft chalk rocks over which it runs? In the latter case, we have not only hundreds, but thousands, of years at our disposal. It is, however, most likely that the explanation of the formation of the Somme valley is to be found in connection with other natural forces."*

Professor Duns quotes also from a paper by Sir Roderick Murchison, "On the Distribution of the Flint Drifts of the South-east of England," from which I take the following paragraphs:—

"No analogy of tidal or fluviatile action can explain either the condition or position of the debris and unrolled flints and bones. On the contrary, by referring their distribution to those great oscillations and ruptures by which the earth's surface has been so powerfully affected in former times, we may well imagine how the large area under consideration was suddenly broken up and submerged. This hypothesis seems to me to be an appeal to a *vera causa* commensurate with the results. As respects the south-east of England,† the operations must have been modern, in a geological sense.

"Alluding to geologists who 'rank all ancient geological phenomena in the category of existing causation,' Sir R. Murchison says, 'The endeavor to refer all former fractures of the strata, as well as their overthrow on a great scale, as in the Alps, to causes of no greater intensity of action than those which now prevail, is in opposition to the observations I have made in every mountain chain as well as in the modest cliffs of Brighton and Dover.' The uniformitarian theory, so strongly condemned here, is that

* Science and Christian Thought, p. 229.
† The same remark must apply to the opposite coast of France, separated from it only by the Straits of Dover.

which Sir Charles Lyell has applied throughout his discussions on this question. He has assigned to Norway 'a mean rate of continuous vertical elevation of two and a half feet in a century,' and assumed this as the standard rate of elevation in most other quarters. But if anything is sure in physical geology, the variable intensity of these agencies is. Indeed, this theory of uniform intensity is contradicted at every point. Many circumstances, for example, influence the rate at which mud is deposited in lakes, in river-courses, and in estuaries. The growth of peat depends much on climatal conditions, which vary in different degrees of latitude. Then what so capricious and so variable in its intensity as the force which makes itself known in the rocking earthquake, or as that which finds expression in the volcanic eruption? Even the introduction and disappearance of zoölogical species, of which so much has recently been made, not only refuse to give that testimony in favor of uniformitarian views, so anxiously sought from them, but bear witness to facts of an entirely different kind. When, then, we sum up the strongest points in favor of an antiquity for man far more remote than is assigned to him in the Word of God, I think the conclusion is warranted, if not irresistible, that *they signally fail* to cast distrust on the biblical historical record." *

Professor Wilson, in his "Pre-historic Man" (vol. i. p. 50), after quoting Sir Charles Lyell on the flint implements and weapons at Abbeville and Amiens, adds, —

* Science and Christian Thought, pp. 276, seq.

"Subsequent investigation by experienced geologists has somewhat modified the ideas here expressed. Professor J. S. Henslow, after minute observations, comes to the conclusion that 'no one can doubt the evidence to be in favor of a cataclysmic action, and rapid deposition of the lower and larger portion of the gravel at the spot near St. Acheul, where the hatchets occur.' Neither does he suppose that the facts witnessed by him indicate, of necessity, that the bones of extinct mammals, found alongside of the flint implements, were contemporary with the unskilled workmen by whom these were wrought; or that the evidence carries man altogether out of the range of human history. The fossil bones and the human implements are mingled in a gravel formed *as a re-disposition by fresh water agency out of older materials, probably belonging to very different periods*, though the most modern of them undoubtedly pertain to a period long prior to the oldest dates of Gaulish history." — *Athenæum*, Oct. 20, 1869, p. 516.

M. Elie de Beaumont, the distinguished French *savant*, concurs in this view. At a meeting of a special commission of naturalists and geologists, French and English, called to examine a human tooth and jaw found in the flint beds at Moulin Quignon, near Abbeville, M. Beaumont "made a statement so positive and so unexpected as, to judge by the contemporary reports, produced an unusual and almost electric sensation on the scientific auditory. His opinion, or decision, was to this effect — that the Moulin Quignon beds are not 'diluvium, they are not even alluvia, deposited by the encroachments of rivers on their banks, but are simply composed of washed soil deposited on the flanks of the valley by excessive falls of rain, such as may be supposed to have occurred exceptionally once or twice in a thousand years. A weck later, this geologist reiterated his opinion to the same illustrious assembly, adding that the age of this formation belongs, in his opinion, to the stone period, or is analogous to that of the peat mosses, and the Swiss lake habitations." — *Edinb. Rev.*, July, 1863, p. 138.

Enough, then, I trust, has been said to show that the facts presented us by the Somme valley do not bear out the conclusions derived from them in regard to the remote antiquity of man on earth. Neither the data themselves, nor the reasoning employed, are to be accepted without question. We dismiss the case, therefore, by citing the following judicious and weighty language of Professor Rogers: —

"To the interrogation, How far are we entitled to attribute a high antiquity to these earliest physical records of mankind, from the nature of the containing and overlying sedimentary deposits?

my response again is, that as the two schools of geologists now named differ widely in their translation of geologic time of all phenomena of the kind here described, this question . . . *does not admit, in the present state of the science, of a specific or quantitative answer.* .

"In conclusion, then, of the whole inquiry, condensing into one expression my answer to the general question whether a remote pre-historic antiquity for the human race has been established from the recent discovery of specimens of man's handiwork in the so-called Diluvium, *I maintain that it is not proven,* — by no means asserting that it can be *disproved*, but insisting simply that it remains *Not Proven.*"— *Blackw. Mag.*, Oct., 1860, p. 438.

The valley of the Somme is confessedly the most important locality in which human relics have been found indicative of a high human antiquity. I shall not, therefore, go into an examination of other similar localities in France, Sicily, and elsewhere, nor of the "bone caverns" in England, Belgium, etc. To the evidence they furnish, the same arguments apply as those which have now been advanced; indeed, the matured opinions of Professor Rogers and others, which we have cited, were professedly given in view of all the facts presented by them.

6. There is another class of facts which is often adduced for the same purpose as the preceding, derived from extensive human remains found in peat beds, in shell mounds, or ancient rubbish heaps, and in the lakes of Switzerland, and other parts of Europe.

These peat beds in the Danish islands are from ten to thirty feet deep, and contain trunks of firs, oaks, and birches, of great size, and of species not now growing in that country. There are found in them flint, bronze, and iron implements, with the bones of man and the various domestic animals. The refuse mounds consist mostly of collections of oyster and clam shells, mingled with bones of quadrupeds, birds, and fish, flint knives, hatchets, and arrows, fragments of pottery, etc. They are called by the Danes *kjökken-mödding*, i. e., kitchen refuse heaps, composed as they are so largely of the remains of animals used for food. The relics found in the lakes indicate the former existence of villages built upon piles in the shallow waters.

All these traces of man prove the existence of tribes of a pre-historic people inhabiting the greater part of Europe, the memorials of which are otherwise lost in remote antiquity. A careful study of these remains has led investigators to divide them into three classes, according to the periods in which they are supposed to have lived, called respectively the stone, the bronze, and the iron age, from the materials and workmanship of the implements then in use.

The question with which we are now interested relates to the time when these primitive people existed. Sir Charles Lyell, after summing up the evidence on this point, and showing that the three ages were of very unequal antiquity, pronounces all the calculations hitherto made by archæologists and geologists of merit respecting it, "as being tentative," and "a rough approximation to the truth." He adds, "They have led to the assignment of 4000 and 7000 years before our time as the lowest antiquity which can be ascribed to certain events and monuments; but much collateral evidence will be required to confirm these estimates, and to decide whether the number of centuries has been under or over rated." — *Geol. Evid.*, p. 273.

M. Frederic Troyon, in his work entitled "Habitations Lacustres des Temps Anciens et Modernes," takes care to say, near the commencement of the volume, "To avoid all mistake, it is well to be understood that the stone age [the oldest of all], of which we find remains in the lakes and tombs, is considered in this work as posterior to the deluge mentioned by Moses." *

But the most important fact relating to this primitive population of Europe is, that whatever be the exact date at which they lived, *they belonged to the Celtic race.* Dr. Keller, than whom there is no higher authority on the subject, remarks as follows: —

"It is very evident that the earliest founders came into Middle Europe as a pastoral people, and possessed the most important domestic animals, such as the dog, the cow, the sheep, the goat, and the horse. All these animals have their origin not in Europe, but in Asia, and were brought here by the settlers through all their long wanderings from the east. They understood agriculture, and cultivated grains (wheat and barley), also flax — plants which, in like manner, they did not meet with in Europe, but brought with them out of Asia, or received them by commerce from the south." (p. 310.)

"It has already been remarked, that on comparing the implements of stone and bronze from the lake dwellings with those of the Swiss museums, some of which were found in graves and tumuli, and others met with by chance in the fields, we are not able to discover the smallest difference, either in material, form, or ornamentation, and we consequently consider ourselves authorized in ascrib-

---

* Quoted in Appendix to "The Lake Dwellings," by Dr. Keller, p. 14.

ing all these specimens, which appear to have come from the same factories to the industry of one and the same people. The identity of the inhabitants of the main land and those of the lake dwellings appears still more striking if we compare the settlements founded by both classes of the people as well as their whole arrangement." (p. 311.)

"In the very same graves and tumuli, implements of stone and bone, precisely alike in form, have been found lying together, and the same remark will apply in other graves to implements of bronze and iron. The products of the potter's art, also, are seen with all their characteristic peculiarities, through all the stages of their development, and form links in the outward phenomena of the different periods." (p. 312.)

"Knowing that history makes no mention of any other people but the Celts, who, in the very earliest ages, possessed the middle of Europe, and, in the later times, received their civilization from the Romans, we believe that it would be contrary to all the facts adduced, to arrive at any conclusion but this — that the builders of the lake dwellings were a branch of the Celtic population of Switzerland, but that the earlier settlements belong to the prehistoric period, and had already fallen into decay before the Celts took their place in the history of Europe." (p. 313.)*

As to who the people of these earlier settlements

* The Lake Dwellings of Switzerland and other Parts of Europe, by Dr. Ferdinand Keller, Pres. Antiq. Assoc. of Zurich. Translated by John Edward Lee, F. S. A., F. G. S., etc.

were, Dr. Keller remarks, in a section entitled "Origin and Age of the Iron Implements of Marin," "We can not refrain from once more repeating what we have stated in the previous parts of this volume. There can be no doubt that *from the earliest ages* the above mentioned country, and also the land beyond the Jura, was inhabited by races of a Celtic origin." (p. 262.) *

I am not aware that this author has assigned, even by conjecture, any specific date to the relics which he describes, other than "a very high antiquity." (p. 292.)

M. Troyon's opinion is that "the population of the first period were a primitive people, perhaps belonging to a Finnish or Iberian race, which came out of Asia several thousand years before our era, and, following the course of the Rhone, or the Rhine, wandered into the valleys of the Alps." †

If these opinions may be accepted, — and I know of none more probable, or freer from objections, — they go to confirm, rather than to weaken, the scriptural chronology as to the antiquity of man. These primitive people were a branch of the great Indo-European family, the origin of which was in Asia, as was that of the domestic animals they brought with them. As to the "several thousand years before

* Appendix N. † Appendix to Lake Dwellings, p. 395.

our era," "one or two thousand are sufficient to meet all the exigencies of the case.

In view, then, of all the facts adduced by geology, we are warranted, I think, in the following definite conclusion, viz., that in order to account for every case of the existence of human relics in Western Europe, whether bones, implements, or dwellings, whether in caves or French drift, we do not *need* an antiquity of more than six or eight centuries before Christ, while we *may* go back twenty centuries and be still more than a thousand years distant from the Noachian deluge — a time sufficient to permit man to wander a long way, and do a great many things.

APPENDIX.

A. Page 25.

CHRONOLOGY OF BUNSEN.

The conception of Bunsen's work is a vast one. "Egypt's Place in Universal History!" Egypt! that land of pyramids; whose kings are enumerated in history under thirty distinct dynasties; whose monuments antedate the oldest historic records; whose language has consumed the lives of some of the greatest scholars; the source whence the wisest of the ancient Greeks drew their wisdom; whose empire had extended from the Nile to the Indus, before Greece and Rome had even a name! And can Egypt's place in history be determined and described? Bunsen has attempted it. He has placed himself on her ancient monuments, and surveyed the immense periods of her historic existence, and, as he thinks, ascertained her "place" in the history of man.

To his own great industry and learning he has joined that of all the learned Egyptologers from Champollion to Lepsius; in short, what human learning and industry could do to fix Egypt's place in history, it would seem has been done by Bunsen in these five volumes.

It is with his system — that of chronology — that we are now concerned. We shall give that system, and the principal facts and reasons on which it rests, as near as we can, in the author's own words. In general, we think these facts and reasons need only to be stated in order to be discarded as insufficient for the basis of such superstructure: —

"SYNOPSIS OF THE FOUR AGES OF THE WORLD.

"First Age of the World.

"Ancient Antediluvian History — from the Creation to the Flood; Primitive Formation of Language; and the Beginning of the Formation of Mythology.

"The Historical Primitive World (I., II., III.). (1-10,000 Year of Man; 20,000-10,000 B. C.).

"First Period (I.). — *Formation and Deposit of Sinism* (20,000-15,000 B. C.).

"Primitive language, spoken with rising or falling cadence — elucidated by gesture — accompanied by pure pictorial writing; every syllable a word, every word a full substantive, one representable by a picture.

"Deposit of this language in Northern China (Shensi), in the country of the source of the Houngho-Sinism. The earliest polarization of religious consciousness: Kosmos or Universe, and the Soul of Personality. Objective worship, the firmament; subjective worship, the soul of parents, or the manifestation of divine in the family.

"Second Period of the World (II.). — *Formation and Deposit of Primitive Turanism:* The eastern polarization of Sinism (15,000-14,000 B. C.).

"Pure agglutinative language: formation of polysyllabic words by means of unity of accent (word accent).

"Origin of particles, words no longer substantive and full, but denoting the mutual relation of persons and things; finally, of complete parts of speech.

"Deposit of this stage of formation in Thibet (Botya language).

"Germ of mythology in substantiation of inanimate things and of properties.

"THIRD PERIOD (III.). — *Formation and Deposit of Khamism and the Flood:* Western polarization of Sinism (14,000-11,000 B. C.).

"Formation of stems into roots producing derivative words; complete parts of speech beyond the distinction between full words (nouns, verbs, and adjectives) and formative words (14,000).

"Declensions and conjugations with affixes and endings; stage of the Egyptian (13,000).

"Commencement of symbolical Hieroglyphics, i. e., picture writing; but without the introduction of the phonetic element or designation of sound (12,000).

"Deposit of this language in Egypt, owing to the earliest immigration of West Asiatic primitive Semites. Invention of, or advancement in, hieroglyphic signs: primitive syllabarium (11,000).

"THE FLOOD. — *Convulsion in Northern Asia.* Emigration of the Aryans out of the country of the sources of the Oxus (Gihon) and Jaxartes, and of the Semites out of the country of the sources of the Euphrates and Tigris (11,000-10,000).

"SECOND AGE OF THE WORLD.

"Ancient Postdiluvian History — from the Emigration after the Flood down to Abraham in Mesopotamia. Formation of the historical tribes and empires of Asia (10,000-2878 B. C.)." *

We will not occupy space with the details of this

---

* Egypt's Place in Universal History, vol. iv. pp. 485-497.

"age." Suffice it to say, the author exhibits the same wonderful knowledge in regard to the history of the "Egyptian deposit" from 10,000 down to 4000 B. C., as in reference to the preceding age. He gives definite dates for numerous events in the civil and religious history, e. g. : —

	B. C.
The formation of Osirism,	10,000
Close of the republican period,	9,086
Duration of the sacerdotal kings, according to Manetho, 1855 years; end of the sacerdotal kings,	7,231
Beginning of hereditary kings in Lower Egypt,	5,413
Duration of them according to Manetho, 1790 years; end,	3,624
Perfect formative language,	4,000
Menes, the first king of the first dynasty,	3,623
Abraham,	2,878
The exodus,	1,320

It is safe to say, in general, that such a mass of pure assumption as our author has here put forth is nowhere else to be found in any professedly historical or chronological work. He frequently says, "According to Manetho," while Manetho affords not the least support for the declaration put forth on his authority.

The following sentences are valuable, as showing our author's manner of assuming his premises and drawing his conclusions, as well as exhibiting a cardinal principle of his work : —

"But if we find, almost four thousand years before our era, a mighty empire possessing organic members of a very ancient type, a peculiar written character and national art and science, we must admit that it required thousands of years to bring them to maturity in the valley of the Nile. If, again, its language be shown to be a deposit of Asiatic, and by no means the oldest formation, it will be admitted upon reflection to be a sober conclusion that we require some twenty thousand years to explain the beginnings of the development of man, which have been only once violently interrupted in its primeval birthplace." (Vol. iv. p. 21.)

"The question as to the place of Egypt, in historical chronology, is thus at once changed to that of its place in the whole development of man. We pass out of the domains of chronology and history into that of pure philosophy." (Vol. iv. p. 22.)

We have here a statement of a fundamental principle of the author — a principle by which he is guided, and which underlies his whole work. It is the founding of a system of chronology on the principles of philosophy. We are fond of philosophy when it is sound and in its place; and we do not assert that it has no connection with chronology. When the materials for a strict historical chronology do not exist, we have no objections to philosophy doing her utmost to elucidate and present probable truth. But the danger is, that she will transcend the limits of her just domain. This we think she has done under the guidance of Bunsen. She magnifies the difficulties arising from the received chronology of Bible history, and then resorts to expedients that destroy the truthfulness of that history. Certainly in such a work as this she should be watched, and her supposed facts and her expedients be severely scrutinized. If our faith in Bible history is to be undermined by philosophy, let us know what is proposed in its place.

The principal facts on which the author rests his system, and the mode of argumentation, are foreshadowed in the following extracts: —

"Philosophy has discovered the existence of two vast branches of cognate organic languages, the Semitic and Iranian. The stage anterior to Semism is Khamism. This antecedent stage is antediluvian. People history is postdiluvian. We find in it, thousands of years before Menes, first of all a world-wide empire — the realm of Nimrod, the Kushite, . . . which probably embraced Egypt as well as Western Asia, the district of the Euphrates and Tigris.

"If we connect these views with the historical development before us, we shall find, in the first place, ancient history divided into antediluvian and postdiluvian. For the former we require ten thousand years, which we can prove proximately to be the extent of the latter period before Christ." (Vol. iv. p. 24.)

"The legends of the classics about colonies from Egypt, in so far as they have any historical foundation, are explainable, just as are the expressions in the Bible that Kanaan, who was driven back out of Lower Egypt, was the son of Kham."* (Vol. iv. p. 30.)

"I must, on the other hand, repudiate all historical connection between the Helleno-Italic mythology and the Indians, or even their patriarchs, the Iranians and Bactrians." (Vol. iv. p. 31.)

"We start, therefore, with this premise, that in the Egyptian we have obtained a fixed chronological point, and, in fact, the highest in general history. In it we find a perfectly formed language which we can prove to have been in existence about the middle of the fourth millennium B. C. We have, moreover, the means of determining approximately the epoch of the beginnings of regal government immediately before Menes. We therefore

---

* A reference to the expulsion of the Shepherds from Egypt.

arrive at the very threshold of the foundation of language." (Vol. iv. p. 45.)

With regard to "the premise" here named, with which the author starts, we simply remark here, that we do not admit it. Nor do we admit the existence of the "perfectly formed language" which he says he "can prove to have existed in the middle of the fourth millennium B. C." See remarks on this point below.

"The result of criticism goes to prove, however, that we can not compute, by the ordinarily received chronology, the interval between the above starting-point of the present life of man and the oldest conquests in Asia, — those of Nimrod, — or the interval between them both and Abraham, the first historical personage in the Semitic reminiscences.

"On the other hand, the period of twenty-one thousand years, which has been adopted by all the great astronomers of the day, for the deviation of the earth's axis, brings us to two resting-places. The consequence of the deviation is a change of the proportion of the cold and heat at the poles, the greatest of which gives eight days more cold or heat.

"At the present time, in the northern temperate zone, spring and summer are seven days longer than autumn and winter; in the southern hemisphere, consequently, the proportion is reversed.

"In the year 1248 this favorable change in our hemisphere had reached its maximum, namely, eight days more warmth, and therefore the same number of days less cold. Consequently, after a gradual decrease during five thousand two hundred and fifty years, in the year 6498, the two seasons will be in equilibrio, but in the year 11,748 (five thousand two hundred and fifty years more) the hot period will have reached its lowest point.

"Now, if we calculate backward five thousand two hundred and fifty years from 1248, we shall find that in the year 4002

B. C. the two seasons must have been in equilibrio in our hemisphere. In the year 9252 B. C. the cold season had attained its maximum. The opposite or most favorable division of heat and cold took place, therefore, in the year 19,752 B. C.

"This epoch explains very simply the reason why the north pole is surrounded with perpetual ice only from about the seventieth degree, when at the south pole it is found at the sixty-fifth. In other words, the history of progressive human civilization, with which we are acquainted, is comprised within one hemisphere, and under climacteric accidents the most favorable to advancement.

"Now, as we must suppose that the date of the commencement of our race was the most favorable both for its origin and continuance, and as, on the other hand, the catastrophe which we call the flood would have arrived at the next unfavorable period for our hemisphere, that epoch, the central point of which is the year 9250 B. C., would seem the most probable one for the change in climatic relations. This assumption is confirmed by the most ancient monuments and traditions.* The chronology of Egypt shows still more clearly than traditions preserved in the Rabbinical Book of the Origines, that the flood of Noah could not have taken place later than about 10,000 B. C., and could not have taken place much earlier.

"The only question, therefore, is, whether the history of the human race, and consequently the origines of the primitive world, date from the above-mentioned favorable epoch, about 20,000 B. C., or whether we are justified in going back to the last epoch but one, or about 40,000 B. C." (Vol. iv. 52-54.)

The following extracts show an important part of the argument adopted to maintain these assumptions : —

---

* What monuments and traditions? As far as we know, even our author has failed to specify them; unless such a specification is intended by his brief allusions to the mythological periods of some of the ancient nations.

"The formative words in the Egyptian mark the transition from Sinism to Khamism — from the particle language to the language of parts of speech. . . . The earliest Turanism to the east of Khamism marks the first stage of organic language, i. e., of language with the parts of speech. The second is Khamism, i. e., the stage of language we meet with in Egypt." (Vol. iv. p. 558.)

"The shortest line from inorganic language to organic is that of Sinism through primitive Turanism to primitive Semism, the deposit of which in the valley of the Nile we have in Egyptian. The last emigration was probably that of the Aryans to the country of the five rivers. The oldest hymns in the country of the Punjaub go back to 3000 B. C. This community of language must then, at all events, be supposed to have existed much earlier than 3000 B. C. They had, consequently, at that time long got over the stage of underived Iranism and Semism. Between 10,000 and 4000 B. C., the vast step in Asiatic advancement from Khamism to Semism, and from Semism to Iranism, was made. If the step from Latin to Italian be taken as a unit, this previous step must be reckoned at least at ten or at twenty." (Vol. iv. p. 562.)

"From all this it appears that the period of one great revolution of the earth's axis (twenty-one thousand years) is a very probable time for the development of human language in the shortest line; and that the double of this, which we should be obliged to suppose, would be a highly improbable one." (Vol. iv. p. 563.)

"It has been shown at the commencement of this volume, that we may hope by a combination of researches and observations to establish that mankind has only terminated one astronomical period, and commenced the second in the year 1240 of our era; and there are reasons for placing the intermediate catastrophe in the most unfavorable part of that period, or about 10,000 B. C. As to subdivisions, if too large a space has been assumed in this one, there is room enough for it in the other. We see no reason for going back to a preceding epoch of twenty-one thousand years; but less than one period is impossible, were it only because of the stubborn fact of the strata of languages. To what point, then, is Egypt brought back by this calculation? To the middle, at least, or the ninth millennium of man, as the period of the immigration of the western branch of our race into the valley of the Nile. But this is the very close of the primitive world in the strict sense, that is to say, of the history of our race before the great convulsion of that part of Central Asia to which we turn as the cradle of mankind. This convulsion, which we know as the flood of Noah, in all probability coincides with that epoch of the northern hemisphere when the temperature was lowest, or from 9000 to 10,000 B. C., just as the origin of our race coincides with that period of it when the temperature was highest, which was ten thousand five hundred years earlier.

"If this principle be correct, the Egyptians can have known nothing of the flood, allusions to which we find everywhere among the Iranians and Semites; and in truth no such tradition is current among them, any more than it was among the old Turanians and Chinese." (Vol. iv. p. 564.)

In regard to the above hypothesis of the great antiquity of man on the earth, and the arguments in support of it, we think little needs to be said by way of confutation. We must, however, briefly state the reasons why we do not receive the hypothesis, and think the arguments inconclusive. We might use the words "absurd," "irrational," and other stronger disparaging epithets, in relation to the author's reasoning, and think ourselves justified in their use. But the use of such terms generally weakens an argument. For what one calls absurd, another regards merely as inconclusive, a third, fair reasoning, and a fourth, sound argument. We, therefore, will endeavor to meet the argument of our author in a sober, matter-of-fact style of reasoning.

And first as to his astronomical argument. The substance of the argument is this: On account of " the deviation of the earth's axis," the northern and southern hemispheres enjoy unequal degrees of heat and cold. When this difference is at the extreme, the seasons of " spring and summer are eight days longer than autumn and winter." But " the history of progressive human civilization with which we are acquainted is comprised within one hemisphere, and under climacteric accidents the most favorable to advancement." These " favorable climacteric accidents " are the seasons of spring and summer being longer than autumn and winter. Therefore, as man has mostly lived in the northern hemisphere, his creation must have taken place when the heat was greatest in this hemisphere, i. e., about 20,000 B. C., and the flood must have taken place about 10,000 B. C., when the cold was at its maximum.

In regard to this argument, we remark: First, we neither admit the premises nor the conclusion. Having passed some fifteen years in the southern part of that belt which has been most densely peopled by the race, we have a little experience that bears directly on the point. We thought and felt decidedly, that the cool season was more favorable to physical and mental vigor, to physical and mental development, than the hot season. And, if we mistake not, such were decidedly the thoughts and feelings of all in that land who had much to do in the various spheres of bodily and mental activity. So that if we were to use Bunsen's premises, we should draw the conclusion the opposite to that which he has drawn. We confess we should never advance this argument to prove that man was created about 10,000 B. C.; but we think it worth as much in support of such an epoch of the creation as that of our author in favor of the higher one of ten thousand years earlier.

Again, in point of fact, in what climate has the race of man attained to the highest degree of development in both body and mind? If we look at the present generation, we certainly cannot point to the mildest parts of the temperate zone as furnishing the best specimens of intellectual and physical vigor. Edinburgh and Glasgow are almost 56° N. Lat.; London is almost 52°; Berlin is farther north, and Paris is about 49° N. It is true that, as we go back into the early historic times, we find the region of human superiority a little further south. Greece is between 37°. and 45° N., and Italy between 40° and 46° N.; and Palestine, and Egypt, and Chaldea were still further south. But the ancients were not equal to the moderns. The reason was, they, through love of ease, delighted in the softness of tropical climates, where a little effort suffices to meet the wants of a degenerate physical nature. They settled along the banks of such streams as the Nile, the Euphrates and Tigris, the Indus and Ganges. It was when they settled in the more northern and cooler climates that the greater strength of body and mind was developed in the race. Where, we would ask, was the garden of Eden? Mount Ararat is in about 40° N. Lat.; and since geologists tell us that the mighty currents which have swept over the earth, the marks of which are now seen on the solid rocks, were from north to south, and that which caused the deluge of Noah was probably in the same direction, the ark floated south during that one hundred and fifty days; hence the garden of Eden was north of the mountain where it rested, and was therefore about in the middle of the temperate zone; whereas, according to our author's theory and argument, it should have been further south. We beg our readers not to spend time to criticise this argument, for in itself considered it will not bear criticism. We only put it forth to meet the reasoning of our author. In fact, the line of argumentation is about parallel to his, and equally conclusive. If we placed any value on the argument from heat and cold as aiding to fix the epoch of the creation of man, we should be inclined to place the epoch at the time when the heat and cold of our hemisphere were in equilibrio, which would be for the last time (according to our author) about 4002 B. C. This differs only two years from the commonly received chronology. But we do not believe in this heat-and-cold argument. Even if we should admit the premises, that the time when spring and summer are eight days longer in our hemisphere than autumn and winter, is most favorable to human development, it would by no means follow that the creation of man took place at that time.

We must devote a little space to our author's chronology of the patriarchs, especially to his era of Abraham. We have here some rich specimens of "philosophy." We need do little more than exhibit the philosopher's theory in his own words: —

"We will now take a glance at dates. Here the first step undoubtedly must be to abandon the views and system adopted by the narrator, from the impossibility of an historian dealing with men who beget children like other people at the age of thirty, and live more than four hundred years afterwards. Those upon whom this consideration fails to make an impression may still be staggered by the fact, that upon this calculation the patriarch Noah lived down to the time of Abraham,* without troubling himself about the history of the world. Neither can we venture, like the authors of the Septuagint, to falsify the text,† and, in order to get rid of the disproportion, add one hundred years to the ages of these geographical patriarchal monsters at the time of their marriage. We have, therefore, but one alternative — to ascertain which of the two is the really traditional date, that of the ages after the birth of the first son, or that of the whole date; to ascertain, in other words, whether the narrator had the authority of tradition for the former date, and, in order to assist his chronology, added, at random, thirty or forty years to their ages when the first son was born; or whether he found the whole sum total recorded, and deducted from it whatever suited his purpose.‡ The fact of his not stating the sum total would incline us to adopt the former view. But in the immediately preceding entries about Noah and Shem, we can prove that the complete sum total is the actual traditional date.

* This is a real objection or difficulty if we adopt the Hebrew chronology, but it entirely vanishes if we adopt that of the Septuagint.

† This is amusing, standing, as it does, in connection with the author's radical alteration of the text of Scripture.

‡ On such suppositions, what becomes of the inspiration of the Scriptures, or even of their authenticity? Yet our author professes great reverence and regard for the Bible. He would not alter a date.

In each case it is six hundred years, which was shown to be the original Chaldaic equation between lunar and solar years. We must, therefore, assume that it is so here also." *

The postdiluvian times to Abraham are thus disposed of (the tabular form being somewhat abridged for the sake of space) : —

"There are three periods or divisions : —

"A. Sem (Arapakithis), i. e., the primeval land of the Kasdim (Chaldees), the frontier mountains of Armenia toward Assyria, four hundred and thirty-eight years.

"B. Selah, 'The Mission,' four hundred and thirty-three years; Heber, the settler over the river (Tigris), four hundred and sixty-four years; Peleg, derivation, partition, four hundred and thirty-nine years; Yohtan (father of thirteen South Arabian races).

"C. RéHu, district of the shepherd country of Edessa (Rohi), two hundred and thirty-nine years; Serug (in Osroëne, Sarug, west of Edessa), two hundred and thirty years.

"D. Nahor goes to Ur of the Kasdim (Chaldees), one hundred and forty-eight years.

"Terah leaves Ur of the Chaldees, and goes to Haran (Karra), a day's journey south of Edessa, two hundred and seventy-five years (70 + 205).

"Nahor sets out from Sarug to Ur of the Chaldees, one hundred and forty-eight years (29 + 119).

"Terah sets out from Ur to Haran, that is, back toward Osroëne, on the way to Canaan. He lives two hundred and five years. At the age of seventy he begets three sons in Ur.

"There is a remarkable closeness between the first three

---

* Our eyes have not fallen on this proof. We know that Josephus (Antiq. i. iii. 9) speaks of a "great year" of six hundred common years; but what has that to do with the six hundredth year of the life of Noah, as the date of the flood, and the duration of Shem's life? It is all assumption.

(geographical historical) dates, Arphaxad, Selah, and Eber: Arphaxad four hundred and thirty-eight years, Selah four hundred and thirty-five, and Heber four hundred and sixty-four.

"Supposing Arphaxad to represent the duration of the Semitic settlement Arapakithis, the mountainous district above Assyria, prior to the memory of man, 'The Mission' would represent the journey towards the plains three years before the close of this migration, and 'Heber' would represent the period when the migrating race passed over the Upper Tigris on their way to the Upper Mesopotamia. The year 464 would, in that case, be the one in which they entered Mesopotamia proper, and the tribe must have remained in a compact body two hundred and thirty-nine years before a portion of them commenced the great migration southward, the result of which was the foundation of the kingdom of Southern Asia." (Vol. iii. p. 367.)

"This would make nine hundred and thirty-three years to Nahor, the grandfather of Abraham" (i. e., $464 + 239 + 230 = 933$ years). (Vol. iii. p. 369.)

Sober criticism on the above would be entirely out of place. We venture to affirm that there is not within the whole compass of literature another such perversion of an evidently plain historical narrative into a monstrous historico-chronologico-geographical jumble.

"Noah was six hundred years old when the flood of waters was upon the earth." (Gen. vii. 6.) This six hundred years is "the Chaldaic equation between the lunar and solar years." "And Noah lived after the flood three hundred and fifty years." This is "half of another equation, with a surplus of fifty years." Only fifty more! "Arphaxad lived five and thirty years, and begat Salah; and Arphaxad lived after he begat Salah four hundred and three years, and begat sons and daughters." (Gen. xi.

12, 13.) This four hundred and thirty-eight years represents "the duration of the Semitic settlement in Arapakithis, the mountainous district above Assyria, prior to the memory of man." And the sacred writer probably, "in order to assist his chronology, added at random the thirty-five years when the first son was born." (!) "And Salah lived thirty years, and begat Eber; and Salah lived, after he begat Eber, four hundred and three years, and begat sons and daughters." (Gen. xi. 14, 15.) Salah means "the mission." "The four hundred and thirty-three years represent the commencement of the journey toward the plains, three years before the close of this migration." "Heber" means "the settler over the river" (Tigris); and "represents the period when the migrating race passed over the Upper Tigris on their way to Upper Mesopotamia. The year 464 would, in that case, be the one in which they entered Mesopotamia proper, and the tribe must have remained in a compact body two hundred and thirty-nine years before a portion of them commenced the great migration southward, which was the foundation of the primeval kingdom of Southern Asia." And so of the other names and numbers. But Bunsen has not told us what was meant, on his theory, by the frequently recurring phrase, "and he begat sons and daughters." This he was certainly bound to do. It is true that in the case of the two sons of Heber, Peleg and Yoktan, he makes the former mean " derivation," " division, two hundred and thirty-nine years," and the latter the real "father of thirteen South Arabian races;" which distinction appears to have been made on some principle of philosophy peculiar to him; but he ought not to have left unexplained so important a phrase so frequently occurring as "sons and daughters."

We must devote a little space to our author's chronology of Abraham and the two or three succeeding generations. For in this his " philosophy " appears to peculiar advantage. After giving the well-known numbers, as in the following table, —

    Abraham lived 175 years,   Isaac, 180 years,
    Jacob, 147 years,   Joseph, 110 years,

Bunsen proceeds to say, —

"Here it is not a question of a solitary exception in the case of one individual. It is true that no instance can be adduced demonstrably of any one reaching the age of one hundred and eighty. Such a case, however, as an exception, would not contravene the laws of nature. But that three patriarchs should have lived, one after the other, one hundred and fifty years, and even more, and the viceroy, Joseph, their successor, one hundred and ten, cannot be historical. There must be some means of detecting some blunder here, or else the historical nature of the narrative will be liable to grave suspicion. None but those who cling to the infatuation that the antediluvian patriarchs, as well as Noah and Shem, lived from six hundred to one thousand years, have any excuse to offer for such purely childish delusions, persistence in which can only be productive of doubt and unbelief.

"But there is no country in which it is so improbable that a man a hundred years old should have a son as in a land of early development, like Syria and Canaan.* But are we compelled,

---

* Our author's " philosophy " likewise sets aside the plain declarations of the New Testament. What becomes, on his theory, of Rom. iv. 19 and Heb. xi. 11, which indorse the account in Gen. xviii. 10-15 and xxi. 5?

on that account, to regard these four ages of the patriarchs as primitive inventions? No one who admits the strictly historical character of the principal branch of the family narrative of this period will come to this conclusion."* (Vol. iii. pp. 340, 341.)

"But, then, this family possessed an era, as was always the case with noble Semitic races; this era must have been that of the immigration." † (*Ibid.*)

"In the history of Abraham we find two predominant numbers, the seventy-fifth year (that of the immigration), and the one hundredth (the birth of Isaac). In this interval, so many events occurred, also, as to require a considerably long sojourn in Canaan prior to his birth.

"We assume, therefore, seventy-five as the year before the birth of Isaac, twenty-five as the duration of the sojourn in Canaan, and, consequently, fifty-one as the first year of the settlement in Canaan.

"But there is also a place for the one hundredth year (which is said to be that of the birth of Isaac), as the year in which Abraham died. This, again, can not be accidental. The computation backward — the turning-point is so historically important and well established — leads directly to the same conclusion. According to this, Jacob died in the one hundred and forty-seventh year, not of his own life, but of the era from the immigration of Abraham. Joseph again, not of his own age, but of the era of Jacob." (Vol. iii. p. 344.)

"*The reader will here find an account taken of every date which occurs in the Scripture narrative.*‡ Whatever is determined upon grounds of internal probability, such as the births of Isaac and Jacob, is placed in brackets. There can not, therefore, be an error of more than two or three years at most.§

---

* Our author distinctly admits that Abraham is strictly an historical person, as well as Isaac, Jacob, and Joseph.
† Mere assumption. ‡ The Italics are ours.
§ Referring to a table which is not copied, the essential part appearing in what follows.

Those which are placed in parentheses are such as arise out of the entries in the Bible in reference to years of marriage. These are, consequently, in themselves thoroughly authentic. All the other dates are taken directly from the Bible." *

Truly, this is taking the subject of chronology "out of the domain of chronology and history into that of pure philosophy." (Vol. iv. p. 22.) An account is taken of every date in the Scripture narrative! Only the date of the son's birth is changed to that of the death of the father, the real date of this latter event being ignored altogether. Is any language, proper for a Christian to use, too severe in reprehension of such a procedure? What! we involuntarily exclaim, was the man insane? Had he become imbecile? Had he so long been groping amid the sepulchral monuments of antiquity that he could not recognize, in the clear light of day which other men use, a plain historical fact?

" And Abraham was an hundred years old when Isaac was born" (Gen. xxi. 5); that is, as our author interprets it, " he was a hundred years old when he died." " And Abraham was seventy-five years old when he departed out of Haran" (Gen. xii. 4); that is, " the seventy-fifth year is the year before Isaac was born." And so of other dates and events in connection with the Scripture narrative. " An account is taken of every date in the Scripture narrative." He might as well have taken the alphabetical letters and figures in the first fifteen chapters of Genesis, and so transposed and arranged them as to make out a story of the creation about 20,000 B. C., and of the flood

* Egypt's Place in Universal History, vol. iii. p. 344.

occurring 10,000 B. C., and the "development" and "strata" of languages, &c., according to his system, and then have claimed the Bible as authority, telling us we should find "an account taken of every letter and figure in the Scripture narrative. If any x's or z's, or other letters, or any figures, had remained unappropriated, he could have found a "place" for them. We say, had he done this, the process would have been about as rational as that which he has adopted in relation to the history of Abraham and his successors in the patriarchal line.

Bunsen lays great stress on the improbability of a man having a son at the age of a hundred years, especially in such a land as Palestine, this improbability being even a corner-stone in his argument. With him, in his "philosophy," the assertion of the sacred writer that the event is miraculous, and the indorsement of the miracle by an inspired apostle (Rom. iv. 19, and Heb. xi. 11), go for nothing. Thus the New Testament suffers alike with the Old under this rationalizing process.

When we first read the following caustic criticism on Bunsen's work, we thought it probably a little extravagant. But we are now prepared to receive it as just.

"Sesostris is the great name of Egyptian antiquity. Even the builders of the Pyramids and of the Labyrinth shrink into insignificance by the side of this mighty conqueror. Nevertheless, his historical identity is not proof against the dissolving and recompounding process of the Egyptological method. Bunsen distributes him into portions, and identifies each portion with a different king. Sesostris, as we have stated, stands in Manetho's list as third king of the twelfth dynasty, at 3320 B. C., and a notice is appended to his name, clearly identifying him with the Sesostris of Herodotus. Bunsen first takes a portion of him, and identifies it with Tosorthrus (written Sesorthrus by Eusebius), the second king of the third dynasty, whose date is 3119 B. C., being a difference in the dates of seventeen hundred and ninety-nine years — about the same interval as between Augustus Cæsar and Napoleon. He then takes another portion, and identifies it with Sesonchosis, a king of the twelfth dynasty; a third portion of Sesostris is finally assigned to himself. It seems that these three fragments make up the entire Sesostris."*

B. Page 27.

CHRONOLOGY OF BOËCKH.

Boëckh makes the duration of the reign of the gods to be seventeen Sothic cycles, beginning July 20, B. C. 30,522, and reaching to July 20, B. C. 5703. The governing principle in his system seems to be the aforesaid cycle, and the distinguished author did not hesitate to make alterations in numbers in order to apply it. His scheme is confessedly artificial. Thus Bunsen says, " We believe that no Egyptologer has ever ventured upon so many and such bold alterations in the dates of Manetho as Boëckh was obliged to propose, in order to make good his assumption that Manetho's chronology was an artificial system of applying cyclical numbers to Egyptian history. There is every reason to suppose that the illustrious master of Hellenic archæology long ago abandoned a

* Sir G. C. Lewis's Survey of the Astronomy of the Ancients, p. 369.

theory so triumphantly refuted by the most stubborn facts of contemporary evidence. On the other hand, it is to be hoped that Egyptologers will not hesitate to admit the instinct of genius which led him to assume a certain connection between Manetho and the Sothic cycles, inasmuch as his three books of Egyptian history were divided according to that cycle of 1460 years." (Vol. v. p. 119.)

The first part of this criticism appears emiently just. We doubt, however, if the " instinct of genius " ever led any one " to assume " anything in chronology or history.

C. Page 29.

CHRONOLOGY OF RODIER.

RODIER places his highest date in human history at about B. C. 24,000. This, however, is not the beginning of history; for before this, at undefined dates, he makes to have taken place the " dissemination of the Proto-Scyths," and the movement of the Japetite or Indo-European races toward Western Asia and Europe. But about B. C. 24,000, he says, took place " the breaking up of the ice at the north pole. The shock which this gave to the crust of the earth was perhaps the cause of the sudden cold which drove the Japetite Aryans from primitive Asia." Intermediate between B. C. 24,000 and 21,778 was the commencement of the period Phta in Egypt, and the outline of Egyptian civilization. At B. C. 21,778 was the commencement of the period of Phre. At B. C. 19,564 was the commencement of the period of Osiris, and his conquests in Ethiopia and Asia. At B. C. 19,337 was the commencement of the period of the "Manouantaras" in India, a "date chronologically precise and approximatively verified by astronomy." At B. C. 14,611 was the "era of Ma. Chronologically the number is 14,606; astronomical verifications, very precise, give 14,611." And here the author places the "origin of the great cycles of fourteen hundred and seventy-five years, and of the vague year of three hundred and sixty-five days." At B. C. 13,901 he places the "era of the Maha-Yuga, the origin of the period called Satya-Yuga, the Institutes of Manu, or legislator Vaivasvata, surnamed Satyavrata, the end of the Vedic epoch, the recension of the Vedas. . . . The exactness of this date is as rigorous as that of the Egyptian date." Omitting the mention of some intermediate dates, at which important historical events are represented to have taken place, we come down to B. C. 9101, a date which is "rigorously verified," at which "Maya compiled the treatise of astronomy called the Suryâ Siddhantâ." At B. C. 4286 is another "date rigorously verified by astronomy," as that when the Egyptian calendar was reformed, &c., &c. These specifications are sufficient to place before the reader the character and pretensions of this remarkable work.

Now, the question arises, How does this author make out these high dates, some of which, he affirms, are verified approximatively, and others rigorously, by astronomy? I need only to indicate his processes in two or three instances. Take first the date B. C. 9101, which he says is "rigorously verified," when the astronomical treatise called the Suryâ Siddhantâ was compiled. Having translated that work from the Sanskrit, while in India, I am pretty well acquainted with it, and with the astronomical literature of the Hindus; and I may state that the treatise itself contains astronomical data which refer the compilation of the work, in its present form, to the latter part of the fifth or the first part of the sixth century after Christ, though it doubtless comprises astronomical knowledge which had existed among the Hindus for centuries before. These are the facts as recognized by all oriental scholars who have given attention to this subject.

Now, how does our author make out the date of B. C. 9101? In this wise: In the commencement of the treatise, it is said it was revealed by the Sun to the Asura Maya, at the close of the Krita or Satya-Yuga (or age) of the present Maha-Yuga, which consists of four million three hundred and twenty thousand solar years. But these are equal to twelve thousand divine years, or years of the gods — one year of the gods being equal to three hundred and sixty years of mortals, i. e., solar years. This is expressly stated in the work itself. Now, our author, setting aside or ignoring the express declarations of the treatise, and of other astronomical treatises, makes the Maha-Yuga to consist of twelve thousand sidereal years, instead of four million three hundred and twenty thousand; and this would bring the end of the Krita-Yuga at B. C. 9101, when the Suryâ Siddhantâ was compiled. The declaration in the treatise itself makes the compilation, or rather revelation of it, to have been at about B. C. 2,163,101. Rodier thinks this a mistake, and, arbitrarily altering the date, makes it to be B. C. 9101, which he says " is rigorously verified," while the treatise itself furnishes unequivocal evidence that its compilation, in its present form, can be dated no earlier than the sixth century before Christ. Rodier might, with equal consistency, have made the epoch of the compilation of the Suryâ Siddhantû to have been 2,163,101, instead of 9101, B. C.

Take another of his dates, " rigorously verified," that of B. C. 13,901, the epoch of the Institutions of Manu, end of the Vedic epoch, the date of the recensions of the Vedas, of the adoption of the Egyptian Zodiac, &c., &c. How does he make this out? Very easily, in this way: There is appended to the Vedas an astronomical part called the *Iyotisha;* in this the position of the *solstitial colure* is given for the time, which a simple calculation shows to have been B. C. 1181 (Rodier says 1500). The original Sanskrit text, in-defining the position, mentions the summer solstice as being at the particular point at that time, or what is equivalent to it. Now, Rodier has the *boldness,* as he terms it, to suppose that it is not the *summer solstice* that is meant, but the *winter;* and this carries back the epoch of the observation a space of time equal to that in which the equinoxes would retrograde through one half the whole circle of the ecliptic, i. e., about twelve thousand nine hundred and sixty years.* This, added to the Vedic date, as admitted by Sanskrit scholars generally, viz., 1181, makes out Rodier's epoch

* Rodier, p. 470.

of B. C. 13,901. (He has mistaken some of his numbers.) He arbitrarily alters a fact — a fact which all oriental scholars recognize as such; i. e., puts the winter solstice for the summer solstice, thus making a clear difference of more than twelve thousand nine hundred years, and then declares the result a "rigorous astronomical verification." Was ever audacity, in a professedly scientific writer, surpassed by this?

Take another of his dates, "the era of Ma," of which he says, "Very precise astronomical verifications give rigorously B. C. 14,611, the date of the origin of the great cycles of fourteen hundred and seventy-five years, and of the vague year of three hundred and sixty-five days, the invention of the zodiac, &c., the institution of the monarchical regime."

Now, how does he make this out? Why, he takes the highest numbers he can find, that are used in giving the duration of the Egyptian empire from Menes to Alexander, and then extends them somewhat, so that he makes the era of Menes at least one hundred and fifty years earlier than any other writer, and a number of hundreds of years earlier than the numbers necessitate, even if we reckon the thirty dynasties consecutive, and about two thousand years earlier than Lepsius and Bunsen, and more than three thousand years earlier than Poole, and others; i. e., he places Menes, the first mortal king of Egypt, at B. C. 5853. He then, from this, mounts up into antiquity on the mythological numbers furnished by Manetho, as interpreted by Eusebius, and corrected by the Turin Papyrus, according to his fancy; i. e., previous to Menes, he makes the kingdom of the *Nekuas* — usually interpreted *Manes*, or *spirits of dead men* (he has another interpretation, which I do not comprehend) — of five thousand six hundred and thirteen years, and then the period of Ma, purely mythological, of thirty-one hundred and forty years: this brings us to the epoch, the " commencement of the period of Ma, B. C. 14,606." This is historical, and the date is verified by astronomy!

His process is short and easy. He says Claudius Ptolemy, the great Grecian astronomer, employed, in his tables, a cycle of fourteen hundred and seventy-five years. Then, starting at the year A. D. 139, — the end of the Sothic period of fourteen hundred and sixty years, which terminated next after the Christian era, — he reckons back by periods of fourteen hundred and seventy-five years — ten such steps bringing him to B. C. 14,611; and as this date differs only five years from 14,606, to which he had arrived historically, the difference of *five years*, as he says, being easily accounted for by the loss of fractions of years in the reckoning of Manetho. And this he calls demonstrating the " precision " of the date B. C. 14,611 by astronomy.

In order to put this matter in its true light, it is scarcely necessary to remark, that there is hardly a datum involved which is reliable. Take the historical part. It is true that a Sothic period, according to Censorinus, terminated A. D. 139. But the Sothic cycle was a period of fourteen hundred and sixty[*]

---

[*] i. e., fourteen hundred and sixty solar years, and fourteen hundred and sixty-one Egyptian or vague years.

years; and on what authority does the writer make this the starting-point for a reckoning with another cycle of fourteen hundred and seventy-five years, if there be such a cycle? And then, again, what becomes of his reckoning, when it is regarded as demonstrable, that the thirty dynasties of Manetho were not all consecutive — that part of them were contemporaneous? by which fact the duration of the Egyptian empire, from Menes to Alexander, is curtailed from two to three thousand years. He had the works of Bunsen, Lepsius, Poole, and Wilkinson, etc., before him, — or ought to have had, — in which the various versions of Manetho are given; but, as far as I am aware, he has not even hinted that different results had been arrived at by those scholars and others. Whereas, in point of fact, there are equally authentic numbers, both historical and mythological, which, if employed, would have varied that date several hundreds, or even thousands, of years; so that, instead of a coincidence between the historical and astronomical numbers within the limits of *five years*, there might have been made a discrepancy of some two or three thousand. But the point of his argument all turns on this coincidence within *five years*.

But the astronomy of Rodier is worse than his history. He says that Claudius Ptolemy made use, in his tables, of a cycle of fourteen hundred and seventy-five years, referring to Syncellus (p. 52) for authority. But his authority does not sustain the assertion. Ptolemy made use of no such cycle; at least, the passage referred to does not prove that he did. But supposing he did, how does that authorize him (Rodier) to take that number, and by it ascend into antiquity, and verify a date fifteen thousand years before? Even if the number were legitimate or true, it could not be available for such a use. Such an application of it is unscientific and absurd. The absurdity may be well illustrated by a reference to the Julian period. The Julian period is formed by multiplying together the numbers of the solar cycle, lunar cycle, and cycle of indiction, i. e., $28 \times 19 \times 15$. The product of these numbers is 7980. This period began B. C. 4713; i. e., the commencements of these three cycles coincide that year, as is found by reckoning backward from any point of time when the cycles were in use in the Roman empire. Now, supposing any one should attempt to maintain from this that the Roman state was in being, and the particular civil matters connected with the cycle of indiction were in vogue, B. C. 4713, his argument would be parallel to that of our French *savant* in the premises before us. I ask, in all soberness, is any language of denunciation too severe properly to characterize such a work? If there is in the whole compass of scientific literature a more inconclusive argument, a more irrational or uncritical process, than that of our author in his astronomical verification, as he terms it, of the date B. C. 14,611, it has not come under my notice.

Others of Rodier's dates, of a high antiquity, are open to the same criticism that I have bestowed on the few above mentioned.

D. Page 68.

MANETHO.

The following is the account of Manetho, as given by Syncellus:—

"It remains, therefore, to make certain extracts concerning the dynasties of the Egyptians from the writings of Manetho the Sebennyte, the high priest of the idolatrous temples of Egypt in the time of Ptolemy Philadelphus. These, according to his own account, he copied from the inscriptions which were engraved in the sacred dialect and hieroglyphic characters upon the columns set up in the Seriadic land by Thoth, the first Hermes; and, after the deluge, translated from the sacred dialect, into the Greek tongue, in hieroglyphic characters; and committed to writing in books, and deposited by Agathodæmon, the son of the second Hermes, the father of Tàt, in the penetralia of the temples of Egypt. He has addressed and explained them to Philadelphus, the second king Ptolemy, in the book entitled Sothis, as follows:—

"'*The Epistle of Manetho, the Sebennyte, to Ptolemy Philadelphus.* To the great and august king Ptolemy Philadelphus, Manetho, the high priest and scribe of the sacred adyta, being by birth a Sebennyte, and citizen of Heliopolis, to his sovereign, Ptolemy, greeting:—

"'It is right for us, most mighty king, to pay due attention to all things which it is your pleasure we should take into consideration. In answer, therefore, to your inquiries concerning the things that shall take place in the world, I shall, according to your commands, lay before you what I have gathered from the sacred books written by Hermes Trismegistus, our forefather. Farewell, my prince and sovereign.'"*

* Syncellus, Chron. p. 40.

Syncellus then, after the letter, thus proceeds: —

"He says these things respecting the interpretation of the books of the second Hermes; he afterwards gives a narrative concerning the five Egyptian nations, called with them gods, demigods, manes, and mortals, of whom Eusebius, alluding to them in his chronological writings, thus speaks: 'The Egyptians have strung together many trifling legends respecting gods and demigods, and with them manes (νεκνῶν), and other mortal kings. For the most ancient among them reckoned by lunar years of thirty days each, but those who came after called the *horas* (ὥρους), periods of three months, years.'"

It should be remarked that this letter to Ptolemy Philadelphus (with the work spoken of by Syncellus, Βίβλος τῆς Σώθεως) is pronounced by many * a forgery executed by some Jewish or Christian writer subsequent to the Christian era. This opinion, however, or charge of forgery, I can not think to be well sustained.

* Kenrick (Anc. Eg., vol. ii. p. 72) says the Book of Sothis " is proved to be spurious by the epithet Σεβαστός, which the introductory epistle gives to Ptolemy, the translation of *Augustus*, and never found among the titles of the Ptolemies." And the writer of the article *Manetho*, in Smith's Dictionary, is equally positive that the letter and *Book of Sothis* are forgeries; and he mentions the occurrence of the epithet *Sebastos* as the principal reason for regarding them as the work of a *pseudo Manetho*.

Though the epithet may not have been used as an official title given to, or assumed by, the Ptolemies, may it not have been applied *occasionally* to those sovereigns, e. g., Philadelphus? I have not yet seen satisfactory evidence that the letter above quoted and the Book of Sothis, spoken of by Syncellus, were not from the pen of the *true* Manetho, the great Egyptian historian.

E. Page 69.

MANETHO'S LISTS,

AS GIVEN BY AFRICANUS AND EUSEBIUS.

THE version of Africanus is reported to us by Syncellus (Chron. pp. 18, 19) under this heading: "*Africanus respecting the Mythological Chronology of the Egyptians and Chaldeans.*" We regard the passage, therefore, as a quotation from Africanus, though Rawlinson (Herod. vol. ii. p. 69) thinks it is from Manetho. The point, however, is not important.

"Manetho, the Sebennyte, priest of the impure sacred rites in Egypt, who lived after Berosus, in the time of Ptolemy Philadelphus, like Berosus weaving lies, wrote to this same Ptolemy respecting the six* dynasties (that is, of the seven gods who never existed), who, he says, reigned through a period of 11,985 years. The first of these, the god Hephaistos, reigned 9000 years. But these 9000 years some of our historians (regarding them as so many lunar months, and dividing the whole number of days in them by 365, the number of days in a solar year) reduce to 727¾ years, thinking they have made a wonderful correction, whereas they have rather confounded truth with error in a manner that is ridiculous."

* So in the original, though there is reason to think that the language as written was *sixteen*, viz., seven gods and nine demigods. The passage, as it stands, does not make sense, and is evidently corrupted.

"THE FIRST DYNASTY.

		Solar Years.	Lunar Years.
1.	Hephaistos (Vulcan) reigned over the Egyptians,	$727\frac{3}{4}$	9000
2.	Helios, son of Hephaistos,	$80\frac{1}{8}$	992
3.	Agathodaimon,	$56\frac{7}{12}$	700
4.	Kronos,	$40\frac{1}{2}$	501
5.	Osiris and Isis,	35	433
6.	Typhon,	29	359
	Sum,	969	11985

		Solar Years.	Quarters of Years.
7.	Horus, demigod,	25	100
8.	Ares,	23	92
9.	Anubis,	17	68
10.	Heracles,	15	60
11.	Apollo,	25	100
12.	Ammon,	30	220
13.	Tithoes,	27	108
14.	Sosos,	32	128
15.	Zeus,	20	80
	Deficiency,	$\frac{1}{2}$	2
	Sum,	$214\frac{1}{2}$	858"

That is, the gods reigned 11985 years = 969 solar years.
The demigods, . . 858 " = $214\frac{1}{2}$ "

Totals, . . . 12843 $1183\frac{1}{2}$

The year of the gods is lunar = 1 month; and the year of the demigods is trimestre, and called ὥρος, four of which make one solar year.

In this table the names with the numbering, and the duration of the reigns in solar years, are as found in Syncellus; in the second column, or that of lunar years (months), only the 9000 of the first god-king are given by Syncellus, with the statement that they equal 727¾ solar years, and that the whole duration of the reigns of the gods was 11,985 lunar years (months); that is, lunar periods of 30 days each, according to the early Christian chronographers. But Syncellus (p. 41) gives additional statements, apparently on the authority of Panodorus, that the 11,985 month-years of the gods are equal to 969 solar years, and that the duration of the reigns of the "two dynasties of nine demigods" was 214½ solar years, deduced from 858 ὧροι or τροπῶν, i. e., tri-monthly periods, the whole amounting to 1183½ solar years. These critical points and computations would not deserve the prominent notice we have given them but for the fact that the result, 1183½ solar years, is an important number with the early chronographers, since by adding it to another number, viz., 1058, the number of years from the creation of Adam to the commencement of the reign of the gods, according to their computation (*Sync. Chron.* p. 41, c.), they make out the sum of 2242 years, the length of the period from the creation to the flood, according to the Septuagint. And this result we regard as worthy of notice.

The ante-historic reigns in Egypt are given by Eusebius, in his Chronology, lib. I, chap. xx. 1. The chapter is headed, "Ex Ægyptiacis Manethonis monumentis, qui in tres libros historiam suam tribuit. De diis, et de heroibus, de manibus et de mortalibus regibus qui in Ægypto præfuerunt usque ad regem Persarum Darium."

"The first god of the Egyptians was Vulcan, who is celebrated as the inventor of fire. After him was Sol, then Agathodæmon, then Saturn, then Osiris, then Typhon, brother of Osiris, and lastly Horus, son of Osiris and Isis; these first ruled over the Egyptians. Afterwards, the royal authority continued in regular succession to Bytis, through a period of 13.900 years. But I understand the year to be lunar, consisting of thirty days; for what we call a *month* the Egyptians formerly indicated by the name of *year*.

	Years.
After the gods, heroes reigned,	1255
Then other kings,	1817
Then other 30 Memphite kings,	1790
Then other 10 Thinite kings,	350
Then followed the rule of manes and heroes,	5813

The whole sum amounts to 11,000, (really) 11,025 years, which are lunar, that is, monthly. But, in truth, the rule of gods, heroes, and manes, which the Egyptians narrate, is supposed to be a period of 24,900 lunar years, which make only 2206 solar years."

Eusebius then, after some remarks to the import that Mizraim of the Holy Scriptures was the founder of the Egyptian race, and that the foregoing chronology can be made to harmonize essentially with that of the Hebrew Scriptures by regarding the year as equal to a lunar month,* proceeds to give, in detail, the thirty dynasties.

* . . . plane æquum est, ut hi *anni* in menses convertantur quot ab Hebræis memorati anni; nempe ut qui menses continentur in memoratis apud Hebræos annis, ii totidem intelligantur Ægyptiorum lunares anni, pro ea temporum summa quæ a primo condito homine ad Mezraim usque colligitur. Etenim Mezraimus Ægyptiaci auctor fuit ab eaque prima Ægyptiorum dynastia credenda est. Quod si temporum copia adhuc exuberet, reputandum sedulo est plures fortasse Ægyptiorum reges una eademque ætate exstitisse: namque Thinitas regnavisse aiunt et Memphitas et Saitas et Æthiopes eodemque tempore alios. Videntur præterea alii quoque alibi imperium tenuisse, etc. . . — *Lat. transl. of the Armenian. etc.*, B. I ch. xx. 3.

THE THIRTY DYNASTIES.

ACCORDING TO AFRICANUS.

DYNASTY I.

After the manes and demi-gods, the first dynasty is reckoned of eight kings, of whom the first was Menes, who reigned 62 years. He was destroyed by a hippopotamus.

2. Athothis, his son, 57 years. He established the kingdom in Memphis. He is said to have been the author of books on anatomy, for he was a physician.

3. Kenkenes, his son, 31 years.

4. Venephes, his son, 23 years. In his time a famine afflicted Egypt. He built the Pyramids, near Kochome.

5. Usaphaidus, his son, 20 years.

6. Miebes, his son, 26 years.

7. Semempses, his son, 18 years. In his time a great pestilence afflicted Egypt.

8. Bieneches, his son, 26 years. In all 253 (263) years.

ACCORDING TO EUSEBIUS.

DYNASTY I.

After the manes and heroes, they reckon the first dynasty of eight kings; of whom the first was Menes, remarkable for his glorious administration. Commencing from him, we carefully record the families reigning in succession, of which the series is as follows:—

1. Menes, the Thinite, and his seven successors, whom Herodotus calls Mina. He reigned 30 (60) years. He went, with his army, beyond the limits of his own country; became illustrious for his exploits. He was destroyed by a hippopotamus.

2. Athothis, his son, enjoyed the regal power 27 years. He cultivated the art of medicine, and wrote books on surgery.

3. Cencenes, his son, 39 years.

4. Vanenephis, 42 years. In his time a famine afflicted the land. He erected the pyramid near Kochome.

ACCORDING TO AFRICANUS.

DYNASTY II.
OF NINE THINITE KINGS.

1. Boethos, 38 years. In his time a chasm opened in the earth, in Bubastus, and many perished.
2. Kæachos, 39 years. In his time the bulls Apis, in Memphis, Mnevis, in Heliopolis, and the Mendesian goat, were declared to be gods.
3. Binothris, 47 years. In his time it was decreed that women might exercise regal power.
4. Tlas, 17 years.
5. Sethenes, 44 years.
6. Chœres, 17 years.
7. Nephercheres, 25 years. In his time the Nile is fabled to have flowed, mingled with honey, for eleven days.

[Both Routh (Rel. Soc. vol. ii. p. 248) and Cory (Anc. Frag. p. 98) add the 8th and 9th kings, according to Eusebius, or as Eusebius has them, but they are not in the text. These writers likewise give the sum of the years of this dynasty as 302 years.]

ACCORDING TO EUSEBIUS.

DYNASTY II.
OF NINE KINGS.

1. Bochus.* In his time a great chasm opened in the earth at Bubastus, and many persons perished.
2. After him Cechous; in which time Apis, and Mnevis, and the Mendesian goat are regarded as gods.
3. Then Biophis, under whom it was enacted by law that women might exercise regal power.
4, 5, 6. Then three others, in whose time no wonderful acts were performed.
7. Under the seventh, the fabulists say the Nile flowed with honey and water for 11 days.
8. Afterward Sesochris, 48 years, whose height, they say, was five cubits and three handbreadths.
9. Under the ninth, nothing worthy of mention occurred.

These reigned 297 years.

---

* In the orthography of the names I follow the Latin of the Armenian version of Eusebius.

ACCORDING TO AFRICANUS.

DYNASTY III.
NINE MEMPHITE KINGS.

1. Necherophes, 28 years. In his time the Libyans revolted from the Egyptians, but through fear, on account of an unnatural increase of the moon, they gave themselves up.
2. Tosorthrus, 29 years. He is called Asklepius by the Egyptians on account of his medical knowledge. He invented house-building with hewn stones, and patronized literature.
3. Tyris, 7 years.
4. Mesochris, 17 years.
5. Soyphis, 16 years.
6. Tosertasis, 19 years.
7. Aches, 42 years.
8. Sephuris, 30 years.
9. Kerpheres, 26 years.

In all 214 years. Altogether, of the three dynasties, according to Africanus, 769 (779).

DYNASTY IV.
OF EIGHT MEMPHITE KINGS OF A DIFFERENT RACE.

1. Soris, 29 years.
2. Suphis, 63 years. He built the largest pyramid, which Herodotus says was constructed by Cheops. He was haughty towards the gods, and wrote a sacred book, which the Egyptians

ACCORDING TO EUSEBIUS.

DYNASTY III.
OF EIGHT MEMPHITE KINGS.

Necherochis, in whose time the Libyans revolted from the Egyptians; but on account of a sudden and immense increase in the size of the moon, they returned to their allegiance.

Then Sesorthus, who, on account of his knowledge in medicine, was called Æsculapius by the Egyptians. He was the inventor of building houses with hewn stone, and gave much attention to writing.

The six remaining kings performed nothing worthy of mention.

These reigned 197 years.

DYNASTY IV.
OF SEVENTEEN MEMPHITE KINGS, FROM ANOTHER ROYAL FAMILY.

Of whom the third was Suphis, author of the greatest pyramid, which Herodotus says was erected by Cheops, who became haughty toward the gods; then, becoming penitent, wrote

ACCORDING TO AFRICANUS.

regard as a work of great importance.
   3. Suphis, 66 years.
   4. Mencheres, 63 years.
   5. Rhatœses, 25 years.
   6. Bicheres, 22 years.
   7. Sebercheres, 7 years.
   8. Thampthis, 9 years.
   In all 274 (284) years. In all of the four dynasties after the flood, according to Africanus, 1046 (1063) years.

DYNASTY V.

OF EIGHT ELEPHANTINE KINGS.

   1. Usercheres, 28 years.
   2. Sephres, 13 years.
   3. Nephercheres, 20 years.
   4. Sisires, 7 years.
   5. Cheres, 20 years.
   6. Rhathuris, 44 years.
   7. Mencheres, 9 years.
   8. Tancheres, 44 years.
   9. Obnos, 33 years.
   In all 248 (218) years, with the 1046 (1063) of the four preceding dynasties, 1294 (1281) years.

DYNASTY VI.

OF SIX MEMPHITE KINGS.

   1. Othoes, 30 years. He was killed by his body-guards.
   2. Phius, 53 years.

ACCORDING TO EUSEBIUS.

a sacred book, which the Egyptians regard as a great treasure.
   Respecting the remaining kings, nothing worthy of record has been related.
   They reigned 448 years.

DYNASTY V.

OF THIRTY-ONE ELEPHANTINE KINGS.

   Of whom the first, Othius, was slain by his body-guards.
   The fourth was Phiops, who, from the sixth year of his age, exercised the regal power till his 100th year.

DYNASTY VI.

   A certain woman named Nitocris reigned. She was the bravest and most beautiful woman of her time, with rosy cheeks (flava rubris genis). It

MANETHO'S LISTS.

ACCORDING TO AFRICANUS.	ACCORDING TO EUSEBIUS.
3. Methusuphis, 7 years. 4. Phiops, who began to reign at the age of 6 years, and reigned till he was a hundred years old. 5. Menthesuphis, 1 year. 6. Nitocris, who was the most beautiful woman of her time, of florid complexion. She built the third pyramid, and reigned 12 years. In all 203 years, which, with the 1294 (1281) of the preceding 5 dynasties, make 1497 (1484).	is said she erected the third pyramid, a huge mass like a hill.* These reigned 203 years.
DYNASTY VII. OF SEVENTY MEMPHITE KINGS, who reigned 70 days.	**DYNASTY VII.** OF FIVE MEMPHITE KINGS, who reigned 75 years.
DYNASTY VIII. OF TWENTY-SEVEN MEMPHITE KINGS, who reigned 146 years; with those before, 1639 years for the eight dynasties.	**DYNASTY VIII.** OF NINE MEMPHITE KINGS (Greek, 5), who reigned 100 years.
DYNASTY IX. OF NINETEEN HERACLEOPOLITE KINGS, who reigned 409 years. The first was Acthœs, who was more cruel than all his pred-	**DYNASTY IX.** OF FOUR HERACLEOPOLITE KINGS, 100 years. The first of these, Octhois, the most cruel of all the kings

* Armen. (Mignes' ed.), speciemcollis præ se ferens — but as given in Cory's Ancient Fragments (p. 107), quæ est moles erecta collis instar.

APPENDIX, E.

ACCORDING TO AFRICANUS.	ACCORDING TO EUSEBIUS.
ecessors. He did much injury to all the inhabitants of Egypt. Being seized with madness, he was killed by a crocodile.	who preceded him, filled all Egypt with dire calamities. He was finally seized with madness, and destroyed by a crocodile.

DYNASTY X.

OF NINETEEN HERACLEOPOLITE KINGS,	OF NINETEEN HERACLEOPOLITE KINGS,
who reigned 185 years.	185 years.

DYNASTY XI.

OF SIXTEEN DIOSPOLITE KINGS,	OF SIXTEEN DIOSPOLITE KINGS,
who reigned 43 years.	43 years.
After whom,* Ammenemes reigned 16 years.	After whom,† Ammenemes, 16 years.
Thus far the first book of Manetho; in all, 192 (200) kings, 2300 (2308) years and 70 days.	Thus far extends the first book of Manetho. There are 192 kings, and 2300 years.

THE SECOND BOOK OF MANETHO.

DYNASTY XII.

OF SEVEN DIOSPOLITE KINGS.	OF SEVEN DIOSPOLITE KINGS.
1. Sessonchosis, son of Ammenemes, 46 years. (Syncellus, 8th.)	Of whom the first, Sesonchosis, son of Ammenenes, 46 years.
2. Ammenemes, 38 years. He was slain by his eunuchs. (Syncellus, 9th.)	Ammenemes, 38 years, who was slain by his eunuchs.
	Sesostris, 48 years, who is said to have been four cubits

---

* μεθ' ὅυς, which Cory (Anc. Frag. p. 108) translates *among whom*. Routh (Rel. Sac. vol. ii. p. 253) has it, quibus Ammenemes succedit, &c. † Post quos.

MANETHO'S LISTS.

ACCORDING TO AFRICANUS.

3. Sesostris, 48 years. He subdued all Asia in nine years, and Europe as far as Thrace. He everywhere erected monuments of his conquests of the nations. He erected pillars, engraven with male emblems, among the people who were brave, and with female emblems among those who were cowardly. By the Egyptians he is held in honor first after Osiris.

4. Lachares, 8 years. He built a labyrinth in Arsenoite, as a tomb for himself.

5. Ammeres, 8 years.

6. Ammenemes, 8 years.

7. Skemiophris, his sister, 4 years. In all, 160 years.

DYNASTY XIII.

OF SIXTY DIOSPOLITE KINGS, who reigned 453 years.

DYNASTY XIV.

OF SEVENTY-SIX XOITE KINGS, who reigned 184 years.

DYNASTY XV.

SHEPHERDS.

They were six foreign Phœnician kings, who took Memphis. The first, Saites, reigned 19 years; after whom, the Saite

ACCORDING TO EUSEBIUS.

three spans and two digits in height. He subdued all Asia in nine years, and parts of Europe as far as Thrace. In all the conquered countries he erected monuments on which he inscribed, among the brave, virilia; among the cowardly, feminea pudenda ignominiæ causa. Wherefore he is held by the Egyptians next in honor after Osiris.

Lampares succeeded, 8 years. He constructed the labyrinth in Arsinois for his tomb.

His successors reigned 42 years.

The duration of all their reigns was 245 years.

DYNASTY XIII.

OF SIXTY DIOSPOLITE KINGS, who reigned 453 years.

DYNASTY XIV.

OF SEVENTY-SIX XOITE KINGS, who reigned 484 years.

DYNASTY XV.

OF DIOSPOLITAN KINGS, who reigned 250 years.

ACCORDING TO AFRICANUS.	ACCORDING TO EUSEBIUS.

Nome was named. They founded a city in the Sethroite Nome, from which, going forth, they conquered Egypt.
  2. Bnon, 44 years. (27 of Syncellus).
  3. Pachnan, 61 years.
  4. Staan, 50 years.
  5. Arehles, 49 years.
  6. Aphobis, 61 years. (29 of Syncellus).
In all, 284 years.	

DYNASTY XVI.

OF THIRTY-TWO OTHER SHEPHERD KINGS,

who reigned 518 years.

DYNASTY XVI.

OF FIVE THEBAN KINGS,

who reigned 190 years.

DYNASTY XVII.

OF FORTY-THREE OTHER SHEPHERD KINGS, AND FORTY-THREE THEBAN DIOSPOLITES.

Altogether, the Shepherd and Theban kings reigned 151 years.

DYNASTY XVII.

OF SHEPHERDS,

who were Phœnician brothers, and foreign kings, who took Memphis. Of whom,
  1. Saites reigned 19 years, from whom the Saite Nome was named. They built, in the Sethroite Nome, a city, from which, going forth, they subdued Egypt.
  2. Bnon, 40 years.
  3. Arehles, 30 years.
  4. Apophis, 14 years.
  In all, 103 years. [The same in the Greek.] It was in the time of these kings that Joseph was in Egypt.

MANETHO'S LISTS.

ACCORDING TO AFRICANUS.

DYNASTY XVIII.

OF SIXTEEN DIOSPOLITE KINGS.

1. Amos, in whose time Moses went out of Egypt, as we show.*
2. Chebros, 13 years.
3. Amenophthis, 24 years.
4. Amersis, 22 years.
5. Misaphris, 13 years.
6. Misphragmuthosis, 26 years. In his time happened the deluge of Deucalion.
7. Tuthmosis, 9 years.
8. Amenophis, 31 years. He is supposed to be the Memnon, the sounding-stone.
9. Horus, 37 years.
10. Acherrhes, 32 years.
11. Rathos, 6 years.
12. Chebres, 12 years.
13. Acherrhes, 12 years.
14. Armeses, 5 years.
15. Ramesses, 1 year.
16. Amenophath, 19 years.

In all, 263 years. [In reality

ACCORDING TO EUSEBIUS.

DYNASTY XVIII.

OF FOURTEEN† DIOSPOLITE KINGS,

of whom
1. Amoses, 45 years.
2. Chebron, 13 years.
3. Amophis (Ammenophis), 21 years.
4. Memphres (Miphres), 12 years.
5. Mispharmuthosis (Misphragmuthosis), 26 years.
6. Tuthmosis, 9 years.
7. Amenophis, 31 years, who is Memnon the speaking (sounding) stone.
8. Orus, 28 (38) years.
9. Achencheres, 16 years. In his days Moses offered himself to the Hebrews as a leader, to take them out of Egypt.‡ [This is put in the time of the 11th king in the Greek.]
10. Acherres, 8 years (Athoris, 39 years).

---

* It is added, apparently by Syncellus, " but by the present reckoning, we are compelled to regard Moses at this time as still a young man."

† So in the Greek likewise; but the Greek, in the detail, gives 16 kings. Josephus has 17 names from Tuthoses (Amoses) to Amenophis included, he inserting a female's name in the fourth place.

‡ Greek, in Syncellus, "led the Hebrews," &c. Syncellus says "Eusebius alone says the exodus of Israel took place under this king, no one agreeing with him, but all before opposing him, as he confesses" p. 72, D.

ACCORDING TO AFRICANUS.

262, without assigning any time to the first king.]

ACCORDING TO EUSEBIUS.

11. Cherres, 15 years (Chencheres, 16 years. In his time Moses led the Jews out of Egypt.) [Acherres and Cherres are the 12th and 13th kings in the Greek, so that Athoris and Chencheres are the two in the Greek which are not in the Armenian.]

12. Armais, who is Danaus, 5 years; after which, being driven from Egypt, and fleeing from his brother Egyptus, he escaped into Greece, and, having conquered Argos, ruled over the Argives. [Armais is the 14th king in the Greek.]

13. Ramesses, who is Egyptus, 68 years. (47 Syncellus.)

14. Amenophis, 40 years. [These last two are 15th and 16th in the Greek.]

Sum of the reigns, 348. [Same in the Greek, but in reality only 317 or 327.]

DYNASTY XIX.
OF SEVEN DIOSPOLITE KINGS.

1. Sethos, 51 years.
2. Rapsakes, 61 years.
3. Ammenephthes, 20 years.
4. Ramesses, 60 years.
5. Ammenemes, 5 years.
6. Thuoris, who is called, by Homer, Polybius, the husband of Alcandra, in whose time Troy

DYNASTY XIX.
OF FIVE DIOSPOLITE KINGS.

1. Sethos, 55 years.
2. Rampses, 66 years.
3. Ammenephthis, 40 years.
4. Ammenemes, 26 years.
5. Thuoris, called, by Homer, Polybius, a bold and brave man, in whose time Troy was taken [Greek: called by Polybius, by

MANETHO'S LISTS.

ACCORDING TO AFRICANUS.

was taken, 7 years (Syncellus, 49).

In all 209 (204) years.

In this second book of Manetho are 96 kings and 2121 (2216) years.

ACCORDING TO EUSEBIUS.

Homer, husband of Alcandra, in whose time Troy was taken], 7 years.

In all, 194 years.

In this second book of Manetho are contained 92 kings and 2121 years.

THE THIRD BOOK OF MANETHO.

DYNASTY XX.

OF TWELVE DIOSPOLITE KINGS, who reigned 135 years.

DYNASTY XXI.

OF SEVEN TANITE KINGS.

1. Smendes, 26 years.
2. Psusennes, 41 (46) years.
3. Nephelcheres, 4 years.
4. Amenophthis, 9 years.
5. Osochor, 6 years.
6. Psinaches, 9 years.
7. Psusennes, 35 (14) years.

In all, 130 years.

DYNASTY XXII.

OF NINE BUBASTITE KINGS.

1. Sesonchosis, 21 years.
2. Osorthon, 15 years.
3, 4, 5. Three others, 25 years.
6. Takelothis, 13 years.
7, 8, 9. Three others, 42 years.

In all, 120 (116) years.

DYNASTY XX.

OF TWELVE DIOSPOLITE KINGS, who reigned 172 (178) years.

DYNASTY XXI.

OF SEVEN TANITE KINGS.

1. Smendis, 26 years.
2. Psusennes, 41 years.
3. Nephercheres, 4 years.
4. Amenophthis, 9 years.
5. Osochor, 6 years.
6. Psinaches, 9 years.
7. Psusennes, 35 years.

Sum, 130 years.

DYNASTY XXII.

OF THREE BUBASTITE KINGS.

1. Sesonchosis, 21 years.
2. Osorthon, 15 years.
3. Takelothis, 13 years.

In all, 49 years.

APPENDIX, E.

ACCORDING TO AFRICANUS.	ACCORDING TO EUSEBIUS.
DYNASTY XXIII.	**DYNASTY XXIII.**
OF FOUR TANITE KINGS.	OF THREE TANITE KINGS.
1. Petubates, 40 years. In his time the first Olympiad commenced. 2. Osorcho, 8 years, whom the Egyptians call Heracles. 3. Psammus, 10 years. 4. Zeet, 31 years. In all, 89 years.	1. Petubastis, 25 years. 2. Osorthon, 9 years, whom the Egyptians called Heracles. 3. Psammus, 10 years. In all, 44 years.
DYNASTY XXIV.	**DYNASTY XXIV.**
Bocchoris, the Saite, 6 years, in whose time a lamb spoke, 99 years.*	Bocchoris, the Saite, 44 years, in whose time a lamb spoke. In all, 44 years.
DYNASTY XXV.	**DYNASTY XXV.**
OF THREE ETHIOPIAN KINGS.	OF THREE ETHIOPIAN KINGS.
1. Sabakon, who, taking Bocchoris captive, burned him alive. He reigned 8 years. 2. Sebichos, 14 years. 3. Tarkus, 18 years. In all, 40 years.	1. Sabakon, who, taking Bocchoris captive, burned him alive, and reigned 12 years. 2. Sebichos, his son, 12 years. 3. Tarakus, 20 years. In all, 40 years.
DYNASTY XXVI.	**DYNASTY XXVI.**
OF NINE SAITE KINGS.	OF NINE SAITE KINGS.
1. Stephinates, 7 years. 2. Nechepsos, 6 years. 3. Nechao, 8 years. 4. Psammeticus, 54 years. 5. Necho II., 6 years. He	1. Ammeris, the Ethiopian, 12 years. 2. Stephinathes, 7 years. 3. Nechepsos, 6 years. 4. Nechaus, 8 years.

* Thus in original.

MANETHO'S LISTS.

ACCORDING TO AFRICANUS.

took Jerusalem, and carried Joachaz, the king, captive to Egypt.
6. Psammuthis (another), 6 years.
7. Vaphris, 19 years, to whom the remainder of the Jews fled when Jerusalem was taken by the Assyrians.
8. Amosis, 44 years (86th of Syncellus).
9. Psammecherites, 6 months.
In all, 150 years and 6 months.

DYNASTY XXVII.

OF EIGHT PERSIAN KINGS.

1. Cambyses reigned over Persia, his own kingdom, 5 years, and over Egypt 6 years.
2. Darius, son of Hystaspes, 36 years.
3. Xerxes the Great, 21 years.
4. Artabanes, 7 months.
5. Artaxerxes, 41 years.
6. Xerxes, 2 months.
7. Sogdianus, 7 months.
8. Darius, son of Xerxes, 19 years.
In all, 124 years and 4 months.

DYNASTY XXVIII.

Amyrteus, the Saite, 6 years.

ACCORDING TO EUSEBIUS.

5. Psametichus, 44 (45) years.
6. Nechaus II., 6 years. He took Jerusalem, and led Joachas captive into Egypt.
7. Psammuthis (another), who is Psametichus, 17 years.
8. Vaphres, 25 years; to whom, Jerusalem being taken by the Assyrians. the remainder of the Jews fled for refuge.
9. Amosis, 42 years.
In all, 167 (163) years.

DYNASTY XXVII.

OF EIGHT PERSIAN KINGS.

1. Cambyses, in the fifth year of his reign, ruled in Egypt 3 years.
2. The Magi, 7 months.
3. Darius, 36 years.
4. Xerxes, son of Darius, 21 years.
5. Artaxerxes Longimanus, 40 years.
6. Xerxes II., 2 months.
7. Sogdianus, 7 months.
8. Darius, son of Xerxes, 19 years.
In all, 120 years and 4 months.

DYNASTY XXVIII.

Amyrtæus, the Saite, 6 years.

ACCORDING TO AFRICANUS.

DYNASTY XXIX.

OF FOUR MENDESIAN KINGS.

1. Nepherites, 6 years.
2. Achoris, 13 years.
3. Psammuthis, 1 year.
4. Nephorites, 4 months.

In all, 20 years and 4 months.

DYNASTY XXX.

OF THREE SEBENNYTE KINGS.

1. Nectanebus, 18 years.
2. Teos, 2 years.
3. Nectanebus, 18 years.

In all, 38 years.

DYNASTY XXXI.

OF THREE PERSIAN KINGS.

1. Ochus, in the 20th year of his reign in Persia, reigned (began to reign) in Egypt, 2 years.
2. Arses, 3 years.
3. Darius, 4 years.

The whole number of years in the third book is 1050. Thus far Manetho. The subsequent history is to be sought from Grecian writers.

ACCORDING TO EUSEBIUS.

DYNASTY XXIX.

OF FOUR MENDESIAN KINGS (REALLY FIVE).

1. Nepheritus, 6 years.
2. Achoris, 13 years.
3. Psammuthis, 1 year.
4. Muthes, 1 year.
5. Nepheritus, 4 months

In all, 21 years and 4 months.

DYNASTY XXX.

OF THREE SEBENNYTE KINGS.

1. Nectanebus, 10 years.
2. Teos, 2 years.
3. Nectanebus, 8 years.

In all, 20 years.

DYNASTY XXXI.

OF THREE PERSIAN KINGS.

1. Ochus, in the 20th year of his reign in Persia, took Egypt, and reigned 6 (2) years.
2. Arses, son of Ochus, 4 years.
3. Then Darius, 6 years, whom Alexander of Macedon slew.

These are the contents of the third book of Manetho. The subsequent history is related by Grecian writers.

Syncellus, pp. 55–78.

F.   Page 74.

THE OLD CHRONICLE.

This is one of the most important fragments relating to Egyptian archæology that have come down to us from antiquity. It is found in Syncellus, pp. 51, 52.

"Reign of the Gods according to the Old Chronicle.

"The time of Hephæstus is not given, as he appeared both night and day.

				Years.
Helius, the son of Hephæstus, reigned,				30,000
Then Kronos, and the other 12 gods, reigned				3,984
Then the 8 demigods,				217
After these, they enumerate 15 generations of the Cynic Cycle, in				443
Then the 16th dynasty of Tanites,		8 generations,		190
" 17th "	Memphites,	4	"	103
" 18th "	"	14	"	348
" 19th "	Diospolites,	5	"	194
" 20th "	"	8	"	228
" 21st "	Tanites,	6	"	121
" 22d "	"	3	"	48
" 23d "	Diospolites,	2	"	19
" 24th "	Saites,	3	"	44
" 25th "	Ethiopians,	3	"	44
" 26th "	Memphites,	7	"	177
" 27th "	Persians,	5	"	124
[" 28th "	Saite,	1	"	6]*

* Supplied from Manetho, according to Eusebius and Africanus. See Müller's Frag. Hist. Græc. vol. ii. p. 534.

	Years.
Then the 29th dynasty of Tanites,	39
Lastly, the 30th " Tanite, 1 generation,	15

In all, 30 dynasties, and 36,525 years.

"This number, resolved and divided into its parts, that is, 25 times 1461, shows the time of the restitution (ἀποκατάστασιν) of the zodiac, as fabled among the Egyptians and Greeks, which is its revolution from a particular point to the same again. This point is the first minute of the first degree of the equinoctial sign which they call the Ram, as is explained in the Genesis of Hermes, and the Cyraunian books."

G. Page 77.

ERATOSTHENES AND APOLLODORUS.

THE testimony of these two eminent writers is so important in Egyptian chronology, that a fuller exhibit should be made of the outlines of their system.

Eratosthenes' list of names is as follows: —

		Years.
1.	First reigned Menes, a Thenite (i. e., a Theban), who is called Aionios (Eternal),	62
2.	Athothis, son of Menes, surnamed Hermogenes,	59
3.	Athothis II.,	32
4.	Diabies, son of Athothis,	19
5.	Pemphos, son of Athothis, called Herakleides,	8
6.	Toigar, the Invincible, a Memphite monocheir, surnamed Tisandros, a giant,	79
7.	Stoichos, his son, called Ares, the Senseless,	6
8.	Gosormies, the Desire of All,	30
9.	Manes, his son, named Heliodorus (gift of the sun),	26

		Years.
10.	Anouphis, the Long-haired,	20
11.	Sirios, named the son of the eye,	18
12.	Chnoubos Gneuros, i. e., Chryses, son of Chryses,	22
13.	Rhanosis, the Supreme,	13
14.	Biuris,	10
15.	Saophis, the Long-haired, called by some the Money-getter,	29
16.	Saophis II.,	27
17.	Moscheres, Heliodotos (given by the sun),	31
18.	Mosthes,	33
19.	Pammes, Ruler of the Land,	38
20.	Apappus, Most Great,	100
21.	Echeskosokaras,	1
22.	Nitokris, a woman, surnamed Athene, the Victorious,	6
23.	Myrtæos Ammonodotos (given by Amun),	22
24.	Thuosimares, the Mighty, the Sun,	12
25.	Thinillos, who increased the power of his father,	8
26.	Semphroukrates, surnamed Hercules Arpocrates,	18
27.	Chouther Tauros, a tyrant,	7
28.	Meures, Philoskoros (Lover of the Eye),	12
29.	Chomaephtha, the World, loving Phtah,	11
30.	Soikunios, the Sharp, a tyrant,	60
31.	Peteathyres,	7 (?)
32.	Sistosis (?) (Palmer supplies Ammenemes I.),	42
33.	Ammenemes II.,	23
34	Sistosichermes, the Strength of Hercules,	55
35.	Mares,	43
36.	Siphoas, who is also Hermes, son of Phtah,	5
37.	Phrouron, or Nilos,	19
38.	Amunthantaios,	63
	Total,	1076

Several points here deserve attention. The first is the alleged commencement of the above list in the year of the world 2900 (ἥτις ἤρξατο μὲν τῷ β =) ἔτει τοῦ κόσμου). Bunsen and Lepsius assume that this date was added by Syncellus; but of this there is no proof. Syncellus' own date for the creation of the world is B. C. 5500, and his era of Menes is B. C. 2776, i. e., in the year A. M. 2724, 124 years earlier than that given in the list of Eratosthenes. The particularity of the date A. M. 2900 creates a strong probability that it was either given expressly by the latter, or derived from some other definite date, which was well known, possibly that of the conquest of Egypt by Cambyses, B. C. 525, or Artaxerxes Ochus, B. C. 341, from which it would be easy to reckon back to the beginning of the list. At any rate, it clearly was not a date given by Syncellus, and it can not be shown that it was not inserted by Eratosthenes himself. This computation places Menes at 638 years after the flood, according to the LXX.

The second point worthy of notice is the reason why Syncellus did not give the names of the fifty-three other kings mentioned by Apollodorus. Bunsen is quite severe upon him for the omission.

"The only natural explanation which suggested itself to us when making the inquiry, was that Syncellus lost his patience in epitomizing that list. With infinite pains he had toiled through the awkward Egyptian names it contained, and the Greek versions of them, which he did not understand. With infinite pains he had made his calculations of the year of the world which coincided with each of the thirty reigns; taking as his starting-point the nearest possible year after the flood, according to his system. In reference to the calculation of the Father of Chronology, he made the epoch from the confusion of tongues down to Abraham as long as he thought admissible, and now, when he had arrived at the end of 1076 years, he was obliged to admit that all his pains had been thrown away. . . . He gives way to his ill humor, throws the list into the fire, and can not refrain from exclaiming, ' Even those names are totally unmanageable; how much more these fifty-three!'" (Egypt's Place, etc., vol. ii. p. 456.)

This charge of " losing his temper," we pass over without more notice. But the cause of it deserves a further remark. Syncellus found the list " unmanageable," and so, " in ill humor," cast it aside when less than half transcribed. The German savant himself finds no little difficulty of the same kind, and finds it much easier to dispose of the fifty-three names that were not transcribed. These, " the hasty words " of Syncellus, " prove most decisively . . . were the kings of the middle empire, who reigned between the downfall of the old empire and the restoration, while the Hyksos had the supremacy, or at least possessed Lower Egypt and Memphis." This is a most remarkable assumption, and Bunsen acknowledges that Lepsius combats the position. The thirty-eight reigns came down to about B. C. 1525, according to Syncellus, bordering on the time of the restoration, as we understand Bunsen; and besides, the chronology of Eratosthenes evidently was, that the whole 91 (= 38 + 53) reigns of Theban kings covered the entire period from Menes till the time Egypt was conquered by Cambyses, about B. C. 526; at least, the eighty-six reigns of Egyptian kings, given by Syncellus, cover the whole of this period, commencing 124 years earlier.

Bunsen compares the names of the kings in this list

with those of Manetho, and of the thirty-eight he claims to find nineteen in the latter, which " are either identical with them, or so nearly so, that to any one moderately versed in the system of Egyptian royal nomenclature the actual or possible correspondence between the two sets will be at once apparent." (Vol. i. p. 124.)

It is true that the two first names, Menes and Athothis, and the twenty-second, Nitocris, are the same in each list. Three or four names are nearly the same, as Stammenemes for Ammenemes, Saophis for Suphis, and two or three others, have some resemblance; but to make Rammes to be the same as Thamphthis, Apappus as Phios, and Gosormies as Sesorthos, is making the " royal nomenclature " a very indefinite affair. A name may be made anything or nothing. Bunsen says, " The occasional discrepancy in the years of the reigns may be satisfactorily explained in various ways." Now, this " occasional discrepancy " is simply this: there is entire harmony in only *three* of the reigns he has identified; the discrepancy is almost universal.

The probability is, that some few of the names in the list of Eratosthenes are those of kings found in the list of Manetho; but still a great difficulty remains, which Bunsen has done little or nothing to remove.

H.

MANETHO ACCORDING TO JOSEPHUS.

"I SHALL begin with the writings of the Egyptians; not indeed of those that have written in the Egyptian language, which it is impossible for me to do. But Manetho was a man who was by birth an Egyptian; yet had he made himself master of the Greek learning, as is very evident; for he wrote the history of his own country in the Greek tongue, by translating it, as he saith himself, out of their sacred records; he also finds great fault with Herodotus for his ignorance and false relation of Egyptian affairs. Now, this Manetho, in the second book of his Egyptian history, writes concerning us in the following manner. I will set down his very words, as if I were to bring the man himself into a court for a witness.

"'There was a king of ours, whose name was Timaus. Under him it came to pass, I know not how, that God was averse to us; and there came, after a surprising manner, men of ignoble birth out of the eastern parts, and had boldness enough to make an expedition into our country, and with ease subdued it by force, yet without our hazarding a battle with them. So when they had gotten those that governed us under their power, they afterwards burnt down our cities, and demolished the temples of the gods, and used all the inhabitants after a most barbarous manner; nay, some they slew, and led their children and their wives into slavery. At length they made one of themselves king, whose name was *Salatis;* he also lived at Memphis, and made both the upper and lower regions pay tribute, and left garrisons in places that were the most proper for them. . . . When this man had reigned thirteen years, after him reigned another, whose name was *Beon,* for forty-four years; after him reigned another, called *Apachnas,* thirty-six years and seven months;

after him *Apophis* reigned sixty-one years, and then *Janias* fifty years and one month; after all these reigned *Assis* forty-nine years and two months. And these six were the first rulers among them, who were all along making war with the Egyptians, and were very desirous, gradually, to destroy them to the very roots. This whole nation was styled Hycsos, that is, *Shepherd-kings;* for the first syllable, Hyc, according to the sacred dialect, denotes a *king,* as is Sos a *shepherd* — but this according to the ordinary dialect; and of these is compounded Hycsos. But some say that these people were Arabians.' Now, in another copy it is said that this word does not denote *kings,* but, on the contrary, denotes *captive shepherds,* and this on account of the particle Hyc; for that Hyc, with the aspiration in the Egyptian tongue again, denotes *shepherds,* and that expressly also; and this, to me, seems the more probable opinion, and more agreeable to ancient history. [But Manetho goes on:] 'These people, whom we have before named *kings,* and called *shepherds* also, and their descendants,' as he says, ' kept possession of Egypt five hundred and eleven years.' After these he says, 'That the kings of Thebais, and of other parts of Egypt, made an insurrection against the Shepherds, and that a terrible and long war was made between them.' He says further: 'That under a king, whose name was *Alisphragmuthosis,* the Shepherds were subdued by him, and were indeed driven out of other parts of Egypt, but were shut up in a place that contained ten thousand acres; this place was named Avaris.' Manetho says, ' That the Shepherds built a wall round all this place, which was a large and strong wall, and this in order to keep all their possessions and their prey within a place of strength, but that *Thummosis,* the son of Alisphragmuthosis, made an attempt to take them by force and by siege, with four hundred and eighty thousand men to lie round about them; but that, upon his despair of taking the place by that siege, they came to a composition with them, that they should leave Egypt and go, without any harm to be done to them, whithersoever they would; and that after this composition was made, they went away, with their whole families and effects, not fewer in number than two hundred and forty thousand, and took their journey from Egypt through the wilderness for Syria; but that as they were in fear of the Assyrians, who had then the dominion over Asia, they built a city in that country which is now called Judea, and that large enough to contain this great number of men, and called it Jerusalem.' Now Manetho, in another book of his, says, 'That this nation thus called *Shepherds* were also called captives in their sacred books.' And this account of his is the truth; for feeding of sheep was the employment of our forefathers in the most ancient ages; and as they led such a wandering life in feeding sheep, they were called shepherds. Nor was it without reason that they were called *captives* by the Egyptians, since one of our ancestors, Joseph, told the king of Egypt that he was a captive, and afterward sent for his brethren into Egypt, by the king's permission; but as for these matters, I shall make a more exact inquiry about them elsewhere.

"But now I shall produce the Egyptians as witness to the antiquity of our nation. I shall therefore here bring in Manetho again, and what he writes as to the order of the times in this case; and thus he speaks: 'When this people, or Shepherds, were gone out of Egypt to Jerusalem, *Tethmosis*, the king of Egypt who drove them out, reigned afterward twenty-five years and four months, and then died; after him his son, *Chebron*, took the kingdom for thirteen years; after whom came *Amenophis*, for twenty years and seven months; then came his sister, *Amesses*, for twenty-one years and nine months; after her came *Mephres*, for twelve years and nine months; after her was *Mephramuthosis*, for twenty-five years and ten months; after him was *Tethmosis*, for nine years and eight months; after him came *Amenophis*, for thirty years and ten months; after him came *Orus*, for thirty-six years and five months; then came his daughter, *Acencheres*, for twelve years and one month; then was her brother, *Rathotis*, for nine years; then was *Acencheres*, for twelve years and five months; then came another *Acencheres*, for twelve years and three months; after him *Armais*, for four years and one month; after him was *Ramesses*, for one year and four months; after him came *Armesses Miammoun*, for sixty years and two months; after him *Amenophis*, for nineteen years and six months; after him came *Sethosis*, and *Ramesses*, who had an army of horse and a naval force. This king appointed his brother *Armais* to be his deputy over Egypt.' In another copy it stood thus: 'After him came *Sethosis* and *Ramesses*, two brethren, the former of whom had a naval force, and in a hostile manner destroyed those that met him upon the sea; but as he slew *Ramesses* in no long time afterward, so he appointed another of his brethren to be his deputy over Egypt. He also gave him all the authority of a king, but with these only injunctions, that he should not wear the diadem, nor be injurious to the queen, the mother of his children, and that he should not meddle with the other concubines of the king; while he made an expedition against Cyprus and Phœnicia, and beside against the Assyrians and the Medes. He then subdued them all, some by his arms, some without fighting, and some by the terror of his great army; and being puffed up by the great success he had had, he still went on the more boldly, and overthrew the cities and countries that lay in the eastern parts; but after some considerable time, *Armais*, who was left in Egypt, did all these very things, by the way of opposition, which his brother had forbidden him to do, without fear; for he used violence to the queen, and continued to make use of the rest of the concubines, without sparing any of them; nay, at the persuasion of his friends he put on the diadem, and set up to oppose his brother; but then he who was set over the priests of Egypt wrote letters to *Sethosis*, and informed him of all that had happened, and how his brother had set up to oppose him; he therefore returned back to Pelusim immediately, and recovered his kingdoms again. The country also was called from his name *Egypt*; for Manetho says that Sethosis himself was called Egyptus, as was his brother Armais called Danaus.'"

The language of the last paragraph gives rise to a doubt as to where the quotation from Manetho should close. We have placed the quotation marks as we find them in the translation of Whiston.

For the sake of convenience in comparing this list of Josephus with those of Africanus and Eusebius for the same period in history, we arrange the names in a concise tabular form: —

OF SHEPHERD KINGS.

	Years.	Months.
1. Salatis,	19	
2. Beon,	44	
3. Apachnas,	36	7
4. Apophis,	61	
5. Janias,	50	1
6. Assis,	49	2

KINGS OF TIJEBAIS, OR THOSE AFTER THE EXPULSION OF THE SHEPHERDS.

	Years.	Months.
1. Tethmosis,	25	4
2. Chebron,	13	
3. Amenophis,	20	7
4. Amesses, his sister,	21	9
5. Mephres,	12	9
6. Mephramuthosis,	25	10
7. Thmosis,	9	8
8. Amenophis,	30	10
9. Horus,	36	5
10. Acencheres, his daughter,	12	1
11. Rathotis, her brother,	9	
12. Acencheres,	12	5
13. Acencheres, another,	13	3

		Years.	Months.
14.	Armais,	4	1
15.	Ramesses,	1	4
16.	Armesses, son of Miammes,	66	2
17.	Amenophis,	19	6
19.	Sethosis, who is Ramesses.		

In comparing these names of Josephus with the corresponding ones of Africanus and Eusebius, the following points of resemblance and discrepancy appear: —

As to the Shepherd kings: Africanus has 81 names, whose reigns (allotting one half of the duration of the 17th dynasty to the Shepherds) covered 877 years; Eusebius gives 4 names, with a period of 103 years; and Josephus 6, with a period of 260 years, saying that the time the Shepherds dwelt in Egypt was 518 years.

Africanus assigns the 15th, 16th, and a part of the 17th dynasty to the Shepherds; Eusebius makes the 17th dynasty only to consist of Shepherd kings.

The 15th dynasty of Africanus, of 6 Shepherd kings, corresponds nearly with the 6 Shepherd kings of Josephus, three or four of the names being nearly alike, and the duration of five reigns being exactly the same, months excepted, the other reign differing by 25 years.

In view of these facts, we think we are warranted in drawing the following conclusion: —

The Manetho of Josephus is not the same person as the Manetho of Africanus and Eusebius; or if, as some suppose (e. g., Bunsen, as we understand him), Africanus made an epitome of the work from which Josephus quotes, or used one made by others before him (Eusebius only having before him the epitome of Africanus), this epitome was so imperfect and erroneous, or is so corrupt through carelessness or design, or both, that it is of little or no critical value, except in its later portions. But the supposition that the lists of Africanus and Eusebius are epitomized from the work which Josephus quotes, can not be sustained on critical grounds. The Jewish historian quotes *in extenso* a number of passages from a work of Manetho in three books, which he says the latter wrote in Greek, translating from the Egyptian language; his extracts are in good Greek, quoted, professedly, *verbatim;* he gives the duration of the reigns in years and months, stating the historical incidents connected with them in historical style. Now, in an epitome of such a work, should we not at least expect an essential correspondence in names (since the language is the same), and in the duration of the reigns, and in the principal historical incidents, that might be noticed? But what is the fact? Why, in regard to the so-called Shepherd kings, where Josephus gives six names, covering a period of 260 years, Africanus speaks of 81 kings, covering a period of about 877 years; of the six names which the latter gives of the Shepherds in his 15th dynasty, none are exactly the same as those of Josephus, three have a near resemblance, and three are almost entirely different, the duration of five of the reigns being exactly the same, the months excepted. The latter fact identifies historically the 15th dynasty of Africanus with the six kings mentioned by Josephus; while the discrepancy in the names, and the additional number of Shepherd kings which constitute his 16th and

17th dynasty, show that the list was not derived from the same work which Josephus quotes, but from other documents and records, which were perhaps but imperfectly understood. The same is true in regard to the succeeding seventeen names given by Josephus, which evidently make the 18th dynasty of Africanus; while some resemblance in names, and a correspondence in duration in reigns, identify the kings historically, yet the discrepancies clearly prove that the list of Africanus could not have been derived from the work which Josephus quotes, but from other sources, perhaps the original records from which that work was compiled, not perfectly understood. Different translators would transfer the same names in a different form; and in regard to such records as those of ancient Egypt, parts would be obscure, and naturally understood differently by different interpreters.

The supposition, then, which best harmonizes with all the known facts of the case, is, that the Manetho of Josephus is not the Manetho of Africanus and Eusebius; that the list of Africanus was derived from another work than that quoted by Josephus, perhaps the so-called Pseudo-Manetho, or some writer who undertook to rearrange the dynasties, and put forth his work under the name of the first leading writer of Egyptian history. He may have stated that his work was mainly compiled from that of the original Manetho, which statement has not been preserved.

I. Page 127.

CHINESE ASTRONOMY.

THE following, from the Shu-King, is the entire original passage on which is based the high claim for the Chinese of a knowledge of astronomy as early as the 24th century B. C. : —

"Thereupon Yaou commanded He and Ho, in reverent accordance with their observation of the wide heavens, to calculate and delineate the movements and appearances of the sun, the moon, the stars, and the zodiacal spaces, and so to deliver respectfully the same to the people.

"He separately commanded the second brother He to reside at Yu-e, in what was called the Bright Valley, and there respectfully to receive, as a guest, the rising sun, and to adjust and arrange the labors of the spring. 'The day,' he said, ' is of the medium length, and the star is in *Neaou*. You may thus exactly determine mid-spring. The people begin to disperse, and birds and beasts breed and copulate.'

"He further commanded the third brother He to reside at Neankeaou, and arrange the transformations of summer, and respectfully to observe the extreme limit of the shadow. 'The day,' said he, 'is at its longest, and the star is *Ho*; you may thus exactly determine mid-summer. The people are more dispersed; and the birds and beasts have their feathers and hair thin, and change their coats.'

"He separately commanded the second brother Ho to reside at the west, in what was called the Dark Valley, and there respectfully to convoy the setting sun, and to adjust and arrange the completing labors of the autumn. 'The night,' he said, 'is of the medium length, and the star is *Heu*; you may thus exactly determine mid-autumn. The people begin to feel at ease, and birds and beasts have their coats in good condition.'

"He further commanded the third brother Ho to reside in the northern region, in what was called the Sombre Capital, and there to adjust and examine the changes of the winter. 'The day,' said he, 'is at its shortest, and the star is *Maou;* thus you may exactly determine mid-winter. The people keep their cosy corners; and the coats of birds and beasts are downy and thick.'

"The emperor said, 'Ah, you! He and Ho, a round year consists of three hundred and sixty and six days. By means of an intercalary month do you fix the four seasons, and complete the determination of the year. Thereafter, in exact accordance with this regulating the various officers, all the works of the year will be fully performed." — *Chinese Classics*, vol. iii. part i. pp. 18-21.

"Now here are He and Ho. They have entirely subverted their virtue, and are sunk and lost in wine. They have violated the duties of their office, and left their posts. They have been the first to allow the regulations of heaven to get into disorder, putting far from them their proper business. On the first day of the last month of autumn, the sun and moon did not meet harmoniously in Fang. The blind musicians beat their drums; the inferior officers and common people bustled and ran about. He and Ho, however, as if they were mere personators of the dead in their offices, heard nothing and knew nothing — so stupidly went they astray from their duty in the matter of the heavenly appearances, and rendered themselves liable to the death appointed by former kings. The statutes of the government say, 'When they anticipate the time, let them be put to death without mercy; when they are behind the time, let them be put to death without mercy!'" — Id. p. 165.

J. Page 198.

SUPERFICIAL CHARACTER OF DIVERSITIES BETWEEN RACES.

The greatest physical difference between any two races is, of course, that which exists between the blacks and the whites, or rather between the Negro and the Caucasian. If this be not sufficient to constitute difference of species, it will be conceded that such difference does not exist. Upon this point the following statements are worthy to be considered: —

"The ablest living anatomist of Germany — Professor Tiedemann — has lately directed his researches with singular felicity to the vindication of the uncivilized man's capacity for improvement. In the works mentioned at the head of this article, and in the translation read at the Royal Society of London, of which the professor is a foreign member, that important question seems to be set at rest forever. The results of a most exact analysis of cases are thus stated by him: —

"'1. The brain of the negro is, upon the whole, quite as large as that of the European and other human races. The weight of the brain, its dimensions, and the capacity of the cavum cranii, prove this fact. Many anatomists have also incorrectly asserted that Europeans have a larger brain than negroes.

"'2. The nerves of the negro, relatively to the size of the brain, are not thicker than those of Europeans, as Soemmerring and his followers have said.

"'3. The outward form of the spinal cord, the medulla oblongata, the cerebellum, and cerebrum of the negro show no important difference from those of the European.

"'4. Nor does the inward structure — the order of the cortical and medullary substance — nor the inward organization of the negro brain show any difference from those of the European.

" ' 5. The negro brain does not resemble that of the orang-outang more than the European brain, except in the more symmetrical distribution of the gyri and sula. It is not even certain that this is always the case. We can not, therefore, coincide with the opinion of many naturalists, who say that the negro has more resemblance to apes than Europeans in reference to the brain and nervous system.' "

And after a minute survey of proofs respecting the intellectual faculties of the negro, Professor Tiedemann concludes in the following words : —

" The principal result of my researches on the brain of the negro is, that neither anatomy nor physiology can justify our placing them beneath Europeans in a moral or intellectual point of view." *

Another distinguished ethnologist, in defining a negro, says, —

" The negroes are referable to an extreme rather than a normal type; and so far are they from being co-extensive with the Africans, that it is almost exclusively along the valleys of rivers that they are to be found. There are none in the extratropical parts of Northern, none in the corresponding parts of Southern Africa, and but few on the table-lands of even the two sides of the equator. Their areas, indeed, are scanty and small. One lies on the Upper Nile, one on the Lower Gambia and Senegal, one on the Lower Niger, and the last along the western coast, where the smaller rivers that originate in the Kong Mountains form hot and moist alluvial tracts."

Again : —

" If the word negro mean the combination of woolly hair with a jetty black skin, depressed nose, thick lips, narrow forehead, acute facial angle, and prominent jaw, it applies to Africans as

* For. Quarterly Review, Oct., 1839.

widely different from each other as the Laplander is from the Samoeid and Eskimo, or the Englishman from the Finlander. It applies to the inhabitants of certain portions of different river-systems, *independent of relationship*, and *vice versa*. The negroes of Kordofan are nearer in descent to the Copts and Arabs than are the lighter-colored and civilized Fulahs. They are also nearer to the same than they are to the blacks of Senegambia. If this be the case, the term has no place in ethnology, except so far as its extensive use makes it hard to abandon. Its real application is to anthropology, wherein it means the effects of certain influences upon certain intertropical Africans, irrespective of descent, but not irrespective of physical condition. As truly as a short stature and light skin coincide with the occupancy of mountain ranges, the negro physiognomy coincides with that of the alluvia of rivers." *

Dr. Livingstone, the great African traveler, is a writer whose opinions few will dare to dispute. He says, —

"All the inhabitants of this region, as well as those of Londa, may be called true negroes, if the limitations formerly made be borne in mind. The dark color, thick lips, heads elongated backwards and upwards, and covered with wool, flat noses, with other negro peculiarities, are general; but while these characteristics place them in the true negro family, the reader would imbibe a wrong idea if he supposed that all these features combined are often met with in one individual. All have a certain thickness and prominence of lip, but many are met with in every village in whom thickness and prominence are not more marked than in Europeans. All are dark, but the color is shaded off in different individuals from deep black to light yellow. As we go westward, we observe the light color predominating over the dark; and then again, when we come within the influence of damp from the sea air, we find the shade deepen into the general blackness of the coast population. The shape of the head, with its woolly crop, though general, is not universal. The tribes on

* Latham, Man and his Migrations, p. 147.

the eastern side of the continent, as the Caffres, have heads finely developed, and strongly European. Instances of this kind are frequently seen, and after I became so familiar with the dark color as to forget it in viewing the countenance, I was struck by the strong resemblance some nations bore to certain of our own notabilities. The Bushmen and Hottentots are exceptions to these remarks, for both the shape of their heads and growth of wool are peculiar — the latter, for instance, springs from the scalp in tufts, with bare spaces between, and, when the crop is short, resembles a number of black pepper-corns stuck on the skin, and very unlike the thick, frizzly masses which cover the heads of the Balonda and Maravi. With every disposition to pay due deference to the opinions of those who have made ethnology their special study, I have felt myself unable to believe that the exaggerated features usually put forth as those of the typical negro characterize the majority of any nation of South Central Africa. The monuments of the ancient Egyptians seem to me to embody the ideal of the inhabitants of Londa better than the figures of any work of Ethnology I have met with." — *Livingstone's Researches in South Africa.* London ed., 1857, ch. xix. p. 378.

The following facts and opinions respecting the negro race are from the work of another recent African traveler.*

Having given a physical description of the negro, which would satisfy any negro-hater, the writer proceeds as follows: —

"Thus it has been proved by measurements, by microscopes, by analysis, that the typical negro is something between a child,

---

* "SAVAGE AFRICA: Being the Narrative of a Tour in Equatorial, South-western, and North-western Africa. . . . By Winwood Reade, Fellow of the Geographical and Anthropological Societies of London, and Corresponding Member of the Geographical Society of Paris. Second edition, London.

a dotard, and a beast. I can not struggle against these sacred facts of science; I can not venture to dispute the degradation of the negro. But I contend that it is only degradation; that it is the result of disease; that it is not characteristic of the African continent; and that it is confined to a small geographical area.
. . . But first I will remove the great stumbling-block of African ethnology. By defining the geography of the negro, I shall pave the way for the elucidation of that mystery which has perplexed the philosophers of all ages — the negro's place in nature.

"Those who deny that the negro type has been produced by natural causes, have alleged that there are two distinct races in Africa, — the red and the black, — and that they inhabit the same localities. The reader will bear in mind that a series of mountain terraces runs along the whole length of Western Africa, and that between them and the sea are low and malarious swamps. These mountains are inhabited by the true African — a red-skinned race. Nations of these, descending into the swamps, have become degraded in body and mind, and their type completely changed.

"The negro forms an exceptional race in Africa. He inhabits that immense tract of marshy land which lies between the mountains and the sea, from Senegal to Benguela, and the lowlands of the eastern side in the same manner. He is found in the parts about Lake Tchad, in Sennaar, along the marshy banks of rivers, and in several isolated spots besides. But he is not found in the vast tracts which are occupied by the Berbers on the north, and the Bitshuanas of the south. He is not found in the highlands of Ethiopia, nor in those of Soudan.

"In Africa there are three grand races, as there may be said to be three grand geological divisions.

"The Libyan stock inhabit the primitive and volcanic tracts. They have a tawny complexion, Caucasian features, and long black hair.

"On the sand-stones will be found an intermediate type.

They are darker than their parents; they have short and very curly hair; their lips are thick, and their nostrils wide at the base.

"And, finally, in the alluvia, one will find the negroes with a black skin, woolly hair, and prognathous development.

"I do not mean to assert that light-colored tribes are never found in the alluvia, and that true negroes can never be met with in the dry plateaus. There is in Africa a continual movement towards the west. It is, therefore, common enough to see Fulas and Mandingos inhabiting the lowlands of Senegambia; and the light-colored Fans are beginning to occupy the banks of the Gaboon. In the same manner, a tribe of negroes migrating across the continent from the east coast might be met with in a sandy desert of Central Africa.

"My assertion that the negro is as exceptional a race in Africa as the livid inhabitants of the Fens in England, or of the Pontine marshes in Italy, and that he inhabits, comparatively speaking, a small geographical area, will excite great surprise. There is a general delusion respecting the negro which is not difficult to explain. The whole western coast, and a great portion of the eastern coast, are inhabited by negroes. It is natural that travelers and coast residents should accept them as types of the races of the continent. The slaves that have been imported into the New World were almost exclusively brought from these regions; and I have always observed that slaves, even among negroes, present a lower type than that of the surrounding population. These also have been examined, and written upon by naturalists as true samples of the African." — pp. 509, 513.

In regard to the cause of color in man, a distinguished French savant * writes as follows: —

"When we seek for the cause of coloration in the human skin, an anatomical analysis presents particulars to which sufficient

---

* De l'Unité des Races Humaines. Par M. Ladevi Roche, Professeur Honoraire de Philosophie à la Faculté de Lettres de Bordeaux.

attention has not been given. In proceeding from the outside, we at first meet with that thin, light pellicle, transparent and colorless tissue, called the *epidermis;* and immediately below, the microscope reveals the colored matter called the *pigmentary body* (from the Latin *pigmentum,* painting), formed of a multitude of granules, and always presenting a yellow, red, or black tint, which is reflected by the transparency of the epidermis. They (the polygenists) have gone further: they have wished to descend even to the true skin of man, to the *dermis,* in which are the roots of the hair, . . . in the hope of finding there the efficient cause of coloration in the pigmentary matter. But, oh, surprise! The dermis, the true skin of man, which they thought to find black, yellow, red, or copper-colored, and, by these different shades, to justify the distinction and plurality of races, — the dermis, I say, turned and returned in every way, examined by the lens and the microscope, in the white, in the black, in the red, and in the yellow, constantly offers itself to the astonished eye with a *uniform* color of faded white, as soon as it is disengaged from the blood that covers it; and we have been forced to recognize — so evident was the fact — that the true skin of man — the two tissues which cover it being removed — was of the same complexion (*d'une teinte unicolorée*) in all men, and that, in this relation, no doubt can be entertained respecting the unity of the human races. Thus the variety of coloration depends solely on the presence of the pigmentary body. This body is a cellular network, of which each cell contains, under the form of granules, the coloring matter. It is very apparent in individuals who are black, red, olive, or tawny; it is less, and sometimes not at all, in those that are white; so that the first observers declared that in the white man there was no trace of it — that which creates a difference between the white race and the other three. And already, taking advantage of this peculiarity, the polygenists cry with an air of triumph (G. Pouchet, p. 74), 'Behold an appendage (*appareil*) which is wanting in the white man, which the negro possesses, and which he alone possesses! Behold a fundamental difference in the name of which we are able to proclaim the non-community of origin in the races!'

"Not so fast (*ne vous pressez pas tant*), Messieurs; you have nothing to proclaim. New researches, made with more care, by M. Flourens in France, and by M. Simon at Berlin, have discovered the *pigmentary* appendage even in the white. It is its presence which gives to the *areole mamelon* its brown color, and it is its appearance which, under the influence of the sun's rays, causes to appear blotches of red so frequent in men of a blond color. It has been found again by M. Flourens throughout the entire skin of a French soldier, who died in Algeria; which would lead one to think that men carry in them the germ of this appendage, and that different outward influences, among which it is necessary to reckon climate, provoke its development (Godron, vol. ii. p. 144.) . . . In the face of these facts, will the polygenists attempt to affirm that between the white and the black there is an impassable gulf?

"The *pigmentum*, or the coloring matter, which covers the surface of the *dermis*, and transmits its color to the *epidermis*, does not exist in the new-born infant, and commences to exist only some time after birth; it is asked, What is the cause of this? To this question several answers have been given. Some have said the formative cause is climate; others, that it is alimentary regime; others, that it is the hygrometric state of the air; others, that it is the excess of carbon, which the blood contains in very warm countries. This diversity of opinions in regard to the true formative agent of the pigmentary substance, proves that science is not yet settled on this point. But let us mark well that the indecision of science on this point does not weaken the certainty, (1.) of the existence of the pigmentary body; (2.) of the uniformity of color in the dermis; (3.) of the infinite variety of colors in each race; (4.) of the generation of the white by the black and the black by the white; and as all these facts concur to demonstrate the unity of the human races, we see that this unity is altogether independent of the different explications proposed, and not yet recognized as true, of the formation of the coloring matter."

Again : —

"They have desired to make the *hair* of the negro a characteristic of the race, saying that they alone have crisped or woolly hair. But they have forgotten to tell us that negroes offer in this, as in all other respects, the greatest variety. There are some with straight, smooth hair, others who have it curled, and others still who have long hair descending to the shoulders. In all cases, where the hair is crispy, it is never woolly. The hair, it is true, presents the appearance of wool, because it combines with it a kind of thick oil, soft to the touch; but its anatomical conformation is different. The filaments of a fleece present small asperities, which permit them to *felt*, that is to say, to be entangled in such a manner as to form a tissue. Their free ends are thicker than the other * — a property that is never met with in the hair of the negro, from which neither cloth, nor anything resembling woolen stuff, can be made. L. Remusat, *Revue de Deux Mondes*, May, 1854."

K. Page 202.

VARIATIONS IN SPECIES AMONG DOMESTIC ANIMALS.

And here I need only allude to a few prominent facts.

1. Swine.

Naturalists are generally agreed that all varieties of swine are descended from the wild boar; † and yet what a

---

* Leur bord libre est plus épais que leur autre extrémité.

† "The hog descends from the common boar, now found wild over the whole temperate zone in the Old World." (Agassiz, in

great variety of races are now known to exist! When transported into different climates, e. g., into South America, the change is sometimes very great. "Some have acquired erect ears, vaulted foreheads, and heads much larger than were found in the original breed. With some the color becomes black, and with others the skin acquires a thick fur, beneath which is a species of wool. Some, again, are red; others have solid hoofs. One breed is found, in Quebaya, with toes half a span long, white ears, pendent belly, and long tusks, crooked like the horns of oxen."

There is a variety of swine in Hungary with solid hoofs, and a breed with the same peculiar characteristics has appeared in the Red River country, in the United States. The difference in the form of the crania of the varieties of swine — especially of the wild and the tame — is greater than is found among the most dissimilar of the human races, e. g., the Negro and the Caucasian.

2. Sheep.

Very marked varieties have sprung up among sheep. And here we need not feel embarrassed in our argument by the fact that it has been, and still is, disputed what was the origin of the sheep;* whether the different varieties sprang from one or a number of primitive distinct species. All we have to do is to consider a few marked cases of a

---

a " Sketch of Natural World, and their Relation to the different Types of Men," published " Types of Mankind," p. lxvii.

* In regard to the single or plural origin of the species of our domestic animals in general, the following opinion of Quatrefages is of great weight: "These examples will suffice to show

change of type in the same stock when subjected to different climatic influences. It is well known that sheep were not found on the western continent till after its discovery in the latter part of the 15th century; hence the cases of marked change in the same stock are perfectly authentic.

"Among those introduced into South America, a hairy breed has sprung up. A breed has been found with monstrous tails; others are found with projecting lips and pendent ears." *

"Several accounts have been published of the change which sheep from Europe undergo in the West Indies. Dr. Nicholson, of Antigua, informs me that, after the third generation, the wool disappears from the whole body, except over the loins; and the animals then appear like a goat with a dirty door-mat on its back. A similar change is said to take place on the west coast of Africa." †

"In some few instances new breeds have suddenly originated. Thus, in 1791, a ram lamb was born in Massachusetts having short crooked legs, and a long back, like a turn-spit dog. From this one lamb the *otter* or *ancon* semi-monstrous breed was raised. As these sheep could not leap over fences, it was thought they would be valuable; but they have been supplanted by merinos, and thus exterminated." ‡ They would breed truly, always

that the profound study of our domestic races always leads more and more to attach to the same species all those which bear the same name, however different they may be." — *Quatrefages, Unité de l'Espèce Humaine*, p. 107.

* Brace, Races of the Old World, p. 455, referring to De Salles.

† Darwin, Variations of Animals and Plants, vol. i. p. 124, who refers to his numerous authorities for these and other facts.

‡ Ibid, p. 126. The same fact is noticed by Cabell (p. 37), Quatrefages and other writers. It is an undoubted case of a new breed or variety springing up from a well-known stock, and hence, in its analogical bearings, is of great importance.

producing *ancon* offspring. "When crossed with other breeds, the offspring, with rare exceptions, instead of being intermediate, perfectly resembled either parent."

"A more interesting case has been recorded in the report of the juries of the great exhibition (1851), namely, the production of a merino ram lamb in 1828, which was remarkable for its long, smooth, straight, and silky wool." *

"The sheep of Yemen introduced into Egypt have acquired a straight, rude hair, with a fine down at its roots. Some of the merino sheep are covered with wool, and others with hair, quite differing in structure; and sometimes the same individual, under new circumstances, shows the changes from wool to hair." †

3. CATTLE.

Darwin remarks, —

"That many breeds of cattle have originated through variation, independently of descent from distinct species, we may infer from what we see in South America, where the genus Bos was not endemic, and where the cattle, which now exist in such vast numbers, are the descendants of a few imported from Spain and Portugal. In Colombia, Roulin describes two peculiar breeds, namely, *pelones*, with extremely thin and fine hair, and *calongos*, absolutely naked. . . . In Paraguay, Azara describes a breed which certainly originated in South America, called *chivos*, 'because they have straight, vertical horns, conical, and very large at the base.' He likewise describes a dwarf race in Corrientes, with short horns; and others, with reversed hair, have also originated in Paraguay."

Darwin then mentions a "*monstrous breed*, called niatas, or natas," two small herds of which he saw on the banks of the Plata. "This breed," he says, "bears the same

---

* Darwin, Variations, etc., vol. i. p. 120.
† Brace, Races of the Old World, p. 455.

relation to other breeds as bull or pug dogs do to other dogs, or as improved pigs, according to Nathusius, do to other pigs. Rütimeyer believes that these cattle belong to the primogenius type. The forehead is very short and broad, with the nasal end of the skull, together with the whole plane of the upper molar teeth, curved upward. The lower jaw projects beyond the upper, and has a corresponding upward curvature. . . . The upper lip is widely open, the eyes project outward, and the horns are large. In walking, the head is carried low, and the neck is short. The hind legs appear to be larger, compared with the front legs, than is usual. The exposed incisor teeth, the short head and upturned nostrils, give these cattle the most ludicrous, self-confident air of defiance." *

Dr. Bachman,† having quoted Darwin's account of this variety, makes the following pertinent remarks: —

"We have here another example in evidence of the fact that, without the slightest intermixture of foreign varieties, new breeds of cattle spring up in America. They made their first appearance about eighty years ago, when one was occasionally brought to Buenos Ayres. Now they have become the only race in an immense region of country where they are nearly wild. What causes have operated to produce this variety? There are no wild animals, not even the buffalo, in that country, from which any admixture could by any possibility have been derived. Were we not positive of their origin, they would unquestionably be regarded as a new species."

These facts, related by naturalists, — many more similar ones might be cited, — are sufficient for our purpose.

* Darwin, Variations of Animals and Plants, i. p. 113.
† Unity of the Human Race, p. 305–6.

But without resorting to extreme cases for illustrations, it would be perfectly legitimate to refer to the common varieties of cattle found in any country, — e. g., England, — the "Durhams," the "Herefords," the "Highland cattle," the "Alderneys," the "Short Horns," the "Long Horns," etc., etc.; for we find varieties arising in the same stock * as marked and apparently distinct as are found in the human race. There are cattle without horns, with one horn, with short horns, with long horns,† with straight horns, and crooked horns, with pendent horns and vertical horns, and of all possible colors; with long legs, and short legs; with crania wide and short, and long and narrow; — exhibiting among themselves a far greater difference than is seen among the crania of the most dissimilar of the human races.

4. Horses.

The following is from Darwin: —

"Whether the whole amount of difference between the various breeds be due to variation, is doubtful. From the fertility of the most distinct breeds when crossed, naturalists have generally looked at all breeds as having descended from a single species. Few will agree with Colonel H. Smith, who believes that they have descended from no less than five primitive and differently colored stocks. But as several species and varieties of the horse existed during the later tertiary periods, and, as Rütimeyer

---

* There are enumerated "19 British breeds" of cattle, and "in the most recent work on cattle, engravings are given of 55 European breeds." (Moll and Gayot, "La Connaissance Gen. du Bœuf," Paris, 1860; Darwin, Variations, etc., vol. i. p. 103.)

† Darwin mentions a specimen 8 feet 8¼ inches from tip to tip, and 13 feet 5 inches as measured on the curve. — *Variations*, etc., vol. i. p. 110.

found differences in the size and form of the skull in the earliest known domesticated horses, we ought not to feel sure that all our breeds have descended from a single species." *

But, admitting the opinion of Colonel Hamilton Smith as correct, — it is only an opinion, — the facts furnished by Darwin himself, in regard to modifications in the same breed from change of climate and other influences, prove that the varieties in mankind may be accounted for without resort to the supposition of a plural origin.

"There can be no doubt," says Darwin, "that horses become greatly reduced in size, and altered in appearance, by living on mountains and islands. . . . There were, or still are, on some of the islands on the coast of Virginia, ponies like those of the Shetland Islands, which are believed to have originated through exposure to unfavorable conditions. The Puno ponies, which inhabit the lofty regions of the Cordilleras, are, as I hear from Mr. D. Forbes, strange little creatures, very unlike their Spanish progenitors." †

"The horses, according to M. Roulin, transported to South America, have formed a race with fur instead of hair, and have changed to an almost uniform bay color." ‡

5. Dogs.

The varieties found among dogs are probably greater and more marked than are known to exist in any other species of animals. There is the St. Bernard dog of the Alps and Mont Blanc, the Newfoundland dog, the bull dog, the "twelve kinds of greyhounds," § and all the way down through the spaniels, terriers, turnspits, pugs, etc.,

* Variations, etc., vol. i. p. 68.
† Ibid., vol. i. p. 69. ‡ Brace, p. 457.
§ Youatt, quoted by Darwin (Variations, etc., p. 49).

to the lap-dog, — all forming an immense variety, in which Cuvier admits " that in form the differences are greater than those of any wild species of any natural genus." — *Darwin, Var.*, etc., p. 49.

We might admit all that any naturalist has imagined — no one has proved anything — in regard to a plural origin of the varieties of dogs, e. g., that they are derived from three, four, five, or six primordial stocks, as the *wolf*, the *jackal*, the *anthus*, the *dingo*, the *d'hole*, or *thus*, etc., etc., to the number of some six or seven.* For Darwin (Variations, etc., i. p. 48) well remarks, " But we can not explain by crossing the origin of such extreme forms as thorough-bred greyhounds, bloodhounds, bull dogs, Blenheim spaniels, terriers, pugs, &c., unless we believe that forms equally or more strongly characterized in these different respects once existed in nature. But hardly any one has been bold enough to suppose that such unnatural forms ever did or could exist in a wild state."

The obvious truth of these remarks makes the illustrations drawn from the varieties of dogs perfectly conclusive.

6. Fowls.

I must not omit to mention the great and marked varie-

---

* As Colonel Hamilton Smith, cited by Dr. Bachman, " Unity, &c.," p. 61, from Dr. Morton.

But the writer of the article *Man*, in the Cyclopædia of Natural History, states, " No one . . . will be inclined to deny that the varieties of dogs (which, according to Professor Owen, are undoubtedly of one species) present far greater differences in form and color, and in some parts of their habits and instincts, than any that are observed in man." — p. 667.

ties that are found among our domestic barn-yard fowls — the more especially since there seems to be little if any doubt that all of them are descended from a single original stock.* And yet how great the difference among the numerous breeds. Darwin enumerates thirteen distinct breeds, and a number of sub-breeds, among which we have the " diminutive elegant Bantam, the heavy Cochin (Shanghai), with its many peculiarities, and the Polish fowl, with its great top-knot and protuberant skull," the Dorking, with an additional toe, etc. There are rumpless fowls and tailless fowls; single-crested and double-crested, and those without crests; frizzled fowls, and silk fowls, and sooty fowls; creepers, or jumpers, with legs so short " that they move by jumping rather than by walking " (Darwin); and those with legs so long that they can feed from the top of a barrel; and with plumage of all varieties of colors — black, white, yellow, mottled, mixed, etc., etc. The time and place of the origin of some of these breeds are well known, and the single origin of the whole not doubted, or scarcely so, by naturalists generally. The analogical argument from the great varieties among domestic fowls is well nigh conclusive in favor of the single origin of all the varieties of mankind; i. e., it completely sets aside the main argument for a plural origin,

---

* " Most naturalists, with the exception of Temminck, believe that all the breeds have proceeded from a single species." (Darwin. Variations, etc., vol. i. p. 280.) This author does not think that the evidence of the single origin of all the breeds of domestic fowls from a single original species is so conclusive as that for the single origin of the pigeon. But he seems to have little or no doubt of the single origin. That original stock was the *Galla Bankiva*.

which is based on variety of color and some differences in physical structure among men.

7. Pigeons.

I will allude to only one more case of great variation among the lower animals for illustration — that of the domestic pigeon; and these illustrations are the more valuable "because the evidence that all the domestic races have descended from one known source is far clearer than with any other anciently domestic animal," . . . and because "from causes which we can partly understand, the amount of variation has been extraordinarily great." *

The original species, as Darwin thinks, is the wild rock pigeon (*Columba livia*). Some authors describe 150 kinds. — *Darwin, Var.*, etc., i. 164.

"I have no doubt," says Darwin, "that there exist considerably above 150 kinds, which breed true, and have been separately named. — *Variations*, etc., i. 165.

Detail is here unnecessary. It is sufficient merely to name a few of the varieties described by Darwin, and other authors — as the *pouter*, the *carrier*, the *runt*, the *barb*, the *fantail*, the African *owl*, the *short-faced tumbler*, the *Indian frill back*, the *trumpeter*, etc. The osteological variations are great; for examples of extremes in the form of the beak and skull, compare the *short-faced*

---

* Darwin, Variations, etc., vol. i. p. 163. A few lines after, Darwin says, "Notwithstanding the clear evidence that all the breeds are the descendants of a single species, I could not persuade myself, until some years had passed, that the whole amount of difference between them had arisen since man first domesticated the wild rock pigeon."

tumbler with the *English carrier*. The variations in the forms of the skull are far greater than are exhibited in the most dissimilar varieties of the human race.

The argument for the unity of the human race, based on analogy from the lower animals, is attempted to be set aside by the allegation that it is only among *domestic animals* that these variations take place. It is *domestication* that produces the change. Man is not a domestic animal; therefore the analogy fails.* Now, what are the facts in the case? Why, simply these: Man is a cosmopolite; his constitution — mental and physical — is such that he can go everywhere, and live in every climate, and in the most diverse conditions. Under the influence of these various climatic conditions of heat and cold, of modes of living, etc., etc., changes take place, and he assumes the various physical types which exist. But he takes the so-called domestic animals with him, which, in the various changed conditions, in the same manner become changed, and assume the various types which we see. This is all. The analogy is perfect. Writers seem to think that domestication is a *power in itself* to produce change of type. Whereas the simple truth is, the animals following man necessarily, in the same manner with him, come under the influence of the various climates, conditions, habits of living, etc., etc., and the result is change of type. The reason why wild animals generally preserve such a uniformity of type is because they have a comparatively

* Pouchet, Plurality of the Human Race, pp. 83, 84. And so with polygenists generally.

limited range. There are a few, however, as the wolf, the bear, and some others, which have a wider range, and consequently exhibit greater varieties. The principle here stated, and the facts dependent upon it, have not, as I think, received a proper attention from naturalists.

L. Page 280.

VISIT OF DIONUSOS TO INDIA.

DIODORUS, in his brief account of India, relates some traditions of the Indians in regard to the expedition of Dionusos to their country. The following extract is of particular importance, as showing that Mt. Meru was the traditional Ararat of the Mosaic narrative, it being kept in mind that Dionusos (the same as Bacchus of the Romans, and Osiris of the Egyptians) was the traditional Noah. Of this there is no room for a reasonable doubt. Diodorus (i. 13) says distinctly that *Osiris* means *Dionusos*, as do others; and the accounts that are given of this deity, as elsewhere stated, leave no room to doubt that he is Noah deified.

"And here it is proper to relate what the most learned among the Indians say respecting these things.

"They say that when the people still dwelt in villages, Dionusos came from the west with a powerful army, passing through all India, there being no city that could resist his power; that on account of the great heat, his army began to perish with a pestilential disease; but he, as a skillful commander, withdrew his army from the plains to the mountainous regions. There, from the influence of the cool breezes and pure water flowing from the fountains, the plague was stayed. The place where Dionusos thus saved his army from the plague was called *Meros*. Hence the Greeks have a tradition respecting Dionusos, that he was nourished in the thigh (μηρὸς).* In addition to these things, he imparted to the Indians a knowledge of the cultivation of fruits, and gave them the invention of the wine, and other things useful to life. He founded cities and villages in healthy places, taught the people to worship the gods, and gave them laws. He established justice among them, and by his favors merited the appellation of a deity, and obtained divine honors. They add that a great number of women accompanied his army, . . . and that at last he died an old man, having reigned over all India fifty-two years." (Diod. ii. xxvii.)

M. Page 280.

CHINESE THEOLOGY.

The following extracts from an able article, entitled "The Chinese on the Plains of Shinar, or a Connection established between the Chinese and all other Nations, through their Theology," by the Rev. T. M'Clatchie, M. A., missionary to the Chinese from the Church Mis-

---

* "Zeus, or, according to others, Hermes (Apollon. Rhod. iv. 1137), saved the child (Dionusos) from the flames. It was sewed up in the thigh of Zeus, and thus came to maturity." — *Smith's Dict.*, article *Dionusos*, p. 1046.)

The coincidence in, or rather the sameness of, the name of the place where Dionusos saved his army, with that of the famous sacred mountain of the Hindus, *Meru*, is truly remarkable.

sionary Society,* are directly to my purpose, as connecting the Chinese in their origin with other nations, especially with the Hindus.

In his prefatory remarks, the author makes the two following general declarations: "1. The chief god of every pagan system, without exception, is designated 'Mind' (Νοῦς, or Mens); 2. This chief god, whose body is the universe, *triplicates*, and also divides into *eight* portions in each system." — p. 369.

He then gives numerous extracts from various Chinese writers, and the Greek and Roman classics, showing the resemblances between the theology of the Chinese and that of other nations. These resemblances are perhaps sometimes a little fanciful, while they are often striking and convincing, especially in reference to the *Triads* and *Ogdoads*. And in the doctrine of Shang-ti, — Deity, the Soul of the World, and Mind, — there is a remarkable identity with the pantheism of the Hindus and more western nations of antiquity. The author claims for the outlines of these doctrines a common origin on the plain of Shinar, before the ancestors of these nations separated from each other, after the confusion of tongues.

The following sentences indicate remarkable coincidences: —

"The first man was Pwan-kou. . . .

"Thus we have in this family of the first man (Pwan-kou, and his hermaphrodite successors) in reality eight persons, viz., Pwan-kou, or Shang-ti, or *Mind*, the Great Father, his wife, three sons, and their three wives; and these eight individuals issue

* In the Journal of the Royal As. Soc. of Great Britain and Ireland, vol. xvi. pp. 368–435.)

forth from chaos, or the *ovum mundi*, and correspond to the prominent characters in the family of Adam.

"Shang-ti is also Fuh-hi.

"It is plain, from what has been already stated, that the first man in his human form is in reality but a *reappearance* of a former first man, viz., animated Chaos; and between these two individuals intervenes a universal deluge, from which the second first man (if I may so designate him) escapes. Now, this first man, who escapes the deluge, and reappears at the commencement of each new world, is Fuh-hi, e. g. : —

"'Fuh-hi is the first (who appears) at each opening and spreading out (of the universe.)' — *Sing-le*, etc., xxvi. 19.)"

"This Fuh-hi, who is but a reappearance of Pwan-kou, or Adam, escapes from the deluge with *seven companions*, and hence, in this material system of the universe, is not only divided into three, but also into eight.

"Here we have a family of eight persons, who issue from the sacred circle, viz., Shang-ti, or Fuh-hi, his wife, and their six children. These 'six children' we find, on reference to the Yih-king, vol. xii. chap. xvii. p. 18, are three sons and three daughters; and these brothers, uniting in marriage with their three sisters, complete the universe.

"In this Fuh-hi and his family, then, we have the prominent characters in Noah's family, who escaped from a general deluge, which destroyed the rest of the human race.

"By the constant succession of similar worlds, the two periods of the world's history, viz., Chaos (or creation) and the deluge are blended together, and consequently the families of Pwan-kou (or Adam) and Fuh-hi (or Noah) are also blended together, the latter being merely a reappearance of the former. . . . (ii. 9.)

"As the deluge occupies so prominent a position in Chinese cosmogony, the first man, or Shang-ti, is rather Fuh-hi than Pwan-kou; yet it is plain that the former is only a reappearance of the latter, or, in other words, the Chinese classical Shang-ti is the same being as the 'Great Father,' worshiped by the whole pagan world, under the different designations of Jupiter, Baal, Osiris, Brahm, &c., *Adam reappearing in Noah.*

"The above system of theology will be found, on examination, to correspond with remarkable accuracy to the general system adopted by the subjects of Nimrod's kingdom before their dispersion, and which was afterward carried by them into the various countries where they settled.

"The Yih-king is the Chinese authority on cosmogony, and the doctrines of the Chinese philosophers are derived from this source. The doctrine of the endless succession of worlds, as drawn from ancient classics, by Choo-foo-tsze (ii. 1), has striking points of resemblance to that taught by the Stoics. Choo-tsye attributes the destruction of each universe to *the degeneracy of the human race*, and also states that each return to chaos is caused by *a general deluge.*

"These rounds of nature are designated 'Great Revolutions,' or 'Years' of the world. The circle in which the universe is supposed to revolve is divided into twelve portions."— pp. 404, 405.

"Each complete revolution of this circle is called a Yuen, and each subdivision a *Hwuy*. A Hwuy is generally supposed to consist of 10,800 years. On this point, however, philosophers differ. In the first Hwuy, which answers to the Fuh diagram of the Yih-king, Heaven (Shang-ti) emerges from the ovum mundi, or chaos; in the second, Earth; in the third, Man — each world commencing with this triad. The deluge prevails during the twelfth and last Hwuy,— that is, the ninth period from the formation of the first man,*— and on the return to the first.

---

* Or the *tenth*, including the period of the first man. Noah was the tenth generation from the first, or Adam; and can there be a reasonable doubt but that the name mentioned in the next sentence of the inventor of the cycle of sixty is that of the patriarch of the Hebrew Scriptures? Let it be noted how the word *Yuen* resembles the Greek *Αἰων*, to which it corresponds in meaning.

Hwuy, the universe is again generated from chaos, as before. The cycle, which is formed by the combination of this circle with another of ten divisions, is said to have been invented by 'Naou the Great,' after the deluge. — See *Kae-peih-yeu-e*, vol. i. pp. 1, 2; also *Kang-keen*, etc., p. 11."

N. Page 324.

THE CELTS IN EUROPE.

The following remarks of the translator of Dr. Keller's work are worthy of notice: —

"With respect to the name and ethnographical determination of the people who lived partly in lake dwellings and partly on the main land, and who at first made use of stone implements, and consequently are considered as aborigines, any one who has a fancy may object to their having any relationship with the Celtic element, and attribute to them a Finnish or Iberian origin, or connect them with the race of men discovered by Boucher de Perthes. Thus far it is certain that they do not differ in the smallest degree, either in their abilities, their manner of life, or their industrial attainments, from the people who were provided with metals, but that in the whole phenomena of lake dwellings, from their very beginning to the end of their existence, a gradual, quiet, peaceful development may be observed.

"From what has been said, it appears certain that there is no foundation for the hypothesis that the inhabitants of the lake dwellings are to be separated into distinct races, because, in the earliest times, they had no metal instruments, and in later times they possessed them. Nothing can be more true than the remark of Lindenschmidt respecting such suppositions as to the change of nationalities, based simply on a difference in implements. 'The simple exchange of material,' he says, ' the transition from the use of stone to that of metal, is in itself not a sufficient ground for inferring a change of population. It is not so important as the change of the spear to fire-arms, and if, at every advance of this kind, an entire change of population were to be supposed, the history of civilization would only have to relate the migrations of nations.' *

"With respect to the immigration of the Celts into Europe, this event belongs to the primitive history of the peopling of our part of the world, and is shrouded in impenetrable darkness. No tradition speaks of the Celts pressing forward toward the countries in the possession of which we subsequently find them; though the Druids, on the other hand, taught that the Gauls were aborigines. At the very first appearance of historical narrative,† they appear in the far west of the Iberian peninsula, and afterward as the first among the great northern nations which pressed forward eastward from their homes in the west." — p. 398.

* Lindenschmidt, Die Vaterländischen Alterthumer, p. 159.
† Herodotus, iii. 33; iv. 49.

INDEX.

Abraham, date of, 25.
Aborigines, 152; of Egypt, 158; of India, 163; of Western Europe, 166, 320.
Abu-Mâshar, 45.
Abydenus. 92.
Abydos, 92.
Adamite race 154.
Ætna, lava of, 313.
Africanus, 54, 68, 77, 78.
Agassiz, his views, 172; discussion with Bachman and Smyth, 172; his Natural Provinces, 173, 175, 183; on unity of species, 177; estimate of his theory, 179; plural origin of man exceptional, 205.
Agglutinative languages, 222.
Alpa Camasca, 240.
American Fauna, peculiar, 204.
Amiot, 123, 124.
Anamim, 160.
Anianus, 55, 96.
Antediluvian generations, 33; myth of, 277.
Antesemitic period, 156.
Antiquities of Egypt, 49.
Apamea, 249.
Apollodorus, 55, 74; Bunsen's testimony of, 75.
Arabic languages, 217.
Aram, 171.
Aramaic languages, 217.
Ark, myths of the, 281.
Armenian version of Eusebius, 69.
Arphaxad, 147.
Aryan languages, 215.
Ashkenaz, 148.
Asiatic Society at Calcutta, 213.
Astronomical inscriptions in Egypt, 61.

Astronomy of the Chinese, 130.
Asshur, Assyrians, 146.
Augustus, name on the zodiacs, 64.
Autochthons, 153.
Avataras, 254.

Bachman's discussion with Agassiz, 172; his doctrine of unity, 184, 187; on monumental figures of animals, 200; on the single origin of species, 204.
Beaumont, de, on Somme valley, 317.
Berosus, 92, 94.
Biot, M., 66.
Birch, Dr. S., 57.
Boëckh, 71; his chronological system, 25.
Bone fossil near Natchez, 293.
Book of the dead, 57.
Bopp's comparative grammar, 214.
Borings in the Nile valley, 287.
Brahma, legend of, 241.
Brasen-nose College 265.
Brick in Nile valley, 288, 293.
Brugsch's chronology, 66. 71.
Bryant on mythology, 266.
Bundehesh, the book, 245.
Bunsen's chronology 24; his sneer, 59; identifies one hundred and ten Egyptian kings, 79.

Cabiri, myths of the, 283.
Cain and his wife, 171, 180.
Cainan, 35, 44.
Calepin of Egypt, 67.
Calippus, period of, 134.
Callisthenes, 92, 101.
Canaan, 151.
Canon of Ptolemy, 40.

INDEX.

Caphtorim, 151, 160.
Casluhim, 160.
Castes in India, 242.
Castor, 55.
Chaldean chronology, 91; tradition of the deluge, 250.
Chalmers on Chinese astronomy, 130.
Champollion, 64.
Changes in races, 195; in languages, 229.
Charles X., 63.
Chinese astronomy, 130; characters, 131; chronology, 120, 133; language, 220; traditions of the flood, 252; year, 126.
Chronology of the Scriptures, 31; of antediluvian generations, 33; from flood to Abraham, 34; Abraham to exodus, 35; exodus to the temple, 36; temple to birth of Christ, 40.
Chronology of Chaldeans, 91; of Chinese, 120; of Egyptians, 48; of Greece and Rome, 85.
Chronological systems, 24; of Bunsen, 24; of Boëckh, 25; of Rodier, 27.
Cimbri, Cimmerians, 148.
Claims of modern science, 23.
Clemens Alexandrinus, 50.
Clinton on O. T. chronology, 37.
Comparison of Hebrew and Septuagint, 23.
Confucius, author of Shu-king, 137.
Confusion of tongues, 224.
Copts, 151, 160.
Coxcox, legend of, 246.
Creation, date of, 25; myths of, 275.
Curse of Ham, 174.
Cush and his family, 150.
Cycle of sixty years, 122, 126, 129.
Cynocephali, myth of the, 269.

Dana, on unity of species, 186; on hybrids, 187; definition of species, 193; single origin of species, 203.
Dasyas, 164.
Date of creation, 25, 44; of the flood, 25; of Menes, 25, 26; of Abraham, 25; of the exodus, 25; of earliest monumental record, 40.
Dates, Egyptian chronology without, 67.
Deluge, traditions of, 246, Mexican and Peruvian, 246; of Ogyges, 247; of Deucalion, 248; myths of, 279.
Demetrius Phalereus, 46.
Demetrius Soter, 46.
Demigods, reign of, 60.
Denderah, zodiac of, 61.
Deucalion and Pyrrha, 249.
Diodorus Siculus, 50, 51, 52.
Diogenes Laertius, 52.
Discrepancies in Egyptian annals, 56.
Diversities in races superficial, 183.
Dodanim, 149.
Domestic animals, changes in, 202.
Dove, myths of the, 282.
Duns, on the growth of peat, 313.
Dupuis, 65.
Dynasties of Egypt, 69.
Dynasties, contemporaneous, 82.
Dyacks, traditions of creation, 240.

Earlier and later departures from the primitive seats, 155.
Egyptian history, 48; books, 50; aborigines, 158; language, 161; tradition of flood, 253.
Egyptians, physical features of, 150.
Elam, Elamites, 146.
Elishah, 149.
Era of the Trojan war, 88.
Eratosthenes, 74; director of Alexandrian library, 75; Bunsen's testimony of, 75; his date of Trojan war, 88.
Ethnology, argument from, 144.
Ethiopian can change his skin, 199.
Eudoxus, 58.
Eupolemus, 46.
Eusebius, 53, 59, 68, 78.
Exodus, date of, 25, 36.

Feridun and his sons, 284.
Flint implements, 304, 315.
Forgery of early annals, 61.

Fossil bone near Natchez, 203; skeleton near New Orleans, 295; skeleton on Florida coast, 300.
Fossils in valley of the Somme, 301; not contemporaneous, 304.
Fuh-hi, 122.

Garden of Eden, tradition of, 243.
Gaubil, 119.
Gayatri, 111.
Genesis consistent with geology, 20; tenth chapter of, 145.
Geology, argument from, 286.
Greek and Roman chronology, 85.
Greek mind practical, 51, 86.
Greek writers on Egypt, 50; on mythology, 266.
Godron on difference in races, 184.
Gods, kings of Egypt, 56.
Gomer, 148.
Gutzlaff, 121.

Hale's dates, 42.
Ham, early name of Egypt, 159; curse of, 174; his family, 149.
Hamitic languages, 217, 228.
Havilah, 150.
Hebrides, growth of peat in, 313.
Hebrew once thought the original language, 209.
Hercules, 53.
Herodotus, 51, 53, 71; date of Trojan war, 88.
Hesperides, garden of, 243.
Hieroglyphics, key to, 49.
Hindus, character of, 107; compared with Greeks, 109.
Hindu traditions of creation, 240; of the flood, 254.
Historic times in Egypt, 67.
History, argument from, 48.
Hitchcock on date of creation, 20; on growth of peat, 312.
Hoang-ti, 122.
Hybrids, fertile and infertile, 187.
Hyksos, 79.

Inachus, 89.
Indian aborigines, 163.

Indo-European languages, 216.
Infidel rejoicing, 63.
Inflectional languages, 223.
Institutes of Menu, 105.
Irej, 218, 264.
Irish, changes in features of, 196.
Iyotisha, 115.

Jablonski on traditions, 238.
Jackson's dates, 42; on the word *yomim*, 97.
Japheth and his family, 147.
Javan and his family, 149.
Jesuit missionaries in China, 118.
Jews, change in features of, 197.
Joktan, 147.
Jones, Sir W., 104, 213.
Josephus, the Greek Livy, 77; against Apion, 77; citation of Manetho, 78.

Kali-Yug, 46.
Keller on Swiss lake remains, 322.
Khamism, 228.
Kittim, 149.
Kjokken-modding, 320.

Lake settlements in Switzerland, 320.
Language, argument from, 209.
Languages, classification of, 215; Aryan, 215; Semitic, 216; Hamitic, 217; Turanian, 218; monosyllabic, 222; agglutinative, 222; inflectional, 223; confusion of, 224; have much in common, 226; approximate as better known, 227; rapid changes in, 227.
La Peyrère, 170.
Latham, 96, 198.
Legge's Chinese classics, 120; on the Chinese year, 127, 132.
Lehabim, 160.
Lenormant on date of Menes, 71; on prehistoric archæology, 22.
Lepsius, 66, 77; identifies one hundred and ten kings of Egypt, 79.
Letronne, 64.
Lewis on Chaldean antiquities, 99.
Lists of Manetho, 69.
Literary remains of Egypt, 50.

Lud, Ludim, 147, 150, 159.
Lunar years in Egypt, 59, 60.
Lyell's geological evidences, 289; on the date of creation, 21.
Lydians, 147.

Ma, the Egyptian period, 28.
Madai, 149.
Magog, 148.
Mahabharata, 105, 254.
Makrizi, on changes in the Nile valley, 291.
Manes, kings of Egypt, 56.
Manetho, 54; his history, 68; his lists of dynasties, 69; his authorities unknown, 71; his lists corrupt, 71; different versions of, 72; internal evidence against them, 72; contradicted by the old chronicle, 73; by Eratosthenes, 74; by Josephus, 77; by the monuments, 79.
Mantchus, features of, changed, 198.
Manu, legend of, 255.
Manuscripts of the Septuagint, 32.
Mariette, on the dynasties, 82.
Measures of time among Chaldeans, 95.
Medes, 149.
Median kings, 98.
Megasthenes, 45.
Menes, mythological, 52; first king of Egypt, 67; date of, 70, 71.
Meshech, 149.
Methuselah's age, 34.
Metonic cycle, 129.
Mexican tradition of the flood, 246.
Milman's version of Manu, 255.
Mississippi, delta of, 297.
Mizraim, 150; early name of Egypt, 159.
Monboddo's speculations on language, 211.
Monosyllabic languages, 222.
Months, reckoned as years, 58.
Monuments, against Manetho, 79.
Monumental figures of animals, 200.
Monumental records of Egypt, 49.
Moral characteristics of men, 207.
Moral relations of men, 207.

Mount Olympus, myth of, 267.
Müller, 109; on date of the Vedas, 114; on changes in language, 231; on unity of languages, 233.
Mythology, argument from, 261; the Roman, 271; Greek, 271; Egyptian, 271; Phœnician and Chaldean, 272; Hindu, 272.
Mythologies have a common origin, 270; in Bible events, 274.
Myths founded on fact, 262; modern examples of, 264; of Mount Olympus, 267; of the Omphalos, 268; of the Cynocephali, 269; of creation, 275; of the fall, 276; of the antediluvian generations, 277; of the flood, 279; of Noah, 279; of the dove, 282; of the Cabiri, 283; of the ark, 281.

Naphtuhim, 159.
Natchez, fossil near, 293.
Nau (or Nao) the great, 137.
New Orleans, skeleton, 295.
Nile, flowing with honey, 72; borings in the valley, 287; annual increase of sediment, 289; changes in the bed of, 291.
Nimrod, 146, 150.
Nineveh, 146, 150.
Noah and his family, 146; myths of, 279.
Nott and Gliddon's types, 173; history of man, 173.

Oa, Oanes, 283.
Ogyges, deluge of, 247.
Old Chronicle, 53, 59, 73.
Olympiad, the first, date of, 86.
Omphalos, myth of, 268.
Orpheus, 51.
Osborn on contemporaneous dynasties, 82; on Egyptian language, 161.
Owen on difference in races, 185; on changes in features of the Jews, 197.

Palmer's chronicles, 57.
Pandora, myth of, 244.
Pankou, 121; same as Hindu Manu, 121.

Pandorus, 55.
Papyrus rolls, 49.
Parian marble, 88.
Pathrusim, 150.
Pauthier's History of China, 120; view of Chinese chronology, 124.
Peat in Somme valley, 309; its rate of growth, 312.
Peruvian tradition of the flood, 246.
Petavius's dates, 42.
Phut, 151.
Physiology, argument from, 169.
Plurality of race, advocates of, 170.
Plutarch, 51.
Polydorus, 96.
Polyhistor, 92, 94.
Pomponius Mela, 53.
Poole's dates, 42.
Portuguese in India, 197.
Prehistoric archæology, 22; times in Egypt, 52; period, how reckoned, 57; races, 158.
Professor, in University of Breslau, 64.
Prometheus, legend of, 239.
Protestant missionaries in China, 120.
Ptolemy Physcon, 46.
Ptolemy's canon, 40.
Puranas, 104.

Quatrefages on La Peyrère, 171; on slavery, 173.
Quietists in geology, 311.

Raamah, 150.
Races of men, 183.
Ramayana, 105.
Rawlinson, Sir H., 156.
Reade on the negro, 198.
Riphath, Riphæan mountains, 148.
Rock temples of India, 163.
Rodier's chronology, 27, 71.
Rogers on new discoveries in geology, 22; on contemporaneousness of fossils, 305, 307, 318.
Rome, time of its foundation uncertain, 89; three theories, 89.
Rosetta stone, 49.
Rousseau, 172.

Sabtah, 150.
Sabtechah, 150.
Sacred words of the Hindus, 111.
Samaritan version of the Pentateuch, 32.
Sanskrit, discovery of, 103, 210; contains no history, 106; estimate of its value, 106; scholars, 213; key to classification of languages, 214.
Saros, a measure of time, 95, 99.
Satya Yuga, 28.
Schlegel's work on Sanskrit, 214.
Scripture chronology, 31; language not always literal, 153.
Scyths, migrations of, 156.
Seasons in Egypt, 58.
Seba, 150.
Sebennytus, 68.
Selim, 284.
Semitic languages, 216.
Septuagint version, 32.
Sexagenary cycle in China, 122, 126, 129.
Shem and his family, 146.
Shepherd kings in Egypt, 79.
Shishak, 80.
Shu-king, 130; ascribed to Confucius, 137; how mutilated, 139; burning of, 139; how recovered, 140.
Simeto, wearing of the bed of, 313.
Skeleton, near New Orleans, 295.
Smith, Philip, date of destruction of temple, 41; on the Sarus, 90.
Smyth's discussion with Agassiz, 172; on primitive traditions, 236.
Somme valley, 301; history of changes in, 308.
Species, unity of, 183.
Stobart's tablets, 65.
Stewart, Dugald, 210.
Syncellus, 53, 68, 74, 77, 78.

Tablet of Abydos, 80.
Tablets, Egyptian, 65.
Tahitian tradition of creation, 240.
Tarshish, 149.
Temple, date of, 36, 38.
Temptation and fall, tradition of, 244; myth of, 276.

424 INDEX.

Tentyris, 160.
Theology, opposed to plurality, 206.
Thompson, J. P., 65.
Tiras, 149.
Togarmah, 148.
Tradition, argument from, 235.
Traditions of primitive times, 236; of one god, 238; of the creation, 209; of Eden, 243; of the fall, 244; of the Sabbath, 245; of the flood, 246.
Treta-Yuga, 28.
Trevor, Canon, on the dynasties, 70.
Trojan war mythical, 87; date of, 88.
Troy, siege of, 88.
Troyon on Swiss lake remains, 324.
Tubal, 149.
Turanian language, 215.

Uniformitarians, 311.
Upangas, 105.
Upavedas, 105.
Usher's dates, 42.
Uz, 147.

Vedas, 104; origin of date of, 112; teach one God, 239.

Vedangas, 105.
Versions of the Pentateuch, 32.
Voltaire, 172.

Weeks, time divided into, 245; days of, 245.
Whitney on date of the Vedas, 113; on changes in races, 196; on classification of languages, 221; on unity of languages, 227, 234.
Wilkinson on lunar years, 59.
Williams on Chinese chronology, 121, 126; on the Shu-king, 137.
Wilson on the Somme valley, 316.

Xisuthrus, 94, 250.

Years in Egypt, lunar, 58; in China, 126, 127.
Yu the Great, 136.

Zodiac of Denderah, 61.
Zodiacs, of Greek origin, 65.

APPENDIX.

A. Chronology of Bunsen, 327.
B. Chronology of Boeckh, 348.
C. Chronology of Rodier, 349.
D. Manetho, 357.
E. Manetho's Lists, 359.
F. The Old Chronicle, 377.
G. Eratosthenes and Apollodorus, 378.
H. Manetho, according to Josephus, 383.
I. Chinese Astronomy, 391.
J. Superficial Character of Diversities between Races, 393.
K. Variations in Species among Domestic Animals, 401.
L. Visit of Dionusos to India, 412.
M. Chinese Theology, 413.
N. The Celts in Europe, 417.

www.ingramcontent.com/pod-product-compliance
Lightning Source LLC
Chambersburg PA
CBHW022107290426
44112CB00008B/580